THE MURDER OF LIL MISS

SHEILA KIMMELL

WITH KAY CARPENTER

THE MURDER
of LIL MISS

EAGLE CREST PUBLICATIONS

· 2005 ·

The Murder of Lil Miss
Copyright © 2005 by Sheila Kimmell
Published by Eagle Crest Publications

For further information, contact the author at:
www.eaglecrestpubl@aol.com

Book design by THE FLOATING GALLERY
www.thefloatinggallery.com

Printed in the United States of America

Library of Congress Control Number 2005924357

ISBN 0-9763524-0-0

CONTENTS

• PART I •

Tragedies

PART II

Fourteen Years of Investigations

* PART III *

Catching A Killer

Acknowledgments

A Special Note of Thanks

Over the years, people who knew of our family's struggles would often say, "Sheila, you need to write a book." I wish I had a quarter for every such comment; we'd be rich. I have done a lot of writing, but it was limited to short stories and company publications.

With continued encouragement from family and friends, I decided to write a book. I knew I could not do it alone, because I was too emotionally connected to the story. I began a quest to find an author to help me write the book, a "ghostwriter," as they are referred to in the publishing industry. What does that mean? It means that I would be credited as the author and the author would be credited as the editor. It didn't make sense to me, but that's how it works.

My search, through The Floating Gallery Publishing Company, led me to a remarkable, talented woman by the name of Kay Carpenter, some 1,400 miles away. Her resumé was impressive, and she was willing to take on this task. She worked with me for many months and even attended portions of the murder trial. She was committed to telling our story our way. She went beyond the call of duty, seeking interviews and conducting independent research to help answer some baffling questions that have lingered in people's minds, including mine. That was more than our contract called for.

Yes, it is our story, but Kay Carpenter wrote this book on my behalf. She is not a "ghostwriter" from my point of view. She had to *live* every aspect of our ordeal in order to put the book together. Aside from being a talented author, Kay gave me the strength and courage to follow through with telling our story. I found another blessing in Kay, and I found another lifelong friend. Thank you, Kay.

—SHEILA KIMMELL

ADDITIONAL ACKNOWLEDGMENTS

I've heard about phone calls that can change your life, but I never expected to get one. Nevertheless, I did on February 16th, 2004. The Floating Gallery hired me to help Sheila Kimmell write a book about the murder of her daughter, Lisa. My first reaction was concern. Why would anyone be interested in a 1988 murder? When I spoke to Sheila, I understood. The story spans sixteen years, and the plots twists are so odd, it could be fiction.

The killer's trial took place in March 2004. I needed to be there for at least part of it. After I arrived in Wyoming, I was astonished. Even in the midst of reliving her daughter's horrible murder, Sheila was thoughtful enough to have a fruit basket waiting in my hotel room.

The first evening I had dinner with Ron and Sheila, and I was impressed by two things. They are so "normal," considering what they went through. Their children and extended family are the focus of their lives, which is heartwarming because my family resides all over the country, and we don't see each other often.

In the three days I attended the trial, Sheila made me feel like family. After a year of working with the Kimmells, I can say this: Sheila, Ron, Sherry, and Stacy are exceptional, compassionate people—Lisa was, too, and I'm sure Ricky would have grown up the same.

Most of my contact was with Sheila, whom I believe to be one of the strongest, most determined women I've ever met. But she's not afraid to show her grief when it hits her. We've both shed tears together while compiling this book. Also, she's organized, intelligent, and sharp. When I needed information, I barely took another breath before it was in my hands. It was a genuine team effort. (She also has a great sense of humor, which was greatly needed at times.)

We had many people helping us out. Many thanks go to Detective

Dan Tholson, Coroner Dr. James Thorpen, and Detective Lynn Cohee from Natrona County for assisting us with research. Additionally, I want to thank the following law enforcement officers for giving interviews and providing invaluable information: Retired ATF Special Agent Don Flickinger, Former FBI Special Agent Greg Cooper, Investigators from Fremont County: Bill Braddock and Roger Rizor, Wyoming Game and Fish Warden Bill Long, Detective Rich Haskell from Sweetwater County, and Inspector Jim Broz from the U.S. Mint.

Other thanks to Judy and Gary Mason, Shannon and Scott Breeden, and Dixie Brewbaker for speaking out. Thanks to Airwolf fans Steven Stull and Ron "Chichio" for their assistance. Thanks to Becky Holman, Wanda Lee, Mark Eagleton, Karen Kimmell, and Kevin Krayna for their time and helpful comments.

I want to say a special "thank you" to writer Ann Rule for her encouraging words and expert advice to me when I first embarked on this writing adventure. Sometimes the details were upsetting, and Ann's e-mails helped me get through emotional moments.

In conclusion, Sheila Kimmell has challenged me and changed my life for the better. She's given me the nerve to write in a field I've always wanted to pursue. I hope to write more books similar to this because I find it rewarding to give victims a final say. Best of all, I know I have Sheila as a friend for life.

—KAY CARPENTER

INTRODUCTION

S heila! Your daughter's missing!"

Those were terrifying words to hear. Twenty-four hours earlier, our oldest daughter, Lisa Marie Kimmell, had left her job in Denver, Colorado and headed for Cody, Wyoming, to spend time with her new boyfriend and visit a friend in a Billings, Montana, hospital. She never arrived.

My husband, Ron, and I panicked as we placed calls to Lisa's friends and answered calls from those who had not heard from her.

The only thing we could imagine was a serious car wreck. Three months earlier, she had had a minor collision during a snowstorm when another driver ran her off the road. She had called us immediately.

This time the weather was clear, and we heard nothing from her—not for hours, which turned into excruciatingly long days.

With little sleep and no rest, my husband, our family, and friends drove her highway route, stopping to search ravines and ditches. We chartered planes in hopes of spotting her car. Law enforcement agencies in three states issued bulletins.

Nothing.

Eight days after her disappearance, our worst nightmare materialized. Two fishermen found Lisa's body early Saturday afternoon, April 2nd, 1988. She hadn't had a wreck. At the tender age of eighteen, Lisa had been raped repeatedly, held hostage for six days in an old school bus without electricity or running water, subjected to untold torture, hit on the head so hard that it caused a four-inch skull fracture, and stabbed six times. Her body had been dropped from the Old Government Bridge

1

near Casper, Wyoming, into the cold North Platte River. Our beautiful daughter was gone.

It took fourteen years to find her killer: Dale Wayne Eaton. It took two more years to try him for her murder. On March 20th, 2004, a jury gave him the death penalty.

———

Our tumultuous journey began the day Lisa vanished, and ever since then we've been asked the same questions over and over.

Who was Lisa? Who was the pretty girl in the picture? People knew *of* her, but they didn't *know* her.

Who is the Kimmell family? How did we get through the horrors of knowing Lisa had been murdered? Our emotional and spiritual welfare has been tested repeatedly.

How did we deal with all the law enforcement agencies? Her case involved three states. Countless officers at local and federal levels became involved.

Who was the monster who killed Lisa? How could someone inflict such heinous acts on an innocent young woman? Few people know about Dale Eaton's dark side.

Ron and I were encouraged to write a book to answer these questions. Now that we're writing the book, people are asking us why. This is not a therapeutic experience for us—we're still not over the pain, but our story is one that needs to be told. There are lessons for law enforcement about how jurisdictional issues can hinder an investigation. Helping us get past the tragedy is our anticipation of better laws for victims in the future, improved cooperation among law enforcement agencies, and advanced technology in forensics.

We also hope that the information we pass on will comfort others who have been direct or indirect victims of violent crimes.

Additionally, we want to recognize the goodness of friends, family, and strangers. Small gestures of kindness touched us deeply, often to the point where it seemed to outweigh the evil, even if nothing can. Frequently people have said that they admired our family's courage. The truth is that we have good days and many unrelentingly bad days. The

INTRODUCTION | 3

strength and courage we have mustered can be credited to the people who have blessed us over the years.

This book can't answer all of the questions that we've been asked. We can explain some of the who, what, when, where, and how, but we'll never understand *why*.

Billings

MONTANA

Sheridan

Cody

Buffalo

Grand Teton Park

SOUTH
DAKOTA

WYOMING

Shoshoni

Moneta

Casper

Lander

*Waltman
Rest Stop*

Douglas

North Platte River

LISA KIMMEL'S
BODY FOUND HERE

NEBRASKA

Rawlins

Rock Springs

Cheyenne

Red Desert

COLORADO

Greeley

Denver

LISA MARIE KIMMELL'S ROUTE
and other areas of interest

PART I

Tragedies

Chapter 1

Knowing Lisa

The Early Years

M y husband, Ron, and I were idealistic young parents. He was only twenty and I only sixteen when we married. I became a mother fifteen months after our wedding, and it was one of the happiest moments of my life. Of our four children, Lisa was the oldest, born on July 18th, 1969, in Covington, Tennessee. Ron was in the Marine Corps. Our next child was Sherry, born August 24th, 1971. While Lisa was confident and independent, Sherry was shy but full of determination. Ricky, our only son, was born May 27th, 1973. He was an energetic, curious boy (we lost him at the age of three to a tragic accident). Stacy, born on May 24th, 1974, was easy to get along with, diplomatic, and charming.

We named our first baby Lisa Marie at Ron's mother's request. She wasn't a big Elvis Presley fan, as the name might imply; she simply liked the name. Grandma often referred to her as "my little miss Lisa Marie," hence her nickname "Lil' Miss."

From an early age, Lisa was independent, inquisitive, and at times alarmingly mischievous. I remember an incident when she was two years old. I rose at my usual early hour to check on Lisa and her newborn sister, Sherry. My heart lurched when I saw an empty bed and I couldn't find her in the house. Ron and I noticed a chair pushed up near a door that was locked every night. The chain dangled from the latch.

We frantically searched outside. Ron drove around the neighborhood

(I couldn't leave the baby) and saw no sign of her. He raced to the police station for help. Ron was speechless when he arrived. Lisa sat on the police captain's desk in a makeshift diaper that the officer had fashioned from one of his old shirts. Lisa had stripped off her clothes somewhere along the way. Unaware of the trouble she caused, she smiled at her daddy with a mouthful of donuts. Lisa must have had fun and thought that she was a little Houdini, because she tried escaping again and again, despite beefed-up security measures.

I have hard evidence of her creativity at age four. I had put the children down for an afternoon nap in our modest suburban home. Tending to four children under the age of five was demanding. Their naps gave me precious hours to wash dishes, run loads of laundry, and fold the three-dozen cloth diapers I didn't get to the night before. Laundry was my least-favorite chore. With the dishes clanging, the washer swooshing, and the dryer buzzing, I didn't hear any commotion in Lisa and Sherry's room.

I went outside to relocate the water sprinkler—and couldn't believe my eyes. Clothes lay everywhere. I looked up and saw Lisa and Sherry's bedroom window screen pushed out. Exasperated, I stormed to the bedroom and threw open the door. Lisa was busily rearranging her furniture. Her younger sister, Sherry, was lying quietly in her bed with a wide-eyed look that said, "I know better than to get in the middle of *this!*"

An empty closet and dresser met my eyes, and Lisa's mattress lay on the floor, where she had dragged it off the springs. My hands on my hips, I yelled at her, "Lisa Marie, what in the world do you think you're doing?"

Without flinching, she turned, imitated my stance, and said, "Well, Mommy, since *you* were cleaning house, I wanted to clean *our* room."

I couldn't help but laugh. I found our camera to take a picture because I knew Ron wouldn't believe what happened if I didn't document the moment. Sometimes fathers don't appreciate the daily events in a house full of four children. I made sure he would.

I collected the clothes in the front yard—wet by then from the sprinkler—and loaded more laundry with a loud sigh.

Lisa attended schools in Billings. She made "A"s in most subjects and never posed a problem for her teachers. She had already formed a strong set of values. Only once did we need to talk to her school counselors.

Lisa was in the seventh grade when a few girls tried to pressure her into buying drugs. Lisa refused, and then lectured them on why drugs were bad. They taunted Lisa for a couple of days and threatened to beat her up. That was enough. At that point we insisted that the counselors get involved, and the problem was resolved.

In her 1984 sophomore term paper, titled, "Murder spelled with an A," Lisa discussed the controversy of abortion and disclosed her views. "Some scientists believe that life begins at the moment of conception. The egg cell and the sperm cell, when united, produce a unique human being. And since it was produced from two human beings, it must be a human being because it certainly is not a goat, or a frog, or anything else. And even I, at one time, was a fetus, and I certainly am not a goat or frog, and am without a doubt a human being."

Lisa was certainly human, especially around her sisters. Their typical sibling quarrels could drive me crazy. We had our share of family disagreements, but we talked out problems when we could. Lisa was a decent kid, the kind of child most parents wish for. As she matured, her independence and motivation to excel emerged as her strongest traits. She began working as a cashier for Arby's in Billings at the age of fourteen. She enjoyed the restaurant business and charmed many customers.

At the age of sixteen, she asked us to co-sign a loan to help her buy a waterbed. She made the payments herself, ahead of time. She established a better credit rating before the age of seventeen than some people achieve in a lifetime.

She was very responsible for her age. My mother often said that Lisa was a thirty-year-old disguised as a teenager. To others, she was like any sweet teenage girl next door. Lisa exercised at the YMCA with friends, watched popular movies, skied with her family, and shopped at the mall. She admired Michael J. Fox, and her favorite television program was *Family Ties*. Her favorite colors were pink and lavender ("mostly pastels"). She loved lasagna, pizza, and tacos.

In her "Senior Moments" scrap book, her most memorable experiences included being a cheerleader, competing in a "Miss Teen" pageant, and winning an accounting scholarship to Kinman Business University (Trend College) in Washington State.

She dreamed of her future. "In five years I will be graduating from college and working for a large corporation as their top female executive.

I will also be married and will be considering starting a family." Eventually she hoped to get her MBA.

Many of her friends called her a "sweetheart," a "nice girl." In her scrapbook, one young man wrote, "Thanks for making sixth period less boring. I thought it would be a bunch of dipsticks—I was right—except for you." Another message from a girlfriend said: "I admire the way you are able to set your mind on a goal and achieve it. For this reason I know you will do well. Thanks for being a great friend. Put off getting married for a while. You've got all the time in the world."

After high school graduation, Lisa moved into an apartment to prepare herself for living on her own when she went to college. She worked full-time as an Arby's Assistant Manager for the summer so she could save money before going back to school. In mid-September, she and her father had planned to drive to Washington to check out the campus and living arrangements before moving her there.

A few days before departure, Lisa came over to discuss "something important." She sat us both down and informed us that after giving it much thought, she wanted to major in business management, but not accounting.

"I really like working in a people-related business," she said. "I like Arby's, and I can use my business training. It's a good career path, Mom. Look how well you've done. I want your job someday. I plan to run the company."

We were dismayed because we wanted all of our children to get a college education. "Are you sure that's what you want?" I asked.

She nodded her head and gave us her trademark smile. "Yep, I'm sure."

Lisa had a year to use her scholarship. She planned to work and explore other options before committing to an out-of-state college. Ron, Lisa, and I debated the pros and cons of her decision at length, but Lisa had thought through every concern. Eventually we agreed. The trip to Washington? Cancelled.

A short time later, Lisa proudly bought her sporty black Honda CRXsi from a local dealership. It was a special two-seater, fitted with extras such as a sunroof and mud flaps. She purchased it without our help based on her outstanding credit, and she ordered personalized plates with her nickname, "LIL MISS." We had no idea how important those plates would become.

THE LATER YEARS

To understand what led to Lisa's fateful trip and how she ended up missing near Casper, Wyoming, on the night of March 25th, 1988, I need to explain some family history.

In 1979, Ron and I had just built a new home, and our children were old enough for school. I wanted to contribute to our household income, so I applied for a job as an assistant manager of an Arby's restaurant. Inadvertently, I discovered my career. After a few years, I was promoted to Director of Operations for The Bailey Company, owners and operators of a five-state division of Arby's Restaurants. The company headquarters were located in Denver, but my family didn't want to move there. I sometimes commuted to Denver by airplane, but I usually drove the long stretch of highways between the cities. Driving that far is common practice in that part of the country. My car averaged more than 60,000 miles per year.

The Bailey Company had set up two apartments in a ten-unit building in Denver. One unit housed the male management trainees. I shared a two-bedroom apartment with the female trainees. My apartment was cozy, with vaulted ceilings, a fireplace, and modest but comfortable furniture. It was an easy ten-minute drive to my office.

One of my favorite coworkers was Joe Morian, a young man who came to work for me in Billings when he was eighteen. He began his career as my assistant manager. Since he had moved from Pennsylvania, far from family, Ron and I took him under our wing. We jokingly referred to Joe as our "loaner kid" because he often spent holidays and his days off with us. He became a big brother to my girls. He was an energetic, clean-cut young man with a wry wit, and he was good at his job. As I was promoted, Joe came with me. He rose to the position of District Manager for the Denver area. He became a friend and part of our family, and still is.

In December of 1987, we experienced problems in one of Joe's Denver Arby's and needed temporary management. Joe and I agreed to ask Lisa if she would assist us for a few months as a Unit Manager. She had proven her skills in Billings. She and I could share the company apartment, and I was thrilled to have her with me during the week. When we asked Lisa if she would help us out, she agreed.

Before she took the position, we discussed our "boss" rule. Learning how to separate "Mom" issues from "Boss" issues was something I had insisted on when each of my three daughters worked for Arby's. They were to settle their work disputes with the person they had the problem with *at work*. They were not to expect special treatment as the boss's daughters. The only exception was if they caught someone lying, cheating, or stealing, and then they were to inform me immediately.

Lisa moved to Denver and loved the challenge. She decided to move to Denver permanently, where she would have more chances to advance her career.

Before Lisa made her final move, she made trips back to Montana to visit friends and to take care of personal matters. Around Christmas in 1987, as she set off for Billings, a snowstorm developed. Someone ran her off the road in the Wheatland, Wyoming area. To avoid a collision, she hit a guardrail. Her Honda was damaged, and a snowplow driver stopped and called the Highway Patrol. We heard from Lisa immediately.

No matter what time of day or night, our daughters knew then (and now) that if they needed help, they could always call us. They always did.

We retrieved Lisa and got the car to Denver. Lisa made arrangements to have her car repaired. The repair shop offered loaner cars, but not to anyone under the age of twenty-one. Therefore, I signed for the loaner car service as the driver and let Lisa drive my car until her Honda was fixed.

Lisa had about a forty-mile drive from our apartment to her store. On another nasty, snowy evening, she took my car to work. I got a phone call from her telling me that she had almost had another wreck when avoiding a dog in the street. She was crying.

"Are you okay?"

"Yes, I'm fine, and so is the car," she sniffed.

"Oh, my! Did you hit the dog?"

"No. I pulled over and got it off the street. I was afraid that if I didn't, it would have gotten run over."

"Okay. If nothing's hurt, what's the problem?" I sensed a catch.

"Mom. The dog's in your car. I can't bring it into the restaurant, and I can't leave it in the car all night. It's wet and it'll freeze to death. Can you come get it?"

With a sigh, I drove in nearly blizzard conditions to pick up a scared cocker spaniel that was dripping wet, and dripping in *my* car. But that was typical of Lisa. She helped anyone or anything in need. We placed an ad in the lost and found. Fortunately, we located the dog's owner.

I cherish the time we spent together while Lisa stayed in my Denver apartment. When I had special company functions that allowed a guest, Lisa was my date. Occasionally we dressed up for dinner and went to a fancy restaurant simply for the fun of it.

One evening when I came home from work about six o'clock, two trainees sat at the dining room table studying. A young lady looked up and said, "I don't know what's wrong with your daughter, but she's in her room crying."

I set down my briefcase and hurried into the bedroom. Already dressed in her pajamas, Lisa lay on her bed in the dark, crying softly.

I sat on the edge of the bed. "What's wrong, honey?"

"I had a fight with Joe," she said, wiping away a tear.

"Do you want to talk about it?

"Nah, it's not that big of a deal."

"It must be if you're crying. How about you get dressed and I'll take you to dinner?"

She paused. "Will that be as the boss, or as Mom?"

I laughed, patting her shoulders. "Neither. How about as a friend?"

From the light in the hallway, I saw her smile.

"Okay, I'll get dressed." She donned her usual tan Dockers and a sweater and met me in the living room.

We chatted as I drove to Ramone's, a large, cheerful Mexican restaurant in Denver. After we placed our orders, I asked Lisa to tell me about her spat with Joe.

Still frowning, she described how hard she had worked to improve the store. The store had experienced better customer service, cleanliness, and organization since she came on board. I knew that based on my store visits and Joe's weekly reports.

She listlessly dipped a chip in hot sauce. "I told Joe that if he were that happy with the store, he should give me a raise. Do you know what he said?"

"No, tell me."

"He said, 'You're not worth what I'm paying you now.' Then he laughed." Her shoulders sagged and more tears welled up. "It really hurt my feelings."

I took her hand. I knew Joe well enough to know that he was kidding—his humor again causing trouble. Sometimes he was too much like her big brother. He overstepped the line, not realizing how important success was to her. "I'm sorry, sweetie. Maybe I'm listening as a friend, but I'm still Joe's boss. I can write him up or even fire him."

Shocked, she looked at me, and then grinned at my tone of voice. "You wouldn't do that, would you?"

"Yes, I would."

"Oh, Mom. You know Joe. He didn't mean it." Her eyes brightened. "He's just full of himself and a jerk sometimes."

We finished our evening remembering other occasions when Joe got himself in trouble by joking around. We laughed so hard, our eyes watered.

Lisa and I had grown beyond the "love you one day and hate you the next" relationship that mothers and daughters so often experience. We became close friends.

THURSDAY, MARCH 24th, 1988

When an Arby's employee closed a store after midnight and opened a store the next morning (about 6:00 A.M.), I called it a "turnaround" shift. I didn't approve of those hours. I felt it interfered with the employee's quality of life. A tired employee is not as productive. Whether I liked it or not, Lisa had arranged that shift for herself because she wanted a long weekend. She had gotten in about 1:00 A.M. and only had a few hours to sleep.

I woke up around 5:00 A.M. I showered first to allow her a few more minutes of sleep. When I finished, I woke her up. Still groggy, she stumbled into the shower. I began blow-drying my hair. Suddenly the blow-dryer exploded.

I shrieked and jerked the plug from the socket. The stinking smoke from the burning plastic set off the fire alarm. The high pitched screeching caused Lisa to zip out of the shower without turning off the water or grabbing a towel.

"What's going on?" she shouted, dripping on the carpet, naked as the day God gave her to me. We respected each other's privacy, but the racket cast all modesty aside.

"The damn hair drier blew up," I said, fanning the smoke away to make the alarm stop shrieking.

She planted her hands on her hips. "Well, if I wasn't awake before, I sure am now." She returned to the shower.

I hollered into the bathroom, "Lisa! Can I use *your* hair dryer?"

"Yeah, just don't blow it up!"

That afternoon, about four o'clock, Lisa arrived at the apartment after work, and we spent a few hours together packing and talking about our weekend trips home. Lisa had driven from Denver to Montana several times, but it would be her first time on the back highways to Cody, Wyoming. She intended to pick up Ed Jaroch, her new boyfriend, and then bring him to Billings to introduce him to the family late Saturday or early Sunday. She also wanted to visit a friend who was having surgery. I gave her my road atlas to study the new route.

My plans were to fly back to Billings and go skiing Saturday. My flight was booked, but before we left the apartment I hesitated. "I don't have to fly home, Lisa. I can ride with you to Billings. I don't mind staying an extra day."

"No, Mom, that won't work. I only have two seats. There won't be enough room after I pick up Ed."

"We could take my car instead." I offered.

"No, Mom, I want to take *my* car."

I relented. She had driven that far before, and I realized she wanted to be free to spend time with Ed and her friends without her mother tagging along. She wasn't a child anymore.

Lisa drove me to the airport in her Honda. During the hour-long drive, we mostly talked about Ed. He was teaching her to dance the country western "swing," a version of the jitterbug.

"I like him a lot, and he makes me laugh," she said, navigating through traffic to Denver's airport.

I was happy that Lisa had found a fun boyfriend and that they seemed to be intellectually matched. She took life *too* seriously at times. When she was fifteen, she met a young Catholic man named Paul. They became engaged, and she focused on becoming a good wife, even converting to

Catholicism. She devoted herself to him, and she was devastated when he broke up with her during her senior year. She was finally venturing out to explore her new world.

She commented about Paul in her Senior Moments Book. "If I could do it over again, I would not have spent most of my high school years with Paul. I would have dated different people and made more friends. Also, I would have spent more time with my friends. I would not have conformed to what Paul wanted me to be. I would have found out who I was sooner and enjoyed *being* myself."

I gazed at my daughter, relaxed in blue jeans and my coat that I had nicknamed the "Mad Dog Kimmell Coat." It was a black leather motorcycle jacket that suited Lisa.

She grinned when I noticed her wearing it. "I kind of like it, too. I hope you don't mind if I borrow it."

"Of course not," I said.

We chatted more about Ed. She was nervous about introducing him to Ron because Ed was several years older than Lisa. I hadn't met Ed in person, but I had spoken with him many times when he phoned. He sounded like a really nice, well-mannered guy.

"Don't you worry about Dad, sweetie. I'll take care of him. I'll remind him of our age difference."

Lisa smiled. "Thanks, Mom."

After we arrived at the airport, Lisa parked her car and walked me to the gate. We sat in the boarding area and made small talk, confirming our plans for the weekend.

When the boarding announcement sounded, we rose.

Instead of getting the usual quick peck on the cheek and, "Bye, love ya," Lisa gave me a long hug. "Mom, I can't tell you how much I really do love you and Dad."

"I love you, too, sweetie." I embraced her one last time and walked towards my flight. I turned briefly as I stood in line to board the plane, and hollered, "You drive careful!"

She waved and yelled back, "Don't worry, Mom, I will!"

Then I got on that damn airplane, which is something I'll never forgive myself for doing. "If *only* I had . . ." or "*what* if I had . . ." has replayed in my mind a million times. That quick glance, the kind everyone takes for granted, was the last time I saw Lisa alive.

CHAPTER 2

The First Eight Days

SATURDAY, MARCH 26th, 1988

Our youngest daughter, Stacy, Ron, and I rose early Saturday morning to go skiing at Bridger Bowl, a resort in southwestern Montana. We had heard it had more than 1,500 acres to ski on, and it was a short two-hour drive from Billings. The views of the mountains were said to be spectacular.

Sherry had to work that morning, and Lisa was supposed to be in Cody, so only three of us went. The trip was a huge disappointment. The snow was slushy because of a warm day, so we ate lunch and went home.

We returned about 2:30 P.M. Ron began to unload the car, putting away the ski equipment. I walked into the house to a ringing phone. It was Joe Morian, Lisa's boss.

"Sheila! Everyone has been trying to get a hold of you all day!"

"Okay, Joe. What's up?" I assumed it had something to do with one of the stores.

"Your daughter's missing!"

I have to admit that I didn't take him seriously at first because of his past tendencies to play pranks on me.

"Joe, don't worry about Lisa," I said. "She's already told me that she's going to stop and visit with friends before she comes home, and she would call if she ran into any problems."

"No, Sheila, I'm serious. She's missing." He became insistent.

"She's got things to do, Joe. She probably won't get here until tonight or early tomorrow."

We hung up, and in frustration, Joe called Carla, Lisa's close friend. Carla had introduced Lisa to Ed. Lisa and Carla had planned to see each other, too. After hearing from Joe, Carla called me immediately. She confirmed that Lisa didn't make it to Ed's house the night before, and she said that Ed had been trying to reach us all morning. He was en route to Billings, hoping that he might find Lisa. Ed had already called the highway patrol in Montana, Wyoming, and Colorado to report an "Overdue Arrival."

The terror sunk in, and my heart dropped to my feet.

I found Ron and told him about the frightening news. We immediately assumed that Lisa must have had a wreck. Nothing else registered on our radar screen.

Ed arrived at our house about 4:30 P.M. He and Ron decided to drive back to Cody. They planned to organize a search for the next morning, retracing Lisa's route back to Denver. Ron would drive over the roads, and Ed knew local pilots we could hire to search from the air.

Still, our thoughts centered on the fender-bender Lisa had in December of 1987. Had the Honda been repaired properly? Did she hit a deer or have a flat tire? We didn't have cell phones back then; could she be stranded in a remote area between Denver and Cody with no phone? We knew she wouldn't change her mind or go somewhere else. Her practical personality had little tolerance for spontaneity.

After Ron and Ed left for his house in Cody, I called the Highway Patrol to change Ed's "Overdue Arrival" report to an "Attempt to Locate" (ATL), a step up. Ed couldn't file that type of report because he wasn't related to Lisa or just didn't have enough information.

The next step was to file a missing person report. However, seventy-two hours were required in 1988. I was told that seventy-two hours allowed time for troubled or runaway kids to cool off if they were mad at Mom and Dad. Despite my pleas and explanation that Lisa was not a troubled runaway, they wouldn't relent, but they agreed to be on the lookout.

Around 8:30 P.M., I received a call from the Wyoming Highway Patrol after they received the ATL alert. They informed me that Lisa had been cited for driving 88 mph in a 65 mph zone, near Douglas, Wyoming, at 9:06 Friday night. She didn't have enough cash to pay, so Officer Al Lesco led her to a cash machine in Douglas. Her card wouldn't work. In 1988, cash cards only worked at compatible banks. Officer Lesco had two options. He could jail her until she came up with the money, or allow her to sign the ticket with a promise to mail the payment. Officer Lesco decided to let her sign for her ticket and continue on her way because she seemed responsible enough.

Officer Lesco's ticket was important. We knew that Lisa had made it as far as Douglas and that she was on schedule. I called Ron in Cody, knowing that would narrow the search.

About 9:30 P.M., I hurried to a grocery store for cigarettes. I'll admit I'm a smoker, and considering the stress I felt, I wasn't about to go without. My eyes were red from crying, and when I rounded a corner to the checkout counter, I ran into Al Ketterling, a family friend since 1975.

Al was a good-looking man, a shorter version of Tom Selleck. He was also a former cop who had become a private investigator. Al took one look at me and frowned. "What's wrong, Sheila?"

I took a deep breath. "Lisa's missing."

"Oh, my God, what happened?"

"We don't know, Al. She was driving to Cody and didn't make it. No one can find her." I paid for the cigarettes, wiping away a fresh set of tears. "I'm sorry, but I've got to get back home in case someone calls."

"I'll come over and see if there's anything I can do to help."

Al was a former deputy for the Yellowstone County Sheriff's Department—he would definitely be helpful.

Al came over about 10:30 P.M. and called Ron at Ed's house in Cody. After getting more details, Al decided to drive to Cody that night with his stepfather to help Ron search on Sunday.

I didn't sleep much that night. Stacy and Sherry were with me, and they were worried, too. They tried to comfort me and they tried to console each other, but mostly they hid out in their bedrooms, not knowing what to do. They were only teenagers, thirteen and sixteen years old. They were terrified, and so was I!

SUNDAY, MARCH 27th, 1988

Ironically, Lisa had been nervous about introducing Ed to her father. Ed turned out to be a trustworthy young man with a nice family. We never thought Ed was responsible for Lisa's disappearance. He was scared, too. He and Lisa were just getting to know each other, and suddenly she was missing and her father was spending the night with him. What an odd twist of fate!

Sunday was our first full day to focus on the search. We didn't know where she had disappeared, so no one had the legal jurisdiction to organize the search efforts. We were on our own.

While Ron was in Wyoming, I set up a "command post" at home to coordinate our efforts to find Lisa, enlisting all the help we could. My sister-in-law, Karen, opened her typesetting shop to create a "missing" poster.

The night before, Ron and Ed had arranged to charter a private plane through a flying service in Cody. The pilot and plane were ready to go first thing Sunday morning. Ed and Al Ketterling's stepfather took to the air while Ron and Al traveled by car, stopping at every sheriff's office, gas station, ravine, and truck stop.

Because Officer Al Lesco had given Lisa a ticket in Douglas, the search was concentrated between Douglas and Cody. After a full day of searching, there was no sign of Lisa or her car. We couldn't fathom anything but car trouble, and became more fearful as Sunday wore on.

Ron and Al returned from Wyoming late Sunday night and headed directly to the Yellowstone County Sheriff's Department in Billings to file a formal Missing Person Report. Al convinced the deputies that Lisa was not a troubled runaway and not to wait seventy-two hours. They agreed to waive the waiting period and filed the report.

I didn't sleep much that night or many of the nights that followed during our ordeal. When I nodded off, I kept one ear awake for the phone. The most intense memory of each night was the sound of a clock I kept in the living room.

For Christmas of 1987, my three daughters had chipped in and bought me a brass anniversary clock attractively set in a bell jar. I was proud of my treasure. It made a beautiful resounding musical chime at the top of the hour, and chimed every quarter hour. But after Lisa's disappearance, each time the chimes sounded, they became harsh reminders that Lisa was still missing and could be in danger. Time became agonizing. Later in the week, I couldn't bear it any longer. I yanked out the batteries.

MONDAY, MARCH 28th, 1988

Ron made plans to return to Wyoming, but he was waiting for the posters that his sister, Karen, expected to have ready at 10:00 A.M. Earlier that morning, he called his longtime friend and business partner, Steve Kramer, to let him know that he wouldn't make it to work. They had teamed up for years appraising and remodeling homes. When Steve learned of the situation and Ron's plan, he insisted on going with Ron back to Wyoming to help in the search.

Sherry wanted to stay home from school to help any way that she could, and so did Stacy. I said no. I wanted to shield them from the trauma as much as possible and insisted they go to school.

Sherry returned a few hours later, distressed. "Mom," she said, "I just can't concentrate on anything. I *need* to be doing something. I can run errands, deliver posters, or help answer the phone."

There I was trying to protect my girls when in reality they both needed to be involved.

By 10:00 A.M. the first posters were ready. Ron loaded a batch in the car, but he also loaded something else—his revolver. My husband is one of the gentlest men to walk the earth, but by Monday we had begun to suspect something more serious than a car wreck.

Many family and friends had heard of our plight and wanted to help. Law enforcement agencies were doing the best they could, given the jurisdictional boundaries they had to observe. We wanted as much assistance as possible, so I called the media and begged them to help us find Lisa. That afternoon, reporters rushed to our house to get more information. In desperation, I even called the White House.

The days and nights blurred together for Ron and me. I wouldn't leave the house because I didn't want to miss any important phone calls. Ron spent hours on the road searching, again stopping at every sheriff's office in every county from Billings to Douglas, and distributing posters along the way. He talked to the deputies in person. Sometimes they would kindly stop what they were doing and take Ron with them on tours of back roads and ditches. They knew their counties well, and they were helpful and sympathetic.

Searching was tedious. Ron slowly drove along highway shoulders, stopped, and walked the desert or areas surrounding the highways, finding things from purses to duffel bags full of clothes. He discovered an amazing number of items, but nothing of Lisa's.

He spoke to truck drivers and road construction crews. The truckers promised to place the posters along their routes. Road workers, who had been laboring along portions of the highway for several days, helped eliminate the need to search those areas in depth. Everyone he spoke to promised to call Ron if they spotted the car.

THE DAYS THAT FOLLOWED

The media embraced our pleas. Lisa's disappearance made the TV news, and newspapers printed the story on Tuesday's front page. The newspapers printed a copy of our poster and reported details about Lisa's planned trip. The phone rang continuously with sightings of her car and offers to help search.

We arranged to charter another plane for Wednesday, but a storm blew in and snow stranded air traffic. Despite the crummy weather, Ron organized another ground search. Our worries escalated, and we prayed that Lisa wasn't trapped somewhere in the cold. We also worried that the snow would blanket the landscape, hiding her car from our sight. The weather cleared Thursday, and the plane was able to fly. It didn't help.

Ron's searching led him to spend the night in whatever town he found himself at the end of a day. Ron was in Sheridan, Wyoming, at his brother's house Thursday night. I was alone again at home.

That night, something strange happened. People might think it was the result of being a hysterical mother, or hallucinating from lack of sleep. It was very real to me.

Six days had passed since Lisa's disappearance. I went to bed Thursday night mentally, physically, and emotionally exhausted, losing hope that we would ever find her. I fell into a restless sleep, only to be awakened sometime between ten o'clock and two o'clock.

Suddenly, I distinctly heard Lisa's voice call out, "Mom? . . . Dad? . . . Mom!" just as she did as a youngster when she got sick or scared in the middle of the night. I bolted upright and couldn't believe my eyes.

Lisa stood at the foot of our bed.

Before I could shout, "Lisa! Where in the hell have you been?" she vanished.

I stared into the darkness for what seemed to be an eternity, not understanding what I saw, and then I collapsed back to the bed with painful sobs. I knew that Lisa had reached out for us one last time. That's when I *knew* we wouldn't find her alive.

I dismissed my vision as a nightmare and fell asleep out of exhaustion. I didn't share what I saw with anyone then, not even Ron. I didn't want to burden him, and I didn't want anyone to think that I was crazy. But I knew in my heart that she had died that night. It would take years, but evidence would eventually support my vision and belief that Lisa had been kept alive as a hostage until Thursday night.

As the week wore on, we found out that not only our emotional bank account was overdrawn, but also our checking account. We would have sold everything we owned to find Lisa. The search took a huge toll on us financially. The communities around us rallied to assist in any way that they could. We hadn't solicited financial help, yet earlier in the week a "Help Find Lil' Miss" fund was set up by a concerned citizen.

Our bank president called and told us not to worry about the money. "Do what you need to do, and we'll cover it. We'll deal with your checking account later."

After learning of our private plane charters, the Civil Air Patrol called and said they would help with the air searches and could put a grid search together by Monday. Cost? No charge. We were humbled. We vowed never to exploit generosity for personal gain and wondered how we could ever thank people enough.

FRIDAY, APRIL 1st, 1988

One week had passed since Lisa went missing. Possible sightings of Lisa or her car and offers to help us search continued to pour in. About noon, Ron returned home again from Wyoming, physically and emotionally exhausted.

Karen came over late that afternoon and convinced Ron and me that I needed to get out of the house. Only because of my previous night's "vision" did I agree to leave.

About seven o'clock that evening Karen picked me up and took me to a pleasant pub in Billings called the Lamplighter Lounge. Old-fashioned lamps softly illuminated the décor to create an atmosphere of a 1900s downtown street. People mingled and laughed around me. I knew some of Karen's friends, but I wasn't ready to socialize. I had nothing to say; I felt numb and despondent.

Finally I said, "Karen, I'm not dealing with this well. Can you take me home?"

She nodded. "I have another idea. Let's get a couple of drinks to go. I'll take you someplace that's quieter and very special."

We left the pub, and Karen drove up to the Rimrocks.

The Rimrocks are towering cliffs that overlook Billings, nestled in the valley below. The cliffs are the kind of place that lovers often go to catch the view and "park," but that night Karen and I were alone. The sky was black as velvet, and the lights of the city twinkled below like fallen stars. We climbed out of the car to sit on the rocks. The air was cool, but the ridge was still warm from the day's sun.

I stared at my drink and took a sip. "I know we're not going to find Lisa alive, Karen."

"How do you know that?"

"I just know." Feeling wretched, I began crying, but I still didn't tell Karen that I saw Lisa the night before. "I don't want to be one of those parents who never finds their child." Tears spilled out. "Even if we don't find her alive, I want to bring her home."

Karen hugged me. "It's okay. Scream all you want," she said. "I brought you here because the rocks can hear you, but they won't pass judgment. You can say anything you want."

I did. I released my rage over losing Lisa and over losing Ricky twelve years earlier. I stood up and cursed at God. "Taking my son wasn't enough? You had to take my daughter, too? Why, God, why?" I screamed at God, using words I'm not too proud of. I don't know how long I ranted, but when I was done, Karen hugged me again and we shared more tears.

I finally crumpled back onto the rocks, sobbing uncontrollably. When I was all cried out, Karen drove me home.

Letting me vent was her gift to me that night, and it meant a lot because I didn't want to burden my husband and daughters with my pain. They had enough of their own.

SATURDAY, APRIL 2nd, 1988

We wouldn't give up our search on Saturday, even though the next day was Easter. We planned to consult a psychic who had called Ron Friday evening while I was with Karen. We also had another interview set up with newspaper reporters in the afternoon.

Ron and I were skeptical about people who claim powers of ESP or otherwise. We had been raised in our religions with the idea that anything paranormal was evil, rather than perhaps a God-given gift. Ron and I sensed the hopelessness of finding Lisa alive, but we were willing to do almost anything, even if that meant meeting psychics. We'd crawl to hell and back on bloody knees if necessary.

The publicity brought calls from many self-proclaimed psychics, but most came across as opportunistic con artists who promised to find Lisa for thousands of dollars. We ignored them. Then Ron got a telephone call from a soft-spoken elderly man named Clyde Praye, a chiropractor in Laurel, Montana. Ron agreed to meet with him. Clyde didn't want money. He only asked us to bring a toy or something of Lisa's. We met with Clyde early Saturday morning at a local diner. I brought one of Lisa's teddy bears and a tennis shoe.

Mr. Praye was a slight, white-haired man in his seventies. Dressed in a modest business-like tweed jacket and slacks, he hardly resembled my idea of a psychic. The three of us sat in a booth and talked about our ordeal over coffee.

During the course of the conversation he took Lisa's teddy bear and tennis shoe in his hands, held them close to his heart, and closed his eyes. He then studied a Wyoming map and pointed to the Casper area. "She's in the river." Tears welled in his eyes and he paused. "I think you already know—she's not alive."

Ron and I glanced at each other, unsure of what to say.

"What river and where?" Ron asked.

"I'm not sure exactly, but it's somewhere around here." He pointed to North Platte River in an area near Casper. It didn't make sense because it wasn't along Lisa's route to Cody.

"If you're willing, I'll go with you tomorrow and help you look for her," he said. The man seemed too frail to be traipsing around any riverbank. (We would learn later that he had cancer. He passed away a year later.)

"That's very kind of you, Mr. Praye, but tomorrow's Easter, and we don't want to impose or take that time away from your family," I said.

"They'll understand. The important thing is to find your daughter. I know she's there."

Setting skepticism aside, Ron made plans with Clyde to meet at 7:00 A.M. on Easter Sunday. Then Ron and I went home to get ready for our two o'clock meeting with a reporter and photographer from the *Billings Gazette*.

By then, Lisa's story had captured the hearts and interest of many people. One thing I remember was that the reporter wanted to know more about the beautiful girl in the photograph, and us—parents driven to find their daughter. Sensing our agony, the reporter had to occasionally wipe away her tears. She wrote notes, the photographer took pictures, and they left.

The rest of Saturday afternoon was chaotic, much like the past week. Dusk darkened the sky when Sherry and Stacy asked if they could walk to the convenience store to buy candy. Sherry could have driven her car to the store, so I knew their trip had nothing to do with candy. I realized that they needed time to themselves. The store was close by, so I agreed, but I watched them more carefully as they ambled down the sidewalk, worrying if I should let them walk alone. I gazed at my girls through the dining room windows I had opened to let in the cool breeze.

Suddenly a vehicle caught my eye. A distinctive white patrol car with green and gold lettering pulled in front of our house and stopped. My knees grew wobbly. I called to Ron in the next room. Two men climbed out of the Montana Yellowstone County Sheriff's patrol car dressed in casual clothes.

Ron and I greeted them at the door and asked them to come in. They introduced themselves. Ron recognized George Jensen as a former high school classmate, which was somewhat comforting.

After the introductions, George asked, "Would you like to have a family member or a clergyman join you? Maybe a friend?"

I knew they had bad news.

"Yes, we have a friend who lives close by." I called Al Ketterling and asked him to come over as soon as possible. My heart beat loud enough to make my ears ring. Al arrived within minutes. Everyone stiffly sat at the dining room table.

George did most of the talking while his partner jotted down information on his note pad.

"Please tell us that you found Lisa," I said.

"Well, Mrs. Kimmell, we have found a female that matches Lisa's general description. But we aren't certain if it's Lisa. We need physical details. Can you give us more information about her?"

Ron and I grasped each other's hands. "She's about five-foot-three, about a hundred and ten pounds. She has blue eyes and light brownish-blondish hair, about to here." I held my hand to my shoulder.

George and the other deputy nodded.

I continued. "She has a small scar on her left cheekbone from her childhood. And she has a permanent silver retainer on her lower teeth that the dentist put on after her braces were removed."

George sat silently. After a long pause he said, "Based on what you've told me, I'm pretty sure it's Lisa. Can you tell us where we can get a copy of her dental or medical records so we can make a positive identification?"

My eyes filled with tears as I gave him the names of her doctor and dentist. We had avoided the hardest question of all. I finally asked, "Can you tell us what happened to her?"

"Yes, ma'am," George said softly and paused again.

I saw the agony in his face before he answered the question.

"She's been murdered. She was found in the North Platte River this afternoon."

I'm sure our screams of anguish and horror could be heard for miles around. I had to abruptly run to the bathroom and vomit. It took me awhile to compose myself and go back to the dining room.

The deputies were still staring at the floor when I returned. George said it wouldn't be official until they could make a positive ID through medical records, but they were sure enough to tell us that we should notify close family and friends. Her dental retainer seemed to be the most obvious clue.

The only details we learned Saturday night was that Lisa had been stabbed and dumped into the North Platte River about twenty miles southwest of Casper. We would later learn that she was dropped from the Old Government Bridge, an abandoned service overpass only used by county workers and fishermen. The bridge was made of steel, as cold as the water beneath it.

Sherry and Stacy had returned to the house just in time to hear our screams from the street. They were terrified, not knowing what to do. When they finally gathered enough courage to come inside, Al ushered them downstairs until we could gain the strength and composure to tell them what happened.

After the deputies left, we called the girls into the living room and sat them on the couch. We knelt on the floor before them and held their hands, Ron before Sherry, and I before Stacy. We told them that we had bad news. Lisa had been found. She had been murdered. They gasped and began to cry.

After that, we needed to notify our close family and friends before they heard on the ten o'clock news about a body being found. Ron called Clyde Praye to cancel their plans for the following morning. Lisa had been discovered in a river not far from Casper, just as he had visualized.

EASTER SUNDAY, APRIL 3rd, 1988

Sleep had been elusive for us, but Saturday night we barely closed our eyes except to cry. Even our cat, Kisha, mournfully yowled throughout the night as she wandered to each of our bedrooms to check on us.

Those who hadn't heard the news awoke Easter morning to Billings' blaring front-page newspaper headlines, "Lawmen recover body of woman." The reporter speculated that it was Lisa and included the interview with Ron and me from Saturday. In the interview we gave, the reporter had asked us if we had made any plans for Easter. We said, "No, we hadn't even thought about meals most of the week, let alone made any plans for Easter."

The support of family, friends, and the community throughout the week had been a source of strength for us. Easter Sunday took on a new dimension, one of comfort and compassion. It started out with two little neighbor boys who brought us an encouraging card and a homemade Easter basket fashioned out of a cardboard box, covered with construction paper, and filled with candy for the girls. That special gift was followed by countless phone calls. A stream of visitors stopped by the house offering their condolences and sharing portions of their Easter dinners with us. Everyone vowed to help us find who had murdered our precious daughter.

The compassion and generosity of our loved ones shifted our focus from anger about the evil murder to the blessings of loving people.

My Saddest and "Gladdest" Easter

(I originally wrote this story for a children's magazine.)

When I think of Easter, I remember making special preparations days and the evening before for a meal that all would boast and tout. I remember coloring Easter eggs, then hiding them all about. That is the way most of our Easters went, until April 3rd, 1988; it is one I will never forget. It was my saddest, but "gladdest" of all Easters, yet.

The day before the Easter of '88, we learned that we lost our Lisa, a precious child of just eighteen. She was one of the sweetest young people that you could have ever met or seen. The news hit us hard; we were very sad and it made our hearts go wild. Lisa's life should not have been cut so short. She was such a kind, caring, and loving child.

We were asked if we had planned anything for Easter the next day. All we could say was "no, but we'll deal with it the best we can anyway." That evening, I did not color any Easter eggs, because you see, I could barely stand on my own two shaky legs. To celebrate Easter as we had done in the past was now an unbearable and unthinkable task. The news of Lisa's sad and painful passing spread as quickly as the speed of light and we did our best to endure a long sleepless night.

Easter morning I was awakened by a knock at the door. When I answered, there stood two small neighborhood boys that I had never met before. They couldn't have been older than nine or ten. They said that they were thinking about how sad we must have been. They presented me a small handmade Easter basket filled with candy. They thought that for our other kids at home, it might come in handy. They explained that they had plenty of Easter goodies to share. Yet I sensed that they just wanted us to know that they really did care.

I was stunned, speechless, and I must have looked a scary sight with my swollen eyes after a long tearful night. They set down their Easter basket before me on the doorstep, then without another word, they fled off into the Easter morning's sunlight.

I picked up the basket and took it inside. I didn't think I had any more tears left in me, but I couldn't help it, I cried. I still keep the card they enclosed with the smiley face and balloons they had drawn, that was meant to bring us cheer. Those two little boys—I will always hold them dear. I learned a greater lesson of what Easter is really all about, be it humble, meek, and mild. It was a grand life lesson and I learned it from a small, caring child.

Since then, many Easters have come and passed. The memory of those two little boy's generous kindness has and will, forever last. Yes, it was the saddest but "gladdest" Easter we have ever had, because two little boys showed us that the good in us tries to outweigh the bad.

May God bless and keep the little children.

CHAPTER 3

Grief

LOSING MORE THAN ONE

Lightning is not supposed to strike twice, but it struck our family twofold with a brutal force. When we found out that Lisa was murdered, it brought back the pain of losing our only son in a blameless accident. Ricky had been three years old.

In the summer of 1976, life was hectic, with four children, close in age. Ron and I had been married eight years, long enough to feel distanced from each other. Our relationship had shifted into the parental phase. We used Citizen's Band (CB) radios. Our CB "handles" reflected our state of mind. My handle was "Domestic Engineer." Ron picked "Curtain Climber" because sometimes the kids made him want to literally climb the curtains. I had a ton of housework, and Ron worked long hours to care for his big family.

We decided to take a second honeymoon in July to reconnect. We had close friends who could baby-sit for our four active children. Barb and Al Ketterling had three kids about the same ages of ours, and Barb was a natural mother. They agreed to house-sit for a week, caring for the kids and the pets.

Al and Barb made an interesting pair. Barb was an attractive young mother, blonde-haired, somewhat introverted and softhearted. Al had a domineering, outspoken personality. He was a tough, macho cop, but he also had a big heart. We could count on Barb and Al.

We had planned our second honeymoon around our boat, a black Leecraft twenty-five-foot cabin cruiser called the "El Dorado." We hoped for a relaxing week of fishing, and swimming. It would be an inexpensive vacation, and the lake was only a few hours' drive from our house. Ron and I looked forward to our time together.

The week before, Ron had taken the boat to Reiter's Marina to have it serviced. The day we were to leave for the trip, Al, Barb, and their three children came over early in the morning to help us with the last-minute details.

Ron had recently bought a large white construction van to transport his heavy work equipment. We only had a tiny Datsun truck that Ron used on a daily basis, and it wasn't big enough to tow the boat for long distances. We planned to drive the van to the lake.

That warm Sunday morning, Ron had pulled the van into the driveway and opened the back doors so I could load it with our necessities. He and Al drove to the marina to pick up the boat.

Barb said she would feed the kids breakfast and get them dressed while I washed my hair under the tap in the sink. The seven children scurried all over the place, noisy and full of life. That changed in a split second.

Suddenly the kids ran inside, screaming, "The van's rolling backwards!"

Barb's daughter and my son, Ricky, had climbed into the van to play. Somehow the children slipped the van out of gear. When the vehicle moved, Ricky panicked and jumped out the back. That was a long drop for a small child. He couldn't get up in time.

I ran as fast as I could, soap and water streaming down my face. I got to the driveway just in time to see Ricky run over by the dual wheels of the van. A snapshot of that horror is forever burned into my memory. He went limp, and everyone screamed in disbelief.

Panic-stricken, I picked him up, raced him into the house, and frantically called 911. Ricky turned gray as I begged them to hurry. Ron and Al drove up just before the ambulance arrived.

The disaster became a blur. Paramedics arrived and hustled Ricky away. We raced behind the ambulance to the hospital.

Hysterical, I screamed over and over, "My God, Ron. He's going to die!"

Ron tried to remain calm and optimistic. "Honey, he's going to be okay."

I prayed, "Please, dear God, don't let him die."

I knew that a three-year-old's fragile body wouldn't survive the weight of those crushing wheels. I was right. He died from massive internal injuries shortly after arriving at the hospital.

Life went numb. I barely recall the funeral, but I do remember that Ron, the girls, and I each placed a yellow rose on his casket to signify that he had been a ray of sunshine in our lives.

For a while, I lost my faith in God and all that I had believed. I had been raised to think that if I prayed hard enough, God would fix things. I heard the traditional clichés—for example, "God never gives you more than you can handle." Losing Ricky *was* more than I could handle. Why couldn't He give me one of those miracles that the preachers talked about? Why did He take my son? Giving His only son was fine, but why did He take mine? I'm too selfish. What did I do to deserve that?

Those questions churned in my thoughts a million times. It took me years to get over my anger and come to terms with God.

After Ricky's funeral, Ron and I struggled to make amends when our relationship was already stressed. We were both overloaded with guilt. We blamed each other as well as ourselves.

What could I have done differently? Why didn't Ron know that the emergency brake didn't work or wasn't set? Why was he gone? Why did I have to be washing my hair at that moment? Why? Why? Why?

The second honeymoon that we had hoped would fix our problems ended up tearing us apart. Shortly after the accident, Ron and I separated. I needed space to work through my anger, guilt, and grief, and I asked him to leave. Becoming a reluctant bachelor, Ron moved into a small, sparsely-furnished apartment.

At first, Ron and I barely spoke to each other. But as the weeks passed, time healed each of us enough to ease the rage. He still came over frequently to check on the girls and me, and I found myself missing him. He was the only man I had ever loved, and I didn't want to lose him. I knew that he loved me, too. Neither of us wanted a divorce.

We began by dating again, almost like starting from scratch. We would go out to dinner and talk about our feelings. We listened to each other for the first time in years. We wanted to work things out, but we didn't ignore our past problems.

We had made vows when we married. They weren't goals. They were commitments. We also knew that the girls were hurting. They weren't standing at the altar when we vowed, "for better or for worse." Our three young daughters had lost their brother, and they thought they were losing their daddy, too. They weren't old enough to understand.

Letting go of the anger and blame was a process, not a one-time event. If there was a defining moment of reconciliation, it happened when I was at his place on a cold evening in December. Ron had taken only the bare necessities with him to his bachelor pad. One evening I had to stop by his apartment. When I arrived, he had been making a survey of his pitifully bare living room, and he said, "If I have to stay here any longer, do you think you could at *least* help me decorate it?"

I couldn't help but laugh and said, "Yes, you could use a decorator or a change of scenery." Then I paused. "I have a better idea. Why don't you come back home?"

He moved home the next day. The hardship that nearly broke up our marriage ended up strengthening it over the years. However, losing our son did not prepare us for losing Lisa. Nothing can prepare a parent for the death of a child. Each loss has a depth of pain that seems insufferable regardless of the circumstances. Time may decrease the intensity, but the ache remains. We will never got *over* it, but we must get *past it*. We learned to move on with life. We had jobs, children to raise, and birthdays to celebrate.

The most important lesson for Ron and me was that everyone *must* give themselves and their family members permission to grieve at their own pace and in their own way. Sometimes I wanted to talk about Ricky when Ron didn't. I had a tendency to vocalize my feelings, whereas Ron internalized his. Then the next week the feelings might be reversed. We weren't always on the same page at the same time, but that didn't mean that we didn't care about each other's feelings, and eventually we learned not to take the differences personally.

We found that friends and extended family had a difficult time with grieving, too. If Ricky's name came up in a conversation, the room fell silent. People often didn't know what to say. Even though we were greatly saddened by our loss, we didn't want to forget him or pretend that he never existed in our lives. We were heartbroken at the loss, but Ricky also left us with delightful memories that I wanted to share with others who were comfortable talking about it.

I found it difficult to answer the simplest question, "How many children do you have?" In my heart, the answer is four. Ricky died, but his memory didn't. Even though we managed to get *past* Ricky's death, we were not prepared for what was to come.

ANOTHER FUNERAL

Hundreds of people attended Lisa's funeral in Billings at two o'clock on Friday, April 8th, 1988. Former classmates, family, friends, and people we didn't know flocked to the church for the services and to graveyard for the burial. People hugged each other and wept. Many held hands and sang hymns. The day was sunny and clear, but a cold wind blew outside as the mile-and-a-half procession made its way to the cemetery. The services were brief. Before Lisa's casket was lowered into the ground, Ron, the girls, and I each placed a red rose on her casket, then one yellow rose for her brother, Ricky, who was buried a few yards away.

The Bailey Company held a memorial service in Denver for Lisa's coworkers and friends earlier in the day, but we couldn't attend both.

The funeral made me wonder again: what had Ron and I done to deserve losing two children? Why was God angry with us? I was angry with God for allowing this horrible thing to happen to Lisa.

A card we received from a stranger began our healing process and put things in perspective. It read: "The deeds of men are not acts of God, but instead acts of God's gift of free will. What a terrible thing to do with such a gift."

Another friend gave us the book *When Bad Things Happen to Good People*, by Harold Kushner. It explained unresolved issues for us. We finally realized that God wasn't punishing us; He was weeping with us. God didn't *cause* Ricky's accident or let it happen. God is not a magician who rescues people at the last minute, as much as we want Him to. Accidents and violence are part of this life on planet Earth. God comforts us spiritually, not always physically.

God gave all mankind the gift of free will, including the wicked.

Someone chose to murder Lisa, and God was troubled to see His gift of free will abused.

To someone who has lost a child, survived a senseless murder, or witnessed other horrible events, Kushner's concepts are healing words. We believe that God has a *righteous* wrath, but Kushner believes that God does not punish people by making terrible things happen *to* them or to their innocent loved ones.

In one chapter, Kushner says it's okay to be angry with God. That was a relief after my cursing session atop the Rimrocks the night before Lisa's body was found. Kushner says, "Actually, being angry at God won't hurt God, and neither will it provoke Him to take measures against us. If it makes us feel better to vent our anger at Him over a painful situation, we are free to do it. The only thing wrong with doing it is that what happened to us was not really God's fault."

The card and the book helped me finally let go of the anger that I had held toward God for so many years.

The outpouring from people in different cities and states also helped us appreciate the good in the world. We have a cedar chest full of thoughtful cards from friends, Lisa's teachers and classmates, other victims of violent crimes, and people we've never met. A woman wrote, "Lisa's tragic death has touched so many people. We just wanted to let you know we care." She signed it, "the community."

During the first year after Lisa's murder, my family and I spent time trying to recover emotionally. We had learned to allow each person to grieve in different ways; however, there were times when our philosophy flew out the window.

We occasionally snapped and took our anger out on each other. Sherry didn't want to return to school right away, so I ended up home-schooling her for a month. On the other hand, Stacy turned to her friends for comfort. Sometimes every Kimmell was on a different page. There might be a day when someone wanted to talk about Lisa but no one else did. Sherry and Stacy were teenagers, not toddlers as when Ricky died. They went through disagreeable phases, too. We ended up choosing people outside the family to talk to when we didn't want to upset each other. Barb Ketterling was my confidant, and Al Ketterling was Ron's.

Sometimes I felt as though I had a split personality because of my rage at Lisa's killer. Ron and I are nurturing people. We have taken in family and friends when they needed a place to stay or to get on their feet. But I pictured Lisa's killer hanging from a noose in the town square. I wanted him dead—my intense anger scared me. Ron began carrying his gun. We would never act on those feelings, but the fury I often felt made me question my sanity.

People have told us over the years that they admired how strong we were in dealing with the tragedies. There were many days when we didn't feel strong. Our strength came from the people who supported us. During our deepest and darkest times, it was as if a legion of angels had been dispatched to embrace us when we needed them the most.

PART II

Fourteen Years
of
Investigations

CHAPTER 4

The First Year

PRACTICAL MATTERS

After the funeral, Ron, the girls, and I decided to go to my Denver apartment for a few days to get away from the chaos. Not only did we need quiet time, but we also had to attend to practical matters. I had been asked to collect anything relevant to the case and take it to Dan Tholson and Jim Broz, the two Natrona County detectives assigned to our case. They asked for letters she might have received from Ed Jaroch or *anything* that might be helpful.

The day after we arrived at the Denver apartment I had shared with Lisa, Ron took Sherry and Stacy to the Denver Zoo and the Natural History Museum while I sorted and packed Lisa's belongings. It was sickening to see my daughter's life reduced to boxes of stuff. Every item, even her house slippers, took on sentimental meanings that I had not expected.

After a couple of quiet days, we headed back to Billings, stopping in Casper to drop off letters and other items to Dan and Jim. We had met them after Lisa's body was found, but I was distracted, to put it mildly. I was more composed at our second meeting and paid attention to whom we would be working with. Dan was an attractive young man close to the age of thirty. He had thinning blonde hair, a mustache, and a gentle demeanor. He seemed shy for a law officer. In contrast, Jim was outspoken, tall, and lanky, with thick dark hair. Their differences seemed to work for them, and they made a good team.

43

For the next couple of weeks, we had to focus on other matters, such as being legally appointed as executors of Lisa's estate. This would allow us to pay her taxes and debts. The car was considered a stolen vehicle, and her insurance covered that. We met with her bank manager to sort things out. During this process, we discovered that Lisa had also taken out a credit life insurance policy. Who would have thought that our eighteen-year-old daughter would be so sensible or even think about death at such a young age? The credit life insurance covered her funeral expenses almost to the dime. She unintentionally paid for her own funeral.

We spent a month sorting things out. Our checking account was overdrawn from spending money on expenses such as the airplane charters, and long distance phone bills. Most people don't realize how a crime financially affects the families of victims. During the eight days we searched for Lisa, we didn't care what it cost. We weren't rich and we weren't poor, but the expenses eventually caught up with us, and they were shocking. We were grateful to those who offered their help to defray the costs. Some people, like the pilots of the chartered planes, contributed time and only asked for reimbursement of gas and other expenses. Many caring citizens pitched into the "Help Find Lil' Miss" fund.

We came to understand that other families or victims of crime may not get the same media exposure as Lisa's case, and they may not have access to the resources we had. Our hearts go out to families who never find their loved ones, or who don't have either the time or money to search. A crime against an innocent victim is truly a crime against society.

The Investigation Continued

Ron and I did what we could to help Dan Tholson and Jim Broz by forwarding tips to them. We were told that law officers from different agencies were doing the same. Less than a week after Lisa's body was found, more than 350 car sightings had been reported. People from California to Canada had called in. Dan and Jim did the best they could investigating Lisa's case. Both men were committed and caring.

Our first meeting with Sheriff Ron Ketchum was a different story. We attended a Crime Stoppers press conference on May 5, 1988. Ketchum was there, a good-looking man with dark eyes and dark hair, but he was aloof; even in this casual setting, he was all decked out in dress whites with his gun in his holster. He politely shook our hands, but it seemed like he was just doing his public duty.

During the next few weeks, Natrona County law enforcement appeared to be following through, according to the media reports Ketchum released. They used hypnosis on car-sighting witnesses, found pilots to fly over the area to look for the car, and asked ranchers to search their land. Ketchum also had artists create composite sketches of men with whom Lisa was allegedly seen in the Casper area. However, Ketchum elected not to release those because he didn't think they would help the public. One of the pictures resembled a young man who owned another black Honda CRXsi. The man's wife also happened to resemble Lisa. (Eventually this young couple's car would be used by *Unsolved Mysteries* in their TV reenactment of the crime.)

The biggest problem for *all* of the law officers was the vast amount of terrain involved in Lisa's disappearance. She left Denver, she disappeared somewhere between Douglas and Cody, and we lived in Billings. Her planned route spanned more than 600 miles in three states, making jurisdiction a touchy issue.

We didn't realize that jurisdictional boundaries have plagued law enforcement agencies for ages. Computers have brought law enforcement a long way, but they weren't widespread in 1988. Ketchum's office didn't even own one. Ron and I didn't understand the territorial nature of the county sheriff's office versus the city police department versus federal agents. We were frustrated. Who could blame us? Our daughter had been savagely raped and murdered.

To bridge the distance, a "liaison" was formed in Billings. Law officers in Montana, both federal and local, were told to forward tips to Detective George Jensen at the Yellowstone County Sheriff's Office, who would then forward them to Dan or Jim. In our eyes, this created more bureaucracy and wasted time, but it was necessary to keep the information organized. So we thought.

As the weeks passed and no murder suspect was found, Ron and I grew discouraged, and so did many citizens in Casper. A killer was out there somewhere. Would he strike again? People were worried. Rumors spread about cult involvement. Dan later said that he and Jim had to work undercover at the Midsummer's Eve Festival and on Halloween because people were afraid that their children would get snatched up like Lisa had been. An editorial in the *Billings Gazette* called the killer a, "sad, sick, perverted splinter of our society." A reader (Kim) of the *Gazette* wrote: "We as people can only hope and pray that these murderers get the justice they deserve, that all the efforts of the police and surrounding communities pay off and bring the ones responsible for this tragedy to a stop."

Fisher's Construction Company and the *Billings Gazette* started a reward fund to help solve the case. My family is eternally grateful to everyone who pitched in to raise the money. Arby's designated April 24th, 1988, as a day whose sales they would contribute to the fund. We appreciated the support of The Bailey Company, and I'm proud to have worked for such a caring firm. The goal was $3,000, but the drive raised $5,589 among all the Arby's in Billings and Casper. My family and I ate our Sunday meal at the Billings location and planned to help bus the tables, but the employees wouldn't let us. We spent our time getting hugs and words of encouragement from the community. We realized how deeply Lisa's murder had affected others. The emotions were overwhelming.

By the end of April, the reward had grown to more than $10,000, but the money didn't make a difference. Six weeks later, Ketchum reported to the media that the leads had dried up. The only newsworthy suspects in late April were two men, escapees from a South Dakota minimum-security prison, who were caught burglarizing a laundry in Lovell, Wyoming. The two were driving a stolen car containing cash, two guns, knives, stolen license plates and drugs, but they were ruled as suspects in Lisa's murder.

During the summer of 1988 the reward grew to $25,000. We realized that Lisa's murder wasn't Ketchum's only case. Naively, we expected that Sheriff Ketchum would welcome help from other agencies because public pressure was mounting; people wanted results. Crime Stoppers had become involved, and the media kept the story alive. Ketchum responded by saying he wasn't giving up, but there was "nothing concrete" after six months of investigations, and finding Lisa's car was considered to be a critical point.

When we shared our concerns with Natrona County authorities about a lack of suspects, Ketchum's attitude toward us became tense. We began to think he had been elected to an office that was unequipped and understaffed to handle a murder case like Lisa's. We think that when Lisa's death rallied the anger and fears of citizens in his county and from different parts of the nation, Ketchum's personality wasn't suited to deal with the attention.

Determined to get justice and catch someone we believed might kill again, Ron and I decided to call the television show *Unsolved Mysteries*. They received hundreds of calls every year. Some cases were more "interesting" than others, according to the selection process. Would Lisa's case attract their attention? We were relieved when they said yes. In October of 1988, the filming began. We found out quickly that Casper was tuned in. When the cameras filmed the black Honda CRXsi, made up to look like Lisa's car, phones rang the dispatcher at the city police and at the sheriff's office. A city cop unaware of the filming even called in a sighting.

We knew before the show aired that we would meet all kinds of people: good, bad, greedy, and strange. However, we weren't prepared for the afternoon of September 12th, 1988.

About two o'clock I was home alone when a knock sounded at the front door. I answered it. A man, dark-haired, stocky, about six feet tall, and dressed in a gray tee shirt and jeans, introduced himself as "Jethro" and said that he had information that might lead to Lisa's killer. He wasn't threatening, but nervous. I invited him in to sit at the dining room table and tell me about it. In retrospect, I shouldn't have let him in the door, but I would have done almost anything to find out what happened to my daughter. A child's murder often blinds a parent to risk.

Jethro said that he knew about people in a drug ring who might have information about Lisa's death. He said he knew of a woman who allegedly had possession the crystal teardrop that hung from Lisa's rearview mirror. The man said he had been "sent" to us by a reliable source. I took a few notes, his name, phone number, and then told him I would turn the information over to the police. He agreed and left. He wasn't there long, but the incident shook Ron and me up. We weren't familiar with drug rings, and we knew that Lisa was outspokenly opposed to drugs.

We didn't know that the mysterious Jethro would be just one test, merely warming us up for what was to come.

CHAPTER 5

Clues

SPRING 1989

The Montana foliage wasn't the only thing to go dormant during the fall and winter of 1988-89. Few solid leads came in. Dan and Jim focused on investigating tips and criminals with records of sexual assault.

In December, a Casper lawyer demonstrated that good could shine on the dimming case. Hugh Duncan, a former assistant prosecutor and active community member, was so outraged about the crime that he offered a personal $5,000 reward to anyone who could help officials find the missing Honda, above and beyond the Crime Stoppers' reward. The *Casper Star Tribune* quoted Duncan as saying, "Somebody has to do something, so I decided it might as well be me."

Otherwise, the headlines only told of the growing reward fund, how the case was at a "standstill," and that Natrona County was "out of fresh leads." That was about to change.

NBC's *Unsolved Mysteries* aired Lisa's segment on prime time television, Wednesday, March 15th, 1989. Detective Jim Broz had flown to California on behalf of Natrona County, and the segment brought in a record number of 579 calls. The Natrona County switchboard fielded more than fifty local calls.

Sheriff Ron Ketchum needed leads? He got 'em!

Imagine our surprise when the headlines of the Sunday, March 19th, *Billings Gazette* read, "No Clues," and Natrona investigators were said to have "no solid leads in the brutal homicide."

49

What?

By Tuesday, March 21st, more than one thousand tips had been called in. We realized that many were frivolous, such as the man who was reported to say that a "hitchhiker did it," or the woman who saw "teenagers acting suspicious and silly in a grocery store." Ketchum saying that he had no solid leads worried Ron and me—Ketchum would not have had time to sort out what was credible and what wasn't. Furthermore, we were getting frequent calls at work and home from people and law officers saying that no one from Natrona had followed up on their tips.

The wife of a sheriff in Buffalo, Wyoming, was certain she had seen Lisa's car because she said she followed it for several blocks, noting the personalized plates. She even pulled up next to the car to see who was driving. She saw a young woman who fit Lisa's description, alone in the car. She was never interviewed.

A man working at a gas station in Buffalo said that he saw Lisa accompanied by a small-built young man with a dark complexion. Never interviewed.

A woman in Casper insisted that she saw Lisa driving her car the weekend she was reported missing. The woman said she noted the license plates because she had a puppy with the same name. Never interviewed. The list went on.

Had any of these people seen Lisa's car, her killer or killers? Based on facts from the trial, we are doubtful that they saw her after she was abducted, but we wish the tips had been investigated.

On Tuesday afternoon, March 28th, 1989, another clue appeared that—we now know—could have cracked the case.

At that time I carried a pager and had instructed my employees, family, and friends that if something was urgent, to add 911 to the end of their message. About 4:40 P.M., I received a 911 call on my pager from Terry Schlenker, one of Lisa's friends in Billings. I was in Denver working; I called her back as soon as I could from my office.

Terry had become one of Lisa's good friends before Lisa moved to Denver. Terry managed a Billings Arby's and had a charming sense of humor and contagious laughter. She was closer to my age, but age didn't matter to Lisa. Terry was the friend Lisa had planned to see in the hospital.

The Tuesday afternoon that Terry called, she sounded shaken. "I went to Lisa's grave today with some flowers and I saw something taped to her headstone. Sheila, it was so weird that I didn't even leave the flowers. I didn't want to touch anything."

"What was it, dear?"

"A very strange note."

Terry told me that she couldn't remember everything it said, other than that it was signed "Stringfellow Hawke." We were accustomed to finding flowers or cards when we visited Lisa's grave, but the note sounded disturbing, and I became concerned. Ron had a car phone, but that old dinosaur only reached Ron if he was in the car. By the time I returned to my apartment in Denver and I found Ron at home, it was late. I told him about the note. It was too dark for Ron to drive out to Lisa's grave that evening. He said he would go first thing in the morning.

Early Wednesday, Ron drove to the gravesite. The peaceful cemetery it's in is filled with lush green grass and budding trees in the summer. In the harsh Montana winters, however, it turns bleak and gray. That morning it was bitterly cold. Ron parked the car and walked apprehensively to the headstone. What he found was more chilling than the gusts of wind.

Someone had securely taped a handwritten note to Lisa's headstone and sealed it in clear plastic as though attempting to weatherproof it. It was dated 11-13-88, but Ron knew it had not been there since November. We had been to the grave within the past few weeks and we would have seen it.

It read:

Lisa -   11-13-88
    There are'nt words to
say how much you're missed
The pain never leaves
it's so hard without you
you'll alway be alive in
me.
Your death is my painful
loss but heavens sweet
gain   Love Always
        Stringfellow Hawke

Ron was uneasy. The spelling and punctuation suggested that the writer lacked education. Lisa's friends were educated. It also implied an intimate relationship. The note wasn't threatening, but it was odd and out of place. It simply didn't "fit." Ron knew it was significant, and his heart raced as he returned to his car.

The cemetery was within the city limits, so he called the Billings police. The dispatcher simply said, "Sir, if it's a problem, take it off."

Ron tried to explain, but he couldn't get through to the dispatcher that this might be a murder clue. Lisa's murder wasn't their case—another jurisdictional dilemma. Ron called Detective George Jensen at Yellowstone County, but Jensen wasn't in. Ron didn't want to leave without the note. Frustrated and cold to the core, Ron called Al Ketterling from his car phone.

Al said, "Go ahead and take it off, Ron, but be careful not to touch it. Put it in an envelope or something and hand-deliver it to George Jensen."

Ron took Al's advice. He returned to the headstone and carefully peeled it off with a penknife, his trembling fingers numb without gloves. His eyes watered in the wind. Touching only a corner, he placed it in a company envelope from his glove compartment and drove to the Yellowstone County Sheriff's Office.

By then, George had returned and processed the evidence. After Ron left, George wrote a report and sent it to Natrona County.

We soon discovered that Stringfellow Hawke was a reclusive character that Jan-Michael Vincent played in the 1980s hit TV series *Airwolf*. Hawke was a loner and had a chauvinistic attitude toward women. People he loved either died or abandoned him, particularly his love interest in each episode. He always emerged as a hero. At the end of the hour, he would play his cello as an eagle sailed above him on the wind. How on earth did that fit into Lisa's relationships, or perhaps her murder?

Dan said that he and Jim would look into the matter. They found a teenager in Billings who called himself Stringfellow Hawke, but the kid was too young and had been living in an institution for more than a year. That ruled him out.

It's a shame they didn't pursue the clue further. We would find out fourteen years later that the writer was indeed the killer.

THE BACKGROUND OF STRINGFELLOW HAWKE

For readers who are interested, the following describes the premiere of *Airwolf,* a TV movie/series pilot that debuted January 2nd, 1984, after the Los Angeles Raiders beat the Washington Redskins 38-9 in Super Bowl XVIII. Stringfellow Hawke was the protagonist of the show. Ron and I have no clue why Lisa's killer related to Stringfellow Hawke or how she fit into his fantasy world. We'll let you draw your own conclusions.

Airwolf's opening scene spotlights the eerie sounds of wind and chopper blades echoing off barren canyon walls of a desert. A haunting theme song plays as the camera cuts to weapons mounted on the supersonic helicopter, then to three men who resemble alien pilots. The men board Airwolf and punch menacing buttons. The turbo engine rockets the helicopter to the speed of sound. The three men are bad guys who blow up Americans and then escape to Libya to party.

When the audience meets Stringfellow Hawke, the reclusive hero of the series, he's strumming a sad melody on his Stradivarius cello to a lone American eagle circling a beautiful lake. Stringfellow lives in a cozy mountain cabin nearby. He's content with the company of wild animals and his dog, Tet.

Airwolf targeted a male market with its war stories involving the high tech helicopter that could repel blasts from tanks and blow up the worst of Middle Eastern terrorists. Similar shows were popular, *Blue Thunder* and *The A-Team,* but none featured a handsome but morose mountain hero like Stringfellow Hawke.

Jan-Michael Vincent was born on July 15th, 1944, in Denver and later struggled with bad publicity over alleged use of drugs and alcohol and abuse of women.

"String" was a hunter of few words; when he spoke, he had a gruff but sexy voice. He fished on the lake and sometimes sustained himself on trout.

The emotional appeal of *Airwolf* was rooted in the romantic plot of the movie. After the bad guy hijacked the helicopter, the "secret" CIA agency's (F.I.R.M.) contact man, Archangel, asks Stringfellow to help get it back. Stringfellow is the only man besides the bad guy who can fly Airwolf. When Archangel makes his proposal to Stringfellow, he brings along a beautiful F.I.R.M. woman, Gabrielle (Belinda Bauer), to help persuade Stringfellow to take the assignment. The moment Gabrielle steps out of the F.I.R.M. helicopter, she shakes her long, wavy brown hair. Stringfellow rudely resists her charms, chuckling when Tet looks up Gabrielle's dress. Despite String's crude nature, Gabrielle is attracted to him.

While Archangel is alone with Gabrielle, he explains Stringfellow's background.

"Gabrielle, don't get interested in Stringfellow Hawke. There's no future in it for you or any woman."

"Why not?"

"When he was twelve, he and his parents were in a boating accident on the lake. They drowned. Just before he shipped out to Vietnam, he and his girlfriend were in a car crash. She died. In 'Nam, he and his brother went down in the same mission. He got picked up; St. John didn't. Stringfellow is afraid that anyone he loves, or might love, will die. That's why, when he was so cold to you yesterday, I knew he liked you." Archangel pauses. "How's that for some paperback psychology?"

Despite Stringfellow's fears, Gabrielle's beauty wins him over, and he falls in love again. She promises not to die like the others, but of course the script calls for her to do something stupid, and she dies in his arms.

A notable dialogue in the *Airwolf* movie takes place when co-star Dom (Ernest Borgnine) brings groceries and other supplies to Stringfellow's isolated cabin.

Dom is introduced to Gabrielle as she walks downstairs (pulling a sweater over her head as though she's just getting dressed), and she offers to carry some of the supplies. Dom refuses, saying he's opposed to women's lib. Gabrielle says he has a right to his views as long as he has brought red meat—String could only offer her helpings of trout that he had caught in the lake. She wouldn't eat the trout—they were too beautiful. As she's helping unpack the groceries, she blurts out, "Bless your heart, I haven't had anything but vegetables for six days."

An old-fashioned Dom pauses. "Six days?" He asks loudly, stunned that Stringfellow and Gabrielle had been sleeping together.

She smiles and nods her head.

Six days was all that Gabrielle and Stringfellow had together before he fell in love, they parted, and she was killed.

CHAPTER 6

Confrontations

A HOSTILE SHERIFF

I'm a sentimental person, and anniversaries are important to me. After the one-year anniversary of Lisa's death passed and no progress had been made, Ron and I grew impatient. Ketchum had said to us, "One hundred people working on the case wouldn't be enough." We agreed!

We would find out later that Ketchum was barely involved in the daily investigations, although when he communicated to the press, he made it sound as though he were in charge. We knew Dan and Jim were working hard, but we didn't know how hard. Dan and Jim spent every day studying the files of known sexual predators in the county and following up the hundreds of tips. Dan had even contacted detectives on the case of the Green River murders to see if anything clicked. However, Ketchum restricted their searching to some degree. Jim told me that Ketchum would not allow them to travel to Denver or Billings to question Lisa's friends. Jim said Ketchum told them, "That's what the telephone is for."

Dan and Jim spoke to us freely in the beginning, but that changed. As the tension mounted between Ketchum and Ron and me, Ketchum demanded that his employees quit telling us about the department's progress. We were livid. This case concerned my daughter's death and could cost the lives of other young women. Ron and I wanted answers, not just for us, but for the community. I had to call Dan and Jim at home when I needed to talk to them. It didn't have to be that way.

I understand Sheriff Ketchum must have felt a lot of pressure from the media and the public as time passed and the case remained unsolved. Only three weeks after Lisa was found, the *Casper Star-Tribune* published an article with the headline, "Sheriff still stymied by teen's murder." The first paragraph read, "Sheriff Ron Ketchum says he has no idea who killed the Billings, Mont., teenager." Other articles read, "Out of fresh leads," or "Kimmell death still unsolved."

Weeks went by, and Ketchum had nothing new to report. Months elapsed. Rumors flew about a satanic cult connection, drug wars, or a car theft ring, and some people "heard" that a law officer was involved. It was unbearable to Ron and me.

The hardest gossip I had to deal with was when someone asked me, "Is it true that they cut Lisa's heart out?" To calm our fears, Ketchum wouldn't tell us what had happened to Lisa. He was adamant about keeping the details about her death a secret. He said it would jeopardize the case. As her parents we had a right to know, but at that point we were more concerned about catching Lisa's killer than forcing Ketchum to divulge his "secrets."

In short, we didn't think Natrona County could solve Lisa's case alone. Ron and I decided that forming a task force might help. In my business management experience, we created task forces frequently when faced with a complex problem. Lisa's case also involved at least two states. In our opinion, that justified bringing in federal agencies that would have the resources that Natrona lacked. We weren't sure where to start.

I called Rita Munzenrider, a *Billings Gazette* reporter who had become a friend and public relations mentor. Rita wisely suggested that I begin by contacting the Wyoming Attorney General's (AG) office in Cheyenne. I met with AG Joe Myer and explained our concerns that Natrona was under-manned and lacked technological resources. He supported our idea. He said he would talk to Governor Sullivan. The Governor was agreeable, as were U.S. Attorneys Peter Dunbar, Richard Stacy, David Kubichek, and the Congressman we contacted.

Natrona's sheriff's office was less enthusiastic. We told Dan and Jim about our goal of creating a task force, and they were obviously uncomfortable, probably knowing Ketchum wouldn't cooperate. I asked them to have Ketchum call us and arrange a meeting with him to discuss the idea. Ketchum called me early the morning of May 11th, 1989. His voice was terse. He agreed to meet with Ron and me the next day.

I was working in Denver and Ron was working in Billings, so we drove to Casper to meet at 1:00 P.M. and go into the meeting together. My instincts had made me distrust Ketchum by then, so I decided to tape the meeting. I stuck a mini-tape recorder in my purse and prepared for the worst.

When we finally faced Ketchum's grim expression, I felt as though I had been sent to the principal's office for bad behavior. Ron and I began trying to explain why we thought Natrona County needed a task force on Lisa's case. I said that after a year, we thought this would be a responsible direction for the investigation. My voice shook as he stared at me.

All Ketchum said was, "Why do you feel that way?"

I repeated myself, saying that Dan and Jim were qualified, but more than a year had passed and the case wasn't solved. "You could do some brainstorming and maximize your resources."

Ketchum's response sounded condescending. "I appreciate your concern. Who is giving you this advice?"

"The Attorney General and the others I have talked to said they would support such a concept but it…"

Ron added, "This was our idea. Nobody put us up to this."

Ketchum glared at us. "Do you know that in this county alone, I have three other homicides that have not been solved? I have a competent staff in this office. We have dealt with 110 different agencies around the United States, and we have followed up on over 3,000 leads. We have talked to or looked at 225 suspects. I will agree with you that this case is limited in information only because of specifics of the crime, but the people I have working for me are competent."

Ketchum continued to defend what Natrona was doing and had even asked Dr. James Thorpen (Doc), the Natrona County Coroner, to attend the meeting. Ketchum wanted someone to back up his statements that giving out information about Lisa's death would jeopardize the case. He focused on the importance of "controlling" the investigation.

Ketchum and I went around in circles. The longer the meeting went on, the angrier Ketchum and I became at each other. He got personal. He said he was "disappointed" that other agencies, including the AG's office, had not contacted him with their concerns. And he was disappointed in *us* for contacting the media.

I said, "I don't mean to interrupt, but we are not trying to attack your department."

"But you are. Let me finish." After more lecturing, he repeated his question, "I just want to know why you feel a task force would be any better than this office?"

Ron and I started over with our arguments. It led us nowhere.

Maybe hindsight is best when analyzing the May 12th meeting. Ron and I suspected that Lisa's murderer had killed before and would kill again. We didn't want other families to lose an innocent young daughter like we had. My instincts made me want to jump up and down on Ketchum's desk and *beg* him to seek outside help. I knew that Dan and Jim were competent, but they weren't trained to flush out this kind of killer. That's not an insult to anyone at Natrona County. Few investigators are trained to deal with a murder like Lisa's.

In his book *Serial Murder: Future Implications for Police Investigations*, Robert Keppel (the chief investigator on the Ted Bundy case), addresses the difficulty small law enforcement agencies have in solving serial murders. His introduction says this:

> Traditionally, police and sheriff departments are organized to prevent burglaries and robberies, intervene in family fights, control traffic and provide other public services. They are not specifically organized to catch serial killers, who typically are not limited by jurisdictional boundaries. The investigation of serial murder is usually unprecedented, an extremely frustrating and difficult task for most police agencies.

Sheriff Ketchum didn't want to face up to the difficulties; he focused on controlling the details of Lisa's case.

"I'm not going to have a task force from here to Montana and down to Colorado that I do not have control over," Ketchum said. "Whether it's me or any other administrator, and it only takes one, and [sic] I'm not going to have this running all over. There is some information that's unique to this case. It has *not* been given to the media; I'm *not* going to give it to the media, and I have control over that information, and it's done for a specific reason. But you want me to form this task force with all these people?

"And policemen are just as bad as anybody else in talking with anybody else about this information. The only reason it has not gotten out is because I have specifically said that I'll terminate anybody who releases the information. And I don't have the power to do that to Al Ketterling. And I guess I'm disappointed in *you*, knowing when you came down to talk to Dan and Jim that you brought Al Ketterling along."

That's when my temper flared. Nobody bad-mouths our friends. Ron and I told Ketchum that Al Ketterling was involved in the investigation *because* he was our friend. He was qualified in law enforcement and as a private investigator.

"Al Ketterling or you do *not* have the authority to ask anybody to be involved in this investigation. You are *not* a police officer," Ketchum said.

I became spitting mad, ready to walk out.

"Okay, I don't know if we really have anything else to go over at this time," I said. "I believe in this concept [the task force], and I'm going to pursue it."

That caused Ketchum and Doc Thorpen to launch into a long discussion about why details about Lisa's death were confidential. They said that only a suspect would know those details. Doc's comments about the limited samples of the DNA made sense. It would take several years before the results would be converted to a computerized file.

However, revealing details to the public was *not the issue*! Ron and I felt as though we were at a choir rehearsal singing different songs. Had it been Christmastime, we would have been belting out, "*Oh, Come, All Ye Faithful*," and Ketchum would have been yelling, "*Silent Night*."

After more lectures, Ketchum began to talk about not caring who solved the case. I didn't believe him. Then Ketchum ranted about Al Ketterling again.

Ron said, "Al's name seems to create animosity in you."

Suddenly Ketchum blurted out, "Do you know anything about Helter Skelter?"

"Yeah," Ron said.

"Do you know that the police department, the law enforcement agencies in that case bungled it? Do you know that?"

"No," Ron and I said simultaneously.

"Do you know about Son of Sam? That they bungled that? I don't want that to happen for *Lisa's*, if for nothing else, for *Lisa's* sake. Whoever did this crime, I want them to pay. I don't want the court over there to say to me that you can't admit this evidence because it wasn't done properly."

We didn't want an open season on the case. We simply wanted a responsible task force. He responded by saying that more people working case couldn't guarantee that the case would be solved. We continued in circles.

At the end of the conversation, we told him that as Lisa's parents, we had the right to know what happened to her, if only to dispel the rumors.

He raised his voice, "You have no rights; you weren't the victims—Lisa was!" He threatened us with "obstructing justice" if we continued to interfere in *his* case.

Ketchum appeared to think our meeting was a personal attack against him, his office, and his control of the investigation. No wonder Dan and Jim had concerns about us meeting with the sheriff.

The meeting was a turning point for Ron and me. Pride is one thing, but threatening a victim's parents like that is another. In our opinion, his obsession with control of the investigation was the primary obstruction to justice. Upon leaving, Ron and I traveled in our separate cars home to Billings. I cried the whole way.

FEDERAL INTEREST

Shortly after we returned home that evening, we received a call from Special Agent Don Flickinger (Flick) from the Federal Bureau of Alcohol, Tobacco and Firearms (ATF). He had been conducting an investigation of a drug trafficking ring and came across information that might be related to Lisa's case. He asked if he could meet with us to ask a few questions. We met "Flick" for the first time on May 12th, 1989, when he came to our house.

We discussed his information. It wasn't likely that it was related to

Lisa's murder, but there were interesting details to pursue. We also told him about our dreadful meeting with Sheriff Ketchum. He was appalled.

I wanted federal agencies to be part of our proposed task force, and suddenly I had a federal agent sitting in my living room vowing to do whatever it would take to help solve this crime. Ron and I interpreted Flick's appearance as a sign of hope.

Ron and I did not know about the numerous investigations already under way by law officers throughout the state. If Ketchum had confided in us, it would have saved everyone a lot of heartache. For example, we were not aware that during the previous summer (1988), a known drug dealer had contacted Flick. The dealer mentioned that he had seen Lisa's car parked near a "cousin's" home. Flick interviewed the drug dealer and his wife, wrote a report, and sent it to Natrona County, as did other law officers in Wyoming when they encountered anyone who said they had information about Lisa's case.

We were also unaware that Flick had spoken to U.S. Attorney Peter Dunbar (from Montana) on May 10th, two days before we met with Ketchum. Ketchum's lack of cooperation with other law enforcement agencies, and complaints about his failure to follow up on leads, had been trickling into the U.S. Attorney's office in Montana and Wyoming since the summer of 1988, long before the idea of a task force crossed our minds.

Flick renewed our optimism about creating a task force. Flick wrote a report and sent it to the U.S. Attorney's office. After U.S. Attorney Dunbar received Flick's report, Flick said he seemed "agitated" when he responded. Dunbar had been hearing repeated complaints about Ketchum. Dunbar promptly called the Wyoming U.S. Attorney's office. He and several officials decided to set up a task force meeting. A brutal, unsolved murder doesn't look good politically. The powers that be wanted it resolved as much as we did.

Before the task force met, Ketchum made a foolish trip to a third grade class in Buffalo, Wyoming. We couldn't believe our eyes when we read *The Blackboard*, a weekly newspaper that reported events in the Johnson County schools.

In an article titled, "*Sheriff Ron Ketchum shares with Sherry ___'s third-grade reading group,*" Ketchum told a class of nine-year-olds how our daughter was killed—details he wouldn't share with us. We were stunned. It was supposed to be confidential. Revealing her fatal injury might jeopardize the case, according to Ketchum.

The article described how a reading group had watched *Unsolved Mysteries* and became intrigued with Lisa's case. They wrote to Sheriff Ketchum to offer ideas about how to solve the mystery. He was so "impressed with the children's interest," he took Dan with him to Buffalo to personally talk to the kids.

I'm no psychology expert, but do nine-year-olds need to hear about blood on a bridge, or how an eighteen-year-old girl had been sexually assaulted? The gruesome details were bad enough, but he let it slip that "Lisa Marie had head wounds" — the same fact he'd kept so closely guarded.

Furthermore, Dan speculated that maybe Lisa had "stopped to pick up a hitchhiker or to help a stranger."

We respect Dan, but we know that Lisa would never have picked up a hitchhiker. When she had the wreck in Wheatland, Wyoming, she barely cracked her window for a state snowplow worker. Would she help a stranger? Maybe, but not on a dark road in the middle of nowhere. That implied to us that Natrona subconsciously believed Lisa's murder was partially her own fault. Blame the victim. Our blood boiled.

The entire incident hurt us deeply and fueled our anger toward Ketchum. Our growing unease would soon become a public battle.

THE TASK FORCE

Assistant U.S. Attorney, David Kubichek, contacted Flick in mid-May. A task force meeting was scheduled for May 23rd, 1989, in Sheridan, Wyoming. Flick wanted to invite Natrona County, but Kubichek was opposed. Because of Ketchum's history of volatile interactions with other law enforcement agencies, Flick reported that Kubichek "did not want the meeting to turn into a shouting match." The intention of the meeting was to compile the evidence and supply a thorough report to Natrona County. Ketchum was *not* going to be left "out of the loop."

Unaware of the approaching task force meeting, Dan Tholson was enthusiastic about the prospect of Don Flickinger's help. That changed when Dan called Flick on May 23rd, *during* the task force meeting. Dan wanted to know why Natrona wasn't invited. I am sure his feelings were hurt because he cared about the case—but Dan wasn't being left out, Ketchum was.

The task force meeting was successful, and furnished information to Natrona County. Flick was appointed as the lead contact for the task force, and yet he insisted on proper protocol before officially heading any investigation. When Ketchum learned of the meeting, he called a press conference for the next day, on Wednesday, May 24th. The politics turned ugly.

In a May 25th *Casper Star Tribune* article, Ketchum accused us ("Kimmell's relatives") of pressuring federal officials to create the task force. We didn't need to pressure anyone; Ketchum had earned his reputation with his bad temper.

Maybe he was upset, but he was wrong about several issues, and he should have kept his mouth shut. The *Star Tribune* article quoted him as saying, "We've been informed this morning that now they (federal officials) want to meet with us. The only reason that they do is because we found out that they had the meeting." That was never the case. The goals were to civilly round up evidence and provide Natrona County with a report. Civility may not have been possible with Ketchum there. The newspaper quoted him saying, "Coming back now, saying 'We have somebody that went up to the meeting and we'll bring (the information) back down to you,' that's *bull—-t*."

Ketchum also "speculated" that we were angry with his not telling us about Lisa's head wound. "I am not going to release that evidence" (to the Kimmells or other law enforcement agencies). "That's the only evidence that will eliminate or substantiate suspects."

Then why did he tell a third grade class about it?

Ketchum rambled to the press about how we hired a private investigator. He was wrong about that, too. Ron and I made that clear in the May 12th meeting. Al Ketterling was *not* conducting a separate investigation the way Ketchum claimed. If Al found any new information, he turned it over the proper agencies.

Ketchum also said that we had threatened him with a lawsuit if we didn't get the answers we wanted from him. We said we would have our private attorney call him after he threatened to arrest *us* for obstructing justice. Suggesting that we might hire an attorney was a statement on our part to distance ourselves from him and avoid further conflict. We never planned to sue him.

We feel that Ketchum's true motive for resenting outsiders ran deeper than his hurt feelings about a meeting. He was emotionally unstable (as he would prove with several suicide attempts), and he wanted to be in control. Ketchum seemed obsessed with control, an issue that came out during our meeting with him, and in his own words, according to the *Tribune*: "I guess I'm real reluctant to say to anybody in law enforcement, 'why don't you come in and help me,' because I don't have control over the case and that's an integral part—knowing what everybody else is doing, and right now I don't have any idea what they're doing."

We weren't the only ones to notice Ketchum's ego. A reader's editorial was published in the Casper newspaper on June 1st, 1989. Titled, "Gigantic crime overshadowed by sheriff's ego," the letter expressed sympathy to the Kimmell family and indignation about Ketchum's press conference. "How unfortunate that the county's top law enforcement official is more concerned about the technicalities of jurisdiction than he is about using any available resource to solve a hideous murder . . . His misaligned priorities underscore the mystery of how nature can build such a large ego into such a small man."

A political cartoon portrayed Ketchum holding a stick horse, a cap gun, and a badge that read "Jr. Sheriff." The caption read, "The feds have got to learn that I'm the law in these here parts."

Eventually the publicity died down, and Flick officially began the federal investigation on June 23rd, 1989. Dan and Jim continued to work hard on the case. Ketchum ignored us.

Despite our long-awaited task force, people still called our house to offer "helpful" information. An employee of Arby's, a young woman I'll call "Holly," told Joe Morian that her boyfriend, "Willie," might have information about the drug connection to Lisa's death. Holly had a few personal problems, but she was a good employee. She had run away from home at the age of sixteen and met Willie, a young Hispanic man with a bad temper. Willie had a drug problem and ended up in an Oregon jail. He called me at home, collect. He wanted to set up a meeting.

I was desperate to find out anything I could. As I mentioned, our desperation sometimes put us at risk. I set up a flight for Oregon, but Flick asked me to wait. I did. He made flight arrangements to Oregon City and agreed to meet Dan Tholson there so they could interview Willie together.

Willie turned out to be insignificant to Lisa's case, but he did know people involved in the Montana drug culture. He offered to "work inside this group of people in order to solve the murder and provide other information about the narcotics scene." Yeah, right. Dan and Flick realized quickly that he simply wanted out of jail.

The trip was not a bust, though. Flick and Dan stayed up late talking about the investigation. They became friends and decided that they would not let the disagreements of their superiors get in the way. Flick later said, "There were ill feelings at the top, but it wasn't at our level. We wanted to solve the case."

In the meantime, Ron and I had received a strange letter from a man in Las Vegas that sounded similar to the Stringfellow Hawke note. Flick flew to Vegas to meet FBI agents. They almost flipped when they drove up to the man's residence. A black Honda CRXsi was parked in his driveway, but it was not Lisa's. The young male owner said he had met Lisa when she worked at Arby's and developed a crush on her to the point of buying a black Honda CRXsi like hers. When he found out about her death, he was upset and wrote the letter to express his feelings. He was eventually ruled out as a suspect.

We received many odd calls and notes over the next thirteen years from all over the country. None panned out, but at least we had more manpower and resources to follow up the leads. We didn't want to miss a *single* one in hopes we would find Lisa's killer before he killed again.

CHAPTER 7

Bringing in the Feds

STRANGE DEVELOPMENTS

As I mentioned, Flick was appointed to head the task force. It was a milestone for Ron and me. Flick, round-faced, gray-haired and solid, a muscular man with an amiable personality, was the kind of person anyone would want as an officer of the law. He would ultimately become another dear and trusted friend of our family.

His qualifications were impressive. From 1970 to 1985, Flick was an agent for the ATF in Minneapolis, Minnesota. He consulted on mob crimes, posed as an undercover agent in illegal gun trade, and investigated fatal arson cases. During presidential campaigns, he worked with the Secret Service.

When Flick's aging parents needed more attention, he requested a transfer back to his home state of Montana. Finally, in 1985, ATF opened an office in Billings and asked Flick to take the lead position investigating illegal firearms and arson cases. The less-populated towns gave him a change of pace and less stress, something he thought he would be content with until his retirement.

Three years after his relocation, Lisa vanished. Flick's youngest daughter had known Lisa from high school. He realized immediately that she wasn't a runaway kid and that the case was unusual.

As the only ATF agent in the region, he was familiar with the local criminals and drug dealers. Statewide media coverage of Lisa's case brought in hundreds of phone calls to various law offices, including the ATF office. Flick sent one of his leads to Natrona County. The tip caught the attention of Dan Tholson and Jim Broz.

I also mentioned that Flick's introduction to Lisa's case began during the summer of 1988 while he worked on drug trafficking in the Billings area and eastern Montana. He was reluctant to get involved because of the jurisdictional issues (that dirty word again), but a certain group of drug dealers would only talk to Flick because they trusted him.

Ron and I were clueless about the narcotics world when our daughter was murdered. We were a Middle American family doing Middle American things. Our children went to school, we held decent jobs, and we attended our daughters' band concerts and track meets. Our children didn't take drugs. Meeting people who sold crack cocaine, heroin, and assorted pills was upsetting, and we didn't know how to deal with the strange characters calling us, writing us, and even showing up at our home. Flick *was* trained; his help was a big relief.

Over the years, it became obvious that two rival drug rings were using Lisa's murder to try to get each other in trouble. I will not use their real names for reasons of personal safety.

The first dealers (a married couple whom I'll call the "Johnsons") were the people who got Flick involved with Lisa's case. The man, "Joseph," thought he was going to be harmed by a rival "cousin." The couple swore they saw Lisa's car parked near the Casper Mountain house of their rival (a man I'll call "Diablo"). They described the Honda and its contents to Flick. They insisted that Diablo was volatile enough to commit murder, and others who knew him agreed. Once Diablo got wind of their accusations, he pointed the finger back at the Johnsons and provided enough "witnesses" to say that *they* had killed Lisa.

Flick spent a lot of time questioning people from both gangs in Montana and Wyoming. He would conduct at least twenty interviews that led to more name-calling and frustrating dead ends. Dan also found himself investigating the possibility of a drug connection. Dan later said that the drug dealers "muddied up the waters." The dealers drained the department of precious man-hours and tax money.

Over the years we got more education into the criminal element's motivation. For example, a few dubious men were reported bragging to their friends (who turned them in, probably hoping for the reward money), saying they knew who possessed the engine to Lisa's car, or they knew who chopped it up and where the pieces were. However, when Flick interviewed these fellows, they quickly denied any involvement.

Several of Flick's sources said they thought that a woman I'll call "Candy" was really the intended murder victim (Lisa resembled Candy). Candy had lived with Diablo either before or after she married a man I'll call "Vince." Vince was in Yellowstone County Jail for drug charges when he requested a meeting with Flick.

Flick met with Vince, who described how he once had marital difficulties with Candy and was expressing his misery to Diablo at a bar. Vince said that Diablo suggested, "Maybe we should do a Lisa Kimmell on her." Vince also said that Diablo and two other men had killed Lisa and they could do the same to Candy. But when pressed for details, Vince got angry and demanded that he be released from jail or he'd quit talking. It was another instance of an inmate hoping for freedom.

Much of Flick's summer in 1989 was spent chasing false leads. *Unsolved Mysteries* aired Lisa's segment again on July 19th. Their show's hotline received another 440 tips claiming sightings of Lisa or her car. We continued to get calls from people who said they called in tips, but were never interviewed.

The DNA found on Lisa had finally been analyzed. Flick began taking blood samples from the drug dealers and other suspects. Lisa's boyfriend, Ed Jaroch, was tested and eliminated, and so was Ed's best friend.

The summer of 1989 ended on a dreary note. Sheriff Ketchum had requested a probe of his investigation by the Wyoming Division of Criminal Investigation (DCI) because of the public criticism he received for not solving the case. The DCI found no outstanding leads or mistakes by Ketchum's office, but the sheriff was criticized for not having installed computers that could have expedited the process. The DCI admitted that Ketchum got behind in the first phases of the case and according to a *Casper Star-Tribune* article quoting Director C.A. Crofts, "staffing shortages also 'created a public relations problem' for the Sheriff's office." That's what Ron and I had said all along. Ketchum lacked manpower and technical resources.

Further along in the article, Crofts was quoted as saying, "Task force is a sexy term, but there was nothing about the Kimmell case to indicate it was part of some serial murder process or anything like that, that would justify a task force.'"

I think Crofts was wrong. An FBI profile that was provided to Natrona County six months after Lisa's death supports that there *were* signs of a serial killer. Special Agent Robert Walker of the FBI's Violent Criminal Apprehension Program (VICAP) wrote this about Lisa's killer: "This is not likely to have been the offender's first crime of this nature. He may have successfully avoided detection for similar offenses in the past. If so, it is likely that he will continue to assault until apprehended." We were disappointed in the DCI's response.

During the summer of 1989, we also moved from Billings to Denver. Denver would provide a bigger market for Ron's work in real estate and construction, and I would have less traveling to do. Sherry had graduated from high school. Stacy didn't want to leave her friends, but given her outgoing personality, we were confident that she would make new friends as she began high school.

Additionally, my commute had led me along miles of Lisa's intended route, not far from the Old Government Bridge, over the North Platte River. It was hard on me. Ron wasn't happy about me driving out there alone, either, with Lisa's killer still at large.

Moving redirected our time and energy for a while. However, Dan Tholson, Jim Broz, and Flick didn't get a break. They stayed busy following up tips.

After we settled into our new home, we refocused on Lisa's case, and our conflicts with Ketchum resumed. Rumors began circulating that Ketchum was involved with Lisa's disappearance. During the evening of Sunday, March 25th, 1990 (the two-year anniversary of Lisa's disappearance), our worries surged again when we heard distressing news.

Sheriff Ron Ketchum had attempted suicide.

CHAPTER 8

Ugly Politics

The second anniversary of Lisa's abduction approached at the same time that the candidates surfaced for the upcoming Natrona County Sheriff's election. Bill Barnes, a Casper police lieutenant, announced his Democratic candidacy and used Lisa's unsolved case as a reason to elect a new sheriff. The *Tribune* printed an article about Barnes' political intentions on March 2nd, 1990. Barnes criticized Ketchum's abilities. The *Tribune* quoted him as saying that Ketchum was "an expert at being scarce."

Barnes had been a police officer in Casper for about twenty years. He vowed to create a better communication system between the city and county law enforcement agencies, which was an issue we strongly supported.

To be fair, the next day the *Tribune* ran Ketchum's opposing view. Ketchum said that he would announce his candidacy soon. Again he defended his staff and his position to withhold "sensitive information" about Lisa's case.

On March 25th, 1990, the *Billings Gazette* published an article that focused on Lisa's reward money, which was rolling into a scholarship fund as of April 1st. As much as we had hoped that the reward would lead to a case breakthrough, we were glad that something good could come out of the tragedy. Ron and I had set up guidelines with *Gazette* editor Richard Wesnick and Billings Senior High School Principal James Rickard. A scholarship would be awarded every spring to a senior interested in business, hotel, and/or restaurant management. Based on the interest earned, the scholarship would be self-perpetuating.

However, our anticipation of the scholarship presentation faded quickly when we heard the shocking news. Ron Ketchum was found unconscious in his home Sunday night, March 25th, from a suicide attempt.

No officials would reveal the facts, other than to say he was in critical condition. Undersheriff Mark Benton was quoted by the *Tribune* as saying, "The sheriff has in the past suffered from some degree of depression. We don't know if that played a part in the situation at this time. We don't know if we have a situation where he may have purposely or inadvertently ingested some type of substance." We heard rumors of a drug overdose (legal or illegal drugs?). Officials were secretive. The hospital wouldn't even acknowledge that he was a patient. Ketchum should have picked another day. It fueled our fear that he was hiding something, and his unexplained "illness" created more rumors in Casper. Was he overwhelmed by the publicity of Lisa's case?

He may have been taking medications for depression; sometimes those don't work as they should. His ex-wife had requested a welfare check the previous fall. Apparently Ketchum had scared her by talking about suicide. Was his defensiveness and his lack of communication with other agencies a result of his depression?

Whatever happened, his hospitalization brought a flurry of negative publicity to the sheriff's office.

After three days, Ketchum left the hospital and took a trip out of state. In the meantime, people wrote editorials to complain. One reader said, "There's a mystery going on in the Natrona County Sheriff's Office at the leadership level . . . It's time for you, Gov. Mike Sullivan, to issue directions to the Department of Criminal Investigation to come to Natrona County and find out what's going on with our public officials."

On April 16th, another editorial read, "I feel that Sheriff Ketchum should step down from office since for the last three years that Sheriff Ketchum has held the office it has been nothing but disaster; i.e., the Lisa Marie Kimmell case, Sheriff Ketchum's refusal to cooperate with other law enforcement agencies, the brutality cases, American Civil Liberties Union lawsuits and your hush-hush methods of running an office."

More names were added to the upcoming sheriff's election. When Ketchum returned to office on April 16th, he confirmed that he suffered from depression but gave no further details. He denied any abuse of alcohol or drugs and was quoted in the *Tribune* as saying, "What took place was strictly a medical issue."

Some people in Casper didn't buy it. Unsympathetic editorial cartoons were printed, and *Tribune* readers questioned Ketchum's emotional ability to hold an office that requires a man to carry a gun.

On May 6th, Deputy Sheriff David Dovala announced his candidacy and said that he planned no major changes for the office and that he would keep Ketchum employed by the county. That stirred up more citizens. A *Tribune* editorial stated, "During the primary election returns, Republican Sheriff Candidate David Dovala, told a television news reporter when interviewed that if elected, he would retain all personnel of the sheriff's office including Ron Ketchum. He had done a 'fine' job. Please, Mr. Dovala!"

Dovala later changed his mind and said he would make changes, such as keeping better records and attending to the issue of jail overcrowding. Apparently he had to promise to change *something* to please his political backers.

On May 18th, the *Tribune* ran an article announcing that Ketchum had chosen not to run for re-election because he didn't want to have to explain his hospitalization and put his family through further stress.

As the election approached in the fall of 1990, Ron and I desperately hoped for fresh leadership that would modernize the sheriff's office. We issued a press release expressing our frustrations and our experiences to four newspapers, five radio stations, and three television stations, and we sent a copy to the sheriff candidates.

The newspapers quoted from our press release. The day the article came out, Lt. Dave Kinghorn called me at work. He didn't call to give me an update on Lisa's case. He called to tell me that he wasn't happy about our press release saying the sheriff's office needed to become more progressive and to cooperate better with other agencies.

"I'm a little bit upset and disturbed. I understand that you're having a problem with Ron [Ketchum] and why. But there are things in your press release that just aren't true. And that upsets me. There are hundreds of agencies that have called and asked for help and we've given information to. It's an ongoing thing. . . . I think you're slighting the whole department and I don't think that was really necessary."

I told Dave that he was entitled to his opinion and we were entitled to ours. We happened to disagree. We liked Dave Kinghorn and still do. He's a nice guy who got involved in our crossfire.

I know Natrona was doing the best they could, but it wasn't enough for a murder case like Lisa's. If Natrona County elected a new sheriff who was happy with the status quo, how could the madman killer ever be caught? He might kill again and again. That was our biggest fear. We wanted a sheriff who would be open to change.

Radio station KQLT asked us to be in their show *Free for All*. The first thing the host asked us was, "why would you make a statement *now* [about the election]?"

I said, "We have an interest in how the sheriff's department will be run in the future. Based on our two and a half years of experience and our relationship with the sheriff's office, we feel compelled to share this with the citizens of Natrona County."

Ron stated our position. "We're just here to give information as to how the department is being run and let the citizens of Natrona County decide for themselves how it should best be run."

We didn't back a particular candidate, and perhaps we should have. Despite our hope for changes, David Dovala was elected in November 1990. We began working with him shortly after. We got along okay, but we still had disagreements with him, most of them involving Ketchum, because by then, Ketchum had become a suspect. For example, even though Ketchum was a polygraph expert, he should not have been allowed to run polygraphs on suspects in Lisa's case.

We also knew that Ketchum had lied to Flick. Ketchum had said he was not working the night of Lisa's disappearance, March 25th, 1988. Flick found out that he *was* on duty, patrolling county roads. The dispatchers gave official statements that they had spoken to Ketchum, and they showed Flick their logbook (that page in the logbook mysteriously disappeared).

Other strange connections to Ketchum trickled in. A woman called after seeing an *Unsolved Mysteries* rerun on TV. She said she was driving to visit a friend on Casper Mountain the night of March 25th, 1988. When she was headed home at 11:30 P.M., she said she saw Ketchum following a small black sports car. When Flick interviewed her, she said, "I knew it was Ketchum because I went to school with him."

The only person Lisa would have pulled off the road for was a law officer. She had received a ticket earlier that night. However, Lisa couldn't have been on Casper Mountain at 11:30 P.M.—it was way off her route. Was the woman seeking revenge, or had Ketchum simply pulled over a small black sports car that resembled Lisa's? Many tips created more mysteries.

Additionally, several women complained to Flick that Ketchum had used his patrol car to pull them over on the pretense of a defective brake light, then suggested that they head out to the boonies and "make out." That was Flick's polite way of wording it.

Ketchum had followed one Casper woman all the way to St. Louis, Missouri. Flick flew there to interview her, and she told Flick that she was so upset when Ketchum knocked on her door that she threatened to call the police if Ketchum did not get back in his taxi and leave. He did.

Another curious tip came from the owner of a pawnshop in Casper. He told Flick that he had seen Lisa's car parked at a car stereo shop across the street. He said he'd walked over to inspect the Honda and admired the design. The CRXsi was a new model, loaded with extras. The pawnshop owner noticed a small detail that would make the sighting significant. It read CRY instead of CRX. Lisa lost part of the X in a car wash. Only Ron, Flick, and I knew that.

The car stereo shop owner turned out to be distantly related to Ketchum, but he denied ever seeing Lisa's car. When Flick interviewed him, the man appeared shaken. Flick found out why when they walked into his office. A bag of marijuana sat on his desk.

Flick would wonder for years what Ketchum's connection had been to Lisa's case, beyond his role as sheriff. Did Ketchum know the killer? Were drugs involved? Flick would retire without learning the answers.

Ron Ketchum must have had a likeable side to his personality, but unfortunately Ron and I never saw it. To this day many county employees are reluctant to discuss Ron Ketchum.

CHAPTER 9

More Dead Ends

HEARSAY

When Flick became involved in Lisa's case, the task force focused on drug dealers and other leads that Dan and Jim had not covered. More than a year after the murder, Flick was the first person to interview some of Lisa's girlfriends. None of Lisa's friends were involved, but Ron and I wondered why they hadn't been questioned.

As I mentioned before, well-meaning citizens called in countless tips. Most of the leads involved car sightings, and some people swore that they had spoken to Lisa at convenience stores or gas stations. Dan and Jim had followed up on hundreds of the sightings, but not all. Flick followed up on a couple of dozen tips that sounded credible at first. People weren't shy to call in with the slightest suspicions. The tips were both a blessing and a curse. Had a tip led to the killer, great! But day after day the tips came in and simply kept the detectives busy and frustrated.

I have two theories about the numerous car sightings. First, Lisa traveled between Denver and Billings several times after she moved to Denver. I'm sure people had seen her as they claimed, but they may have gotten their dates mixed up. Second, a young couple in Wyoming owned a black 1988 CRXsi. The woman resembled Lisa, and the pair traveled around the state frequently.

Some people seemed to have vengeful motives when calling. For example, "Edna" called Flick and said that her daughter and niece told her that they were involved with "real bad people" who did drugs. Edna said the girls thought a composite sketch shown on *Unsolved Mysteries* looked like a drug dealer friend of theirs. When Flick called the girls, they were angry that their mother/aunt had called the police. They called her a "drunk gossip" with an overactive imagination. Flick called the mother back, and she was ashamed that the girls had talked like that. It turned out to be another dead end lead that consumed several hours of Flick's time.

Besides the constant barrage of false leads, Flick had a bigger problem to worry about. Ketchum's suicide attempt on the two-year anniversary of Lisa's disappearance added to the rumors that he was involved in her death. Flick wanted Ketchum to submit his blood for DNA testing.

Ketchum denied involvement, and he refused to give a blood sample to federal authorities. Sheriff Dovala asked if he could take the blood sample from Ketchum and personally transport it to the state lab. Flick agreed in order to stop the bickering.

According to Flick's report, that didn't end the issue. "Later it was learned that when Ron Ketchum came to the Sheriff's office to give the blood sample, he insisted that Sheriff Dovala, as well as Lt. Dave Kinghorn, provide their blood as well. Why this was done is a total and complete mystery to those involved in the investigation."

Flick described the problems that the three samples posed. The blood wasn't packaged properly. No one was sure whose blood was whose, and Flick didn't know why Dovala and Kinghorn would agree to the arrangement. The annoyed lab technician said the FBI was busy enough "without being subject to a logjam." Flick and Dovala exchanged heated words about Dovala's integrity. Flick was close to seeking a federal court order to force Ketchum to submit a proper blood sample. It would take almost another year to obtain it *legitimately*, but it was finally done in 1993. Why was Ketchum so unwilling to give a blood sample to eliminate himself as a suspect?

Everyone else had been cooperative in giving blood samples. Al Lesco, the patrolman who had stopped Lisa for speeding, was the last person known to have had contact with her. When asked to give a sample, he immediately rolled up his shirtsleeve and told them to take all the blood they needed.

Ketchum's blood sample incident would lead to a complete breakdown in cooperation between Natrona County and the Federal authorities in Lisa's case. Sheriff Dovala was angered by Flick's formal report and requested Flick be reprimanded by his superiors.

When I heard about this, I was furious. I called Dovala and told him that I would no longer tolerate this kind of crap. It wasn't Flick who had been messing up blood samples, and if anyone should have been reprimanded, it should have been Dovala for the way it was handled. I told him that I wanted Natrona off our case, now! Ron and I wanted it turned over to the Wyoming Division of Criminal Investigation (WDCI). I warned Dovala that I was one mad mama and I wouldn't back off.

Dovala agreed, and was probably glad to see us go.

In conclusion, I want to set things straight about Ron Ketchum. Ketchum's DNA did not match what was found on Lisa. He was cleared of being a suspect. Today neither Ron nor I think he had anything to do with her death. However, it's still a mystery why he was reluctant to give a blood sample. Was he afraid that a blood test would reveal that he was on depression medications? Drugs, whether they're prescription or illegal, carry a stigma. Or was his ego simply too big, as some people suggested in their editorials?

Either way, Ron Ketchum obviously had emotional issues. I don't think he purposely picked Lisa's disappearance anniversary to attempt suicide. Why would a man worry about a date when he was so deeply depressed that he would try to take his own life?

PUSHING OUR LUCK

After Dave Dovala was voted sheriff in 1990, Flick, Dan, and Jim stayed busy with their investigations. We heard little about Ketchum, and we focused on finding Lisa's killer. Ron and I still got calls from peculiar people saying they had information about Lisa's murder, but they wouldn't talk to law enforcement. We agreed to meet with them, and that got us in trouble more than once.

A memorable episode took place one evening while I was in Casper on business. I agreed to meet with a man I'll call "Brian Williams" in my hotel room (yeah, *now* I know how bad that sounds). He proclaimed to be a "former" drug dealer and thought he might have information about the drug connection rumor surrounding Lisa's death. Brian told me that he wanted to explain how the drug scene worked. He had another dealer's "file" that he thought would prove who was responsible for Lisa's death. He wanted to give me this "file."

When Brian showed up, he seemed pleasant enough. Brian was a tall, slim fellow with short brown hair, dressed in a tee shirt and blue jeans, in his mid-forties. He didn't resemble a drug dealer to me. He looked more like a ranch hand.

After listening to him ramble for nearly an hour, I told him, "I'm sorry, but this isn't making any sense to me. I know you don't want to talk to anyone in law enforcement, but we have a close family friend who's now a private investigator. You can trust him. Would you talk to him?"

Brian agreed.

I picked up the phone and called Al Ketterling at home (Al was living in Casper by that time). When Al answered, I told him about the situation.

"Can you come over and talk to him?"

"Sure, who is it?"

"Brian Williams."

Al obviously recognized the name. He yelled, "Do you have any idea who in the *hell* you are dealing with? I'll be right over!"

I hung up, turned, and grinned nervously at Brian. "Can I get you a glass of water or something?"

"No ma'am, but thanks," he said.

We made small talk, and Al arrived within minutes, giving me a dirty look as he came in my room. He understood what Brian was talking about. Al knew the players involved. I remained clueless.

After Brian left, Al turned and glared at me. "Are you out of your mind, Sheila? Don't *ever* let those people in your room like this. Never! You have no idea how dangerous they are."

"Oh, Al, don't get so hot," I said, pretending to be strong. "You worry too much. I'll be okay."

"Don't worry about it? Let me show you how worried *I* was about it!"
He flung open his jacket and revealed his hidden revolver. "*This* is how
worried I was."

Appropriately humbled, I promised not to let anyone else in my room,
and I promised to bolt the door. Al left, taking a large portion of my pos-
terior with him.

Al wouldn't be the only one to reprimand me. When Flick found out
about my meeting with Brian, he let me have it, too. However, Ron and
I still didn't care about the risks. We wanted to find Lisa's killer.

FLICK DOESN'T GIVE UP

Flick didn't focus exclusively on drug dealers. Sexual predators were also
investigated thoroughly.

The first sexual predator (whom I'll call "Barry") that Flick interro-
gated was in jail for the rape of a young coed from a college in Billings
during the summer of 1989. His modus operandi fit Lisa's case in some
ways. He had bound his victim and shaved her pubic hair. He had confessed to a girlfriend and his ex-wife that he had assaulted other women,
sometimes hitting them over the head. Barry had worked in several
places with different jobs. He had been a short-order cook and a casino
employee, and had worked for a garden nursery. When his employer
told Flick that Barry had not reported to work from March 23rd to April
2nd, 1988 and was fired for it, Barry became a top suspect.

Flick interviewed Barry's girlfriend, ex-wife, employers, and parents.
The girlfriend and ex-wife said that he bound them during sex and was
rough, sometimes forcing himself on them. His girlfriend said that he
played with knives and threatened to cut her up. She moved out of state
to escape him. His ex-wife had encountered much of the same; additionally, he had told her that he transported drugs and guns to Arizona.
Barry would be one of the first suspects to be tested for DNA, and he
wasn't fully eliminated until mid-1993. He was one "bad dude."

Most of the predators that Flick and Natrona County pursued fit
the 1988 FBI profile of a loner and blue-collar worker to some degree.
A man I'll call "Mick" worked for a moving company and lived in a tent

near Pathfinder Lake, Wyoming, not far from where Lisa's body was found. He owned no car and often hitchhiked to town. One of his former girlfriends accused Mick of taking her to his tent, binding her, and sexually assaulting her, using a knife to cut around her breasts. She also said he was into Satanism and had told her it was time for another "sacrifice" like Lisa Kimmell. When Mick was questioned, he denied everything. He was given a lie detector test, on which he performed poorly, but eventually a DNA test cleared him of involvement.

A man I'll call "Rich" was reported by a tipster to have witnessed a videotape of Lisa being murdered at the Government Bridge. Rich said he'd heard of the rumor, but besides the "stupidity" of filming such a thing, he said he had never witnessed a video or told anyone that he did. Rich wasn't seriously considered, but it was another lead that illustrated the strange rumors that the investigators faced.

By September 1991, Flick had earned the nickname "the Vampire," which wasn't surprising given the amount of blood he had drawn, and given the rumors of occult involvement (the media had reported that Lisa's body was found with an odd pattern of stab wounds). There were many calls from people accusing others of being involved in Satanic worship.

Flick interviewed a woman, "Diane," whose name had been supplied by a caller to *Unsolved Mysteries*. Diane wasn't involved with the occult, but she told Flick about her stepson and his girlfriend. (It was interesting to learn how many people were willing to turn in a disliked family member.) In 1987, Diane said the stepson and his girlfriend had joined a Casper group that indulged in ritualistic behaviors. She described the Government Bridge as a site where the group would meet and kill small animals, then drink their blood or smear it on their bodies. The stepson was said to have a robe with a pentagram on the back, and the group had talked about using human victims at some point.

If the event actually happened, the group may have crossed the line one night when they used a young girl in a ritual. According to Diane, the girl was forcibly stripped, tied up by the hands, and suspended from the ceiling in a Casper home. After being raped repeatedly, she was eventually freed, but was told that she would be killed if she reported the incident to anyone. The girl's pubic hair was allegedly shaved and used in a later ritual.

Diane said she was with her stepson and girlfriend when they ran into the victim at a grocery store. Diane said the girl became hysterical and asked why they didn't stop the men from raping her. Diane threatened her stepson that she would go to the police if he didn't stop associating with the group.

The stepson and girlfriend eventually moved to Denver, and Flick interviewed them seven months later, along with "David," who was reported to be the leader of the group. All three denied having witnessed a ritual abuse of anyone, but Flick noticed pentagrams hanging in their apartment and books referencing occult rituals. David admitted to "dabbling" in such groups but wrote it off as a "juvenile adventure." Both David and Diane's stepson had blood taken and tested, but again, it was a dead end.

Flick's investigations were creepy. Flick interviewed at least seven people who admitted to attending Casper rituals, or allegedly knew of others who had. The leads turned up nothing related to Lisa's case, and it was debatable how many were true.

THE PSYCHICS

Not everyone associated with mysticism was creepy. My sister-in-law, another Lisa Marie, married my brother *after* my daughter was killed. She didn't know my Lisa, but the murder bothered her. She heard about two psychic sisters named Delores and Darlene who lived in Great Falls, Montana. My sister-in-law made an appointment to meet with them ("the ladies" or "sisters") in July 1992 to get a reading. The ladies taped the session and gave it to my sister-in-law. A few days later, I arrived in Great Falls to visit family, and my sister-in-law played the tape. The ladies brought up details about my Lisa's murder that were uncanny. Still skeptical, I made an appointment to see them in person the next day.

I was surprised when I met the women. Perhaps I was expecting flowing robes and crystal balls surrounded by a haze of incense. The ladies, in their sixties, were rather grandmotherly, much like any elderly woman one might find in a church pew on Sunday mornings.

Delores was the only one available for my "counseling session." When we got started, she gazed at me and said, "What can I do for you, dear?"

I did not tell her anything about the murder, and I withheld my name. I just sat down and said, "Tell me who did it."

Delores paused in thought, staring into a glass of water she said helped her "see." She began telling me details about Lisa's death, the stab wounds, and the river, and she described Lisa's car. Granted, she could have gotten some of these details from the newspaper, but I didn't tell her who I was or what my question related to. I was shocked.

After our session, she removed her tape from the recorder and handed it to me. I pulled my wallet out of my purse to pay for our session in cash. She refused to accept my payment, explaining that she and her sister did not accept fees when they counseled on murder investigations. How would she know that? She still didn't know my name, and I didn't tell her any details about Lisa's death.

I returned to Billings and took the tape to Flick. After he listened to it, he was also flabbergasted. We both wondered if the ladies could help if they came to Casper. We checked into their background. We found out that they had a good reputation among law enforcement agencies. They had even worked on the Ted Bundy case. They had provided information in Great Falls that resulted in solving two separate homicides. They refused to charge for their services when they involved murder, only asking for the reimbursement of expenses such as food and hotel fees. Obviously, they weren't opportunists.

Flick decided to take a leap of faith and ask the ladies to come to Casper. He knew he would be met by skeptics, but he had chased so many dead ends, what could it hurt? They agreed to meet Flick in Casper. They "saw" the figures "2" and "2," but not together. They obsessed about the numbers being important, but they couldn't get more specific.

Flick wrote in his report after their meeting: "They accurately described the patterns of the stab wounds, and also remarked about Lisa Kimmell's head wound. The stab wounds have been mentioned in the press as simply being stab wounds, but were not described as to the pattern, and the head wound has not been publicized at all. It was also somewhat remarkable that the psychics described Lisa as having been held against her will for a few days before being killed, which is exactly what the pathologist who did the post mortem reported in his autopsy findings. None of this had ever been made public."

The ladies were not warmly received by others in Casper. Although Flick was with them, they told him they felt uneasy. They said they felt "inhibited" and even "intimidated." They sensed a bad "karma" about Ketchum. They told me later that on their way out of Casper, a patrol car trailed them for several miles. They were concerned enough to write a note and place it under the seat of their motor home in case something happened.

I wanted them to return a year later to Casper to try again to find Lisa's car. They were reluctant at first because of the first unpleasant visit, but I assured them that they would not be harmed. They returned in the fall of 1993. This time Ron and I joined them to ensure their safety and comfort.

We met with the ladies along with Lynn Callahan, who was the newly appointed investigator from the Wyoming DCI in charge of Lisa's case after our falling out with Dovala. She was not opposed to using unusual investigative techniques, such as psychics.

This time the atmosphere was relaxed and inviting for the ladies. We drove out to the North Platte River and the Old Government Bridge. They continued to obsess about "2" and "2," perhaps on a street sign or billboard, but not joined.

We drove slowly along a back road to the fishing area where Lisa's body was found and Darlene asked us to stop.

She said, "What's Oly? I'm getting a word, Oly. What does that mean? I'm getting a reading right over there." She pointed to some bushes along the road.

Ron shrugged, pulled over and got out of the car. He looked in the bushes, pulled something out, and grinned. "It's an 'Oly' can. You know? Olympia beer?"

We got a kick out of that since both women were teetotalers and wouldn't know an Oly can from a Bud Light.

They insisted that there was a *back* way, or even a tunnel, from the Government Bridge that would take us to the killer. Hmmm. Interesting.

The afternoon wore on. We drove into Evansville, a suburb of Casper.

Darlene pointed. "There's something in that building. It's black, and it is connected to Kimmell."

Once again, Ron stopped the car. We all got out and wandered around the building.

"I know something's here," Darlene repeated.

Could there be parts from Lisa's car?

Someone must have called the police to report suspicious people milling around the garage, because who would show up in a patrol car? Al Ketterling. (Al had left his private investigation practice, moved to Casper, and taken a job with the Evansville police department.)

He drove up, rolled down his window, and grinned. "What the hell are you guys doing here?"

We explained that our friends were psychics and they saw something black connected to "Kimmell" in the garage.

Al burst out laughing. "For Christ's sake, of course it's connected to 'Kimmell'! It's a part of your old boat that I bought from you five years ago, and this guy's fixing it for me. Now get the hell outta here before I have to arrest you for trespassing on private property and you get me in trouble."

He was kidding, of course.

Al solved that mystery, but other mysteries remained. How did the ladies know that something in that garage belonged to us at one time? Ron and I didn't even know the boat parts were there.

Unfortunately, the sisters weren't able to help us find Lisa's car or the killer, but our day with them was a memorable experience.

CHAPTER 10

Life Goes On

HAPPY OCCASIONS

For the sake of my mental health, I had to ease up on the investigation after 1993. I couldn't emotionally take the false leads year after year. We were forced to face the reality that we might never catch Lisa's killer, but threads of hope remained. In the meantime, our other two daughters needed us. Both girls had graduated from high school.

Sherry went to college for a short time to study accounting. She found a good job in the field and got married in 1991. Sherry had wanted a small, quiet wedding in our backyard. To enhance our back yard, we hung woven crystal-blue decorations throughout our gazebo and fountain. The yard was enchanting. Initially there were to be about thirty people, but it grew to seventy. I don't know how we pulled it off, but we did.

We had expressed to our guests that we would rather they not bring small children. We loved kids, but we had a swimming pool that could pose a safety problem.

People understood, except for good old Joe Morian.

Joe brought his two active youngsters to the wedding. I was busy, occupied with overwhelming hosting duties. Our cameraman, a husky guy more than six feet tall, was photographing the events. What happened? Yep! The kids fell into the deep end of the pool. The cameraman threw his expensive camera to the ground and created a mini tidal wave when he hit the water. After we toweled off the guests, the kids, and our cameraman, the groom's mother suddenly fainted amid the bedlam.

She survived. The kids were fine, but wet. The cameraman was fine, but wet. The camera didn't break, and the wedding pictures didn't perish. The mishaps added amusing memories that I will cherish forever. But an important person was missing—Lisa. I know she would have loved to have shared her sister's special day.

Ron and I celebrated his parents' fiftieth wedding anniversary in August 1995. That same month, we were blessed with our first grandson, Trevor. Two years later, his brother, Alex, joined the family.

After a few years of college Stacy met her future husband. In July of 1998, Stacy was married in a church with a traditional service. Her reception, however, was not traditional. It was held outdoors at a friend's ranch. I guess the Kimmells are destined to occasionally endure turbulence. A huge downpour, flanked by tornados, hit the ranch, but no one let the weather dampen their spirits. We took our shoes off and danced in the rain and mud. What a delightful memory!

That same month, the day before Lisa's birthday, Ron and I held an informal, low-key memorial service on July 17th at the Old Government Bridge. We brought a wreath and twenty-nine vanilla candles for Lisa. Then we visited Conwell Park. We planted a blue spruce tree to thank the community for keeping her memory alive. The next morning, Ron released twenty-nine balloons into the sky and cast her wreath into the river. Another bittersweet day.

MORE LOSSES

Many changes took place over the next few years, and some were heartbreaking. Al Ketterling's fate was one we didn't expect. I don't remember the exact date in 1999, but I remember the tearful afternoon phone call I received from Al. He wanted to speak to Ron. I knew something was seriously wrong because I had never seen or heard this tough guy cry before. I hurriedly found Ron.

Al broke the news. He had been diagnosed with amyotrophic lateral sclerosis (ALS), Lou Gherig's disease, and he didn't have long to live—one, maybe two years.

ALS is a degenerative motor disease that attacks the brain and spinal cord, atrophying every muscle in the body until it reaches the heart. Ron and I were devastated. Ron and Al had formed a special bond over the years. They had shared a lot of good times and tough times, such as losing Ricky. Al was there for Ron when he and I separated briefly after Ricky's death. Ron was there for Al during his divorce from Barb. Al was a pillar of strength when we lost Lisa.

Ron made frequent trips to Casper to see Al and give him moral support and, interestingly, spiritual guidance. They both needed that. Ron helped Al and his new wife with home projects. He built ramps for Al when Al became wheelchair-bound. Ron also remodeled the bathroom so that it would be easier for Al to bathe. Al passed away on March 4th, 2000.

In 2001, The Bailey Company restructured and eliminated my position. I was thrust into early retirement. My first reaction was to find another position in the restaurant industry.

However, Ron asked me to consider other options: "You've been married to your job for twenty-three years, and now I would like to have my wife back."

I decided to take a few months to weigh my options. I told my friends that I had to find out "what I want to do when I grow up."

Life went on, not just for the Kimmell family, but for others involved in our lives. Flick retired in November 1995. Dan Tholson transferred within Natrona County and found his life more peaceful as an investigator in the Youth Division. Jim Broz left to work for the U.S. Mint in Denver. Dave Dovala left the sheriff's office, and Mark Benton was elected.

We rarely heard much about Ron Ketchum after his blood sample eliminated him as a suspect in Lisa's case. We knew that Ketchum continued to work as an elected county commissioner. However, it appeared that he lost his battle with depression on May 20th, 2000. On a Saturday afternoon he drove up Coal Mountain Road and called a friend from his cell phone to say he couldn't take life any longer. The friend wasn't able to talk him out of it.

Ron Ketchum drew his gun and shot himself.

It distressed us to hear the news. As angry as we were with Ketchum at times, we never wished him harm. We were crushed to learn that he left a daughter behind to grow up without her father.

FADING EFFORTS

Ron and I made a last major effort to find Lisa's car in October 2000. We had always wondered if it had been pushed into Alcova Lake near the Old Government Bridge. The lake, a popular recreational area and reservoir, would be a logical place to dispose of a stolen car. Natrona County had divers search the lake in 1991, but they had limited visibility in the murky waters. Was Lisa's car at the bottom of the lake, as so many people had speculated over the years?

On my car radio one day, I heard a news story about Innerspace Exploration, a company out of Washington State that specialized in using high tech equipment to search oceans and lakes for bodies, shipwrecks, missing airplanes, and other items. For my peace of mind, I needed to know whether Lisa's car was in that lake.

I contacted Innerspace, then Natrona County to let them know of our plans to search Alcova Lake. Fortunately, Innerspace had a brief gap in their busy schedule, and they were able to travel to Casper the following week. Ron and I traveled to Casper to meet the exploration team. Sheriff Mark Benton was supportive of our efforts and even came out to observe (what a refreshing experience after Ron Ketchum!). We were happy to let Natrona County take over Lisa's case again after Benton was elected to office.

Lynn Cohee, the Natrona County Detective assigned to Lisa's case, and Doc Thorpen went out on the boat. We wanted to accompany them, but it had limited space. We let the qualified investigators go in case they found something important. Sheriff Benton, Ron, and I stayed close by offshore, watching every move.

We were disappointed. The closest thing to a car they found was an old tire and a picnic table. They said Alcova was one of the cleanest lakes they had seen. It wasn't the answer we hoped for, but it was better than no answer at all.

The years passed, but no one in our family ever forgot Lisa. Our primary reminders would be the anniversaries of her disappearance and death, her birthday, and the annual scholarship awards in Billings.

Thank God the law enforcement agencies had not forgotten Lisa or the case, either. When Wyoming opened its new crime lab in late 2001, their computers began connecting to national data banks. What happened next would turn the Kimmell family upside down once again.

PART III

Catching A Killer

CHAPTER 11

Incriminating Evidence

By the summer of 2002, Ron and I had settled into a quiet lifestyle. The girls were married and working. Our grandsons were growing faster than wildflowers, so we spent time with them and our aging parents. We never lost hope that Lisa's killer would be caught, and we still heard from people we met through the investigations. We kept in touch with Lynn Cohee, the Natrona County detective assigned to our case. Time passed fairly routinely.

Wednesday, July 17th, 2002, was the day before Lisa would have been thirty-three years old. We can only imagine what she would be doing had someone not brutally taken her life. Perhaps she would be an executive for The Bailey Company in Denver, as she once had envisioned. Or she might have been picking up her children—our grandchildren—from school. Lisa's sweet face at age eighteen is one way I'll remember her, but I can't help thinking about what she could have contributed and accomplished, and the fine people she would have brought into our lives.

July 17th was an ordinary Wednesday, a lazy mid-summer afternoon. My in-laws were visiting, and Ron was running business errands with his father. I decided to fire up my computer and show Mom how to play fun Internet games. Just after I logged on, the phone rang.

"Hi, Sheila, this is Lynn." Lynn Cohee was calling from her cell phone.

"Hi, Lynn, how are ya doing?"

"Doin' fine. We're in your neighborhood and thought if you and Ron were going to be around, we'd stop by and visit."

"We?"

"Yeah, Dan and me," meaning Dan Tholson.

"You just happen to be in the neighborhood and wanted to stop by? May I remind you that you're from Casper? Something must be going on. What's up?"

"We'll talk about it when we get there."

"Ron isn't home right now. He's out running errands, but I expect him back shortly," I said, my stomach beginning to churn.

"That's okay, we'll just shoot the breeze till he gets there."

As I hung up the phone, my heart pounded. What could bring Dan and Lynn 290 miles to Denver?

After Dan and Lynn arrived, I introduced them to Mom and invited them to have a seat at our dining room table. I offered them something to drink, but they declined. "Maybe later."

I joined them at our round oak table, sitting across from Lynn. "You must have news for us. It must be good news; I can see it in your eyes, Lynn."

She partially smiled. "We have news, but we'll wait till Ron gets here."

Their timing was perfect; we only had to make small talk for a few apprehensive moments.

Ron opened the front door and hollered, "What's with the car with Wyoming plates out front?"

I rose and hurriedly met him to tell him about our company. Ron seemed surprised and anxious, too.

After Ron and Dad sat at the dining table, everyone stared at the two detectives.

I nervously blurted out, "Okay, Ron's here now. What's the news?"

Lynn's face grew serious. "Sheila, it is good news, or at least we think so. We needed to tell you and Ron together in person, not over the phone." She looked at Dan and paused.

Dan took the cue. "We think we know who killed Lisa. We have a DNA match."

We burst into tears at the bittersweet news.

Once we stopped reeling, Lynn and Dan explained that there was an enormous amount of work still ahead. Throughout the conversation I couldn't focus because my brain was screaming repeatedly, "Oh my God, thank God, a DNA match." It drowned out most of what they said.

Then Ron asked, "Can you tell us his name?"

Everyone fell silent.

Dan's eyes darted to Lynn, then back to Ron's. "Yes. His name is Dale Wayne Eaton."

Lynn explained how the semen sample taken from Lisa's body matched the DNA of a federal inmate in Colorado, a fifty-seven-year-old man incarcerated in 1998 as a felon carrying a firearm. An FBI database program called CODIS (the Combined DNA Indexing System) had been created in the early 1990s to gather genetic samples from prisoners. The technology took about ten years to spread to all of the states. The new Wyoming State Crime Lab had opened in the latter part of 2001, and on July 5th, 2002, they got a hit.

Dale Wayne Eaton owned land seventy-five miles northwest of Casper in a small hamlet called Moneta. It was on Lisa's route to Cody. We didn't learn many details that day. I wouldn't have retained much anyway because I was so stunned.

Dan and Lynn urged us to be patient. They had to obtain search warrants and find additional evidence. They would explore his property and his belongings, and interview his friends, neighbors, and family members. We had to wait for them to build a case. The fairly new DNA technology was strong, but they wanted more.

Before leaving, Dan had asked us if he could break the news to Flick, knowing how deeply the case had affected him. We agreed.

After Dan and Lynn left, we knew we must immediately summon our daughters to tell them the news. I called each one at home and said that I realized that they were probably cooking dinner, but we had an important family matter to discuss with them and I asked them to come over as soon as possible.

I had tried not to panic Sherry or Stacy, but they recognized the urgency. They made it in record time, within seconds of each other. Sherry dashed through the door asking, "What's wrong?" Stacy was at Sherry's heels. "Is everything okay?" Their breathlessness and flushed cheeks suggested they had run a 10k race instead of driving their cars the few miles between our houses.

Mom and Dad knew that we needed one-on-one time with our girls. They went to another room to comfort each other.

We asked our daughters to have a seat on the sofa. Ron knelt before Sherry and me before Stacy, in the same manner we had done over fourteen years before when we told them that their sister had been murdered. Ron and I held their hands.

"Dan and Lynn just left," Ron said. "They told us they have found who killed Lisa."

Disbelief clouded their faces. We had had too many close calls in the past that led to bitter disappointments. After so many years, we had almost given up hope that anyone would find Lisa's murderer.

Trying to hide his emotions, Ron added, "They have a DNA match."

With that, they fell into our arms. We held each other and wept. No matter how much we wanted justice, the news was hard to face. None of us ate dinner that night because we were too shaken up.

Dale Wayne Eaton. His name wasn't familiar. In the thousands of tips that were called in over the years, not one had mentioned him. Strangely, he was in a prison only about ten miles from our home in Littleton, Colorado; Eaton had been in the Englewood Federal Correctional Institution for four months. Answers were so close but so far away.

Who was this monster?

Raw emotions surfaced. The pain of losing Lisa hadn't lessened in fourteen years, and I wasn't sure how strong I could be, but Ron and I had learned to communicate. We would need each other's strength and the support from our daughters more than ever as the investigation continued.

When we discovered more about Eaton, we faced a horrifying truth. Ron and I realized that Ron had driven by Eaton's land or had flown over it probably three or four times while searching for Lisa before her body was found. The hardest part was realizing that she was still alive. The fact that we hadn't saved her made Ron and me suffer worse than had her killer stabbed our own hearts.

The next day, Flick called to tell me about his phone call from Dan. In his retirement, Flick was working part-time for an automobile auction house when he was paged to come to the office. He was told that he had a call on hold and it sounded important. Flick said Dan got straight to the point.

"We got our man." Dan knew Flick would instantly catch on.

Flick told me that when he hung up the phone, he put his head in his hands and cried. Flick would later tell Dan, "When you called, I about fell out of my chair." Flick said he had never heard of Eaton before, and he went home and looked back through six years of his notes to see if he had missed any of the tips that could have connected Eaton to the crime. None did.

After Dan and Lynn returned to Casper, they obtained search warrants to examine Eaton's property. The search began Monday, July 29th. Eaton owned a barren piece of land located in Moneta along a two-lane portion of Wyoming Highway 20-26 that was so isolated it could have served as a landing strip. (Interesting. The psychics had "seen" the numbers "2" and "2," but not connected.) At one time, ten people had lived in Moneta, but in 1988, only three people populated the hamlet. In 2002, when Lisa's car was found, one of the neighbors was reported by the *Tribune* to comment that Moneta could possibly have the highest number of killers per capita in the United States.

Chapter 12

Tireless Heroes

While our family coped with the news of a DNA match and faced the emotional consequences of reliving Lisa's murder, Natrona County Detectives Lynn Cohee and Dan Tholson worked hard behind the scenes. Keeping procedures legal was vital to building a strong case against Eaton.

Dan and Lynn have quiet personalities and never complained to us about their demanding jobs. We later learned about their countless hours on the case from reading their reports. We were amazed at how dedicated they were to making sure Lisa's killer paid for his crime.

Lynn Cohee was a good choice for Lisa's case. She had worked for the sheriff's office since 1981, starting as a dispatcher and working her way up to deputy. She became an undercover officer in 1988, and was assigned to the Investigation Division in 1991. She currently works in Emergency Management, supervises four deputies, and conducts search-and-rescue operations. She has the kind of demeanor that makes people trust her, but she's one tough lady.

Lynn wasn't assigned the case until 1997, when Natrona County got it back from the Wyoming DCI. Since then, she took messages from people who called in about Lisa's car, and she followed up on the few leads that trickled in. The trickles turned to a roaring waterfall on Friday, July 5th, 2002.

Lynn and other investigators often went to breakfast on Friday mornings. At 8:49 A.M., her cell phone rang. Lynn's secretary told her to call Tilton Davis at the Wyoming Crime Lab immediately. Tilton answered the phone, and then got Sandy Mays, the director, on the speakerphone. Lynn said she was curious, thinking it had something to do with a recent crime in Mills, Wyoming.

She was wrong. They had a DNA hit on Lisa's case.

"I almost dropped my phone in my biscuits and gravy," Lynn said. She had broken her right thumb playing softball, so she told Tilton and Sandy to hold while she ripped the metal splint off so she could take notes.

"The first question out of my mouth was 'Who is it?' They said Dale Wayne Eaton, and he was in their penitentiary back in 1998. After I picked my jaw off the floor, I started doing any research I could on Dale Eaton."

When she returned to her office, she told Undersheriff Kinghorn, Sheriff Benton, and District Attorney Kevin Meenan about the DNA hit.

Lynn would later say in an interview, "The best day of my career wasn't the phone call from the crime lab, but when Dan Tholson and I went to the Kimmells' residence in Denver just after our first interview with Dale Wayne Eaton. We all sat at the table and I told them that we finally knew who killed Lisa. I could see life return to Sheila's face."

Lynn's next step was to run a criminal history of Eaton, which revealed a long list of prison times and confrontations with the law. Ironically, he had no records in Casper. Lynn had never heard of the man. However, Eaton had been in a Casper halfway house and had escaped on June 16th, 1998. He was caught on July 30th, 1998, in Grand Teton National Park.

Lynn contacted the Rocky Mountain Information Network to see what they could find. They had plenty of information about Eaton's past addresses and vehicles. She quickly called the Sweetwater County Sheriff's Office to find out more about his 1997 charge of aggravated assault. She spoke to Detective Rich Haskell, who had been involved in Eaton's arrest. She got a full report, but unfortunately almost all the evidence seized had been destroyed, although an inventory list was still intact.

Lynn didn't slow down. She contacted the United States Attorney's Office in Casper to obtain reports about his arrest in Teton County and the charges of "felon in possession of a firearm." She eventually spoke to Fish and Game Warden Bill Long, the officer who had discovered Eaton camping along a Grand Teton Park road.

She checked with a few other sheriff's offices and police departments before she left for the day. Dan wouldn't find out the big news until Monday, July 8th.

Early Monday, Lynn told Sheriff Benton, Undersheriff Kinghorn, and Lt. Lauderdale that there was too much work for one investigator. She wanted Dan Tholson to assist her. Everyone agreed and we were thankful for that.

Dan Tholson doesn't seem to be the toughest cop one will ever meet. He has a quiet voice; he's attractive, of average height. He looks younger than his forty-something years. He wears glasses. He's more like Clark Kent than Superman, yet when he returned to Lisa's case, Dan was relentless in building the case.

When Dan was called into the initial briefing with Lynn and Sheriff Benton, he said he didn't think much about it. Dan told me, "My first thought was, nobody ever heard of this guy; is this real or not? I guess it didn't sink in until we went to the crime lab and talked to them about the DNA stuff. I'm kind of a skeptic, and I just had to be convinced that it was real."

By the time Lynn and Dan drove to Denver to break the news to us on July 17th, Dan was convinced. In addition to the DNA evidence, they had visited Eaton before calling us.

Dan told us, "We ended up interviewing him in a visiting room, with glass in between us, so it was really hard to determine what his demeanor was like. We could only see his face. He seemed calm enough, and then he got pretty upset as it went on."

They said he admitted to hearing about the case on TV. He denied knowing anything about her, but he did say something like, "wasn't she the girl who was driving to Montana?" The media had focused on her trip to Cody, Wyoming. Dan and Lynn suspected that he knew more. They also said that his mouth became so dry when they brought up the DNA match, he lost his voice.

Before searching Eaton's property, the detectives found a couple

(I'll call them the "Smiths") in Glenrock, Wyoming, longtime friends of Eaton's. They were keeping some of Eaton's things in storage. On July 24th, with a search warrant in hand, the detectives made a trip to Glenrock. The reports said that they found three vehicles belonging to Eaton: a pale green 1985 Dodge van, a Ford F600 welding truck, and a 1982 Ford F150 pickup. Other items that he obviously valued were boxed and stored in the friends' trailer and an old freezer while he served his jail time.

Dean and Virginia Smith said they had known Eaton from about 1970, when he and Dean worked in the Gas Hill mines together. Eaton obviously admired and trusted the church-going folks. While Eaton was in federal prison, he wrote to them, citing Bible verses and worrying about his salvation.

I seriously doubt that the Smiths knew what they were storing for Eaton. Goosebumps rose on my arms as I read the inventory list. Eaton owned several weapons that were found in the boxes and in his trucks. Dan and Lynn found an axe, a wooden club, several flex cuffs, and wire ties, along with a pair of handcuffs. They discovered nine knives—some obviously intended for camping, since they also found numerous camping items (such as a canteen, bedding, and tarps). Other knives looked more sinister, including a butcher knife. They also found a blue dildo and a plastic bag containing rope. When Eaton was caught with a firearm in the Teton National Forest, he was carrying a Stevens Model 325-A .30-.30 rifle with the serial number ground off. Had Eaton warehoused part of his "rape and murder kit" with friends, hoping to use it again when he was free? Thank God he was behind bars.

Dan had also immediately requested a search warrant of Eaton's property in Moneta, Wyoming (Fremont County). On Monday, July 29th, 2002, he and Lynn executed the warrant signed by Judge Sullins of the Seventh District Court in Natrona County.

Billings, where Lisa grew up, has a semi-arid climate with mild summers. Elm trees and firs are nestled in a lush valley surrounded by the Rimrocks, sandstone cliffs from 300 to 500 feet tall. Billings consists of numerous suburbs, ideal for raising children. Lisa loved Billings, and we did, too.

By contrast, Moneta lies in the dusty deserts of the Great Basin, a parched climate where few plants and animals thrive. Once a person leaves the comfortable boundaries of Billings, the scrubby terrain becomes inhospitable. On long highway drives, there's little to see but brush and dirt for hundreds of miles. In the early spring, daytime can be a pleasant 50 degrees, but temperatures drop by up to 30 or 40 degrees by nightfall. Nothing breaks the wind as it howls over the flat terrain. What a hellish place for Lisa to spend her last days.

To search Eaton's property, two teams of three Natrona investigators were formed. Team 1, Lt. Stew Anderson, Deputy Mickey Anderson, and Deputy Sexton, were assigned to search a sheet metal shed that stood on the lot. Team 2, Deputies Trey Warne, Sgt. John Becker, and Deputy Paula Thomason, were assigned to seek evidence in the two trailers Eaton had lived in before he went to prison. A briefing was held in the Emergency Operations Center room of the Natrona County Sheriff's Office before the execution of the search warrant. In addition to the teams, an entourage of detectives and staff arrived at Eaton's land about 11:30 A.M. that Monday. Dan and Casper Police Department Evidence Tech Chris Reed took pictures. A total of fifteen people showed up.

From Natrona County, Sheriff Mark Benton, Undersheriff Dave Kinghorn, Coroner Dr. James Thorpen, and District Attorney Kevin P. Meenan were on the scene. Sheriff Roger Millard and Sgt. Roger Rizor from Fremont County also joined the group. It must have been quite an eventful day for tiny Moneta. The few neighbors strained to watch the flurry of activity. The *Tribune* reported that a woman got a headache from peering through binoculars.

The detectives' reports and photos from the scene told the rest of the story.

Like a county dump, ugly sights met the officials' eyes. Three structures rose from the flat land: a partially rusted, metal two-story shed—a cross between a barn and a garage—a decrepit trailer house, and a smaller trailer that might have been used for storage. An old mattress, crates, pallets, tire-rims, broken concrete blocks, twisted metal, and scrap lumber lay in jumbled heaps in the yard, although I wouldn't call it a real yard. Nothing but scrubby weeds dotted the landscape.

A nasty pile of insulation and rusted appliances occupied the inside of the large trailer. The 1970s décor once boasted cheerful orange shag carpeting with a green and gold theme in the striped couch, wallpaper, and curtains. After Eaton lived in it and it was abandoned for four years, the fabrics were torn, and what was left of the couch was filthy with dust and bird droppings. Moldy boxes of old clothes and shoes sat among a pile of wire hangers in one of the small bedrooms. The thin, wood-paneled walls sagged, and most of the cabinet doors hung open by one hinge.

When the teams completed searching the three buildings and found a few items of interest, they turned their attention to sinkholes that showed signs of digging. Neighbors had reported that Eaton once said he was trying to dig a well, and someone else reported that he was trying to dig a septic tank. They decided to start with what appeared to be the "well hole." George DeMarce, a backhoe operator, began with scoops of dirt that were carefully sifted with rakes. The excavators found more junk, but pieces of black metal and orange/red plastic emerged from the dirt. A pair of glasses with one lens also turned up. Dan said his arms prickled when a hubcap appeared with a large "H" on it. He recognized the Honda logo. It lifted the group's morale because they knew they were close to something important.

They didn't leave the property until 6:30 P.M. Deputy Walters guarded the scene all night.

The search resumed about 7:30 A.M. the next day. The "well hole" examination was completed, and the backhoe began digging up the floor of the shop. Nothing was found in there, so excavation began at a site between the trailers and the metal shop where they spotted sunken dirt. A white pipe stuck out as though a septic tank was buried below. Again, George DeMarce lifted dirt and the deputies sifted.

Suddenly, the backhoe hit something. Deputy Mickey Anderson waved his hands and shouted at George to stop. Lynn ordered the digging halted for closer inspection.

Sheriff Millard made a call to request a camera that could be dropped down the pipe. Captain David Good, a Fremont County deputy, arrived at about 12:30 P.M., but the camera couldn't reveal identifying features. George fired up the backhoe again, but slowed his pace. While sifting through a scoop of dirt, Lynn found a tag number on a piece of metal. It was part of Lisa's LIL MISS license plate.

Barely able to contain her excitement, Lynn called the Wyoming State Crime Lab to see if they wanted to be on the scene. Sandy Mays told Lynn, "Keep digging." The lab would arrive the next day to process the findings.

George used the backhoe as long as he could, but the men had to climb into the hole with shovels after the backhoe kept scraping metal. The teams dug, their anticipation rising. Dull black metal peered from under the sandy dirt, drawing everyone's attention. The group gathered at the top of the hole, sweat drenching their clothes in the sizzling sun. Slowly a large flat shape emerged about eight feet below ground level. Elation rose when a car door and bumper surfaced.

The shapes weren't pieces of a car; they WERE the car!

The usually calm, Mr. Unexcitable, Dan Tholson, leapt into the deep hole to sweep the dirt away from the VIN number on the dash (did Clark Kent turn into Superman?). Dan read the numbers out to Lynn. She confirmed what they suspected. The tangled metal at the bottom of the hole was Lisa's Honda CRXsi.

Lynn would later comment on A&E's *Cold Case Files*, "It's really hard to describe. There's the car we've been looking for, for fourteen years. It was very quiet. Everybody that was out there hardly spoke a word. Everyone had their own thoughts, like, 'Oh, my gosh, here it is.'"

Finding her car ended the nationwide sightings, especially after *Unsolved Mysteries* aired her story countless times. Dan had once said that he felt like he was chasing a ghost car. The sightings could no longer haunt us.

Recovering Lisa's car was paramount to the case. We feared Eaton's defense would argue that Eaton either had sex with Lisa consensually or by assault, thus explaining the DNA semen match, but that he didn't kill her. The car buried on Eaton's property, combined with the DNA evidence, would provide the prosecution with a formidable case.

Detectives sifted more items out of the septic hole. Most were parts from the car that had been broken off when Eaton moved it from the well hole. Small things that Lisa had owned surfaced. Lynn found Lisa's jar of Carmex. Lisa had a rash on her shins and used Carmex to sooth the itching. Her dark-red visor caps from Arby's were in the car.

Several of Lisa's religious items were found. A small white porcelain figurine of Mary, her eyes closed, her hands clasped in prayer, was still intact. When I saw that picture, I wanted to hold the figurine, maybe feeling Lisa near me once again. Someone found the rear view mirror with her rosary attached. The beads were dirty, and the metal cross had corroded, but Jesus's form was still unmistakable.

They found her other eyeglass lens and pages from my atlas—the same one we had studied so carefully the day before she vanished.

A shell casing from Eaton's .30-.30 rifle was found in the car, creating another mystery. How did a casing get there?

The second day of the crime scene investigation didn't end until 6:30 P.M. No wonder Lynn sounded exhausted when she called. The desert heat had assailed them for almost eleven hours.

Once again, a deputy stood guard all night. Tireless heroes, a dozen strong, arrived at 7:00 A.M. Wednesday to continue.

Sheriff Roger Millard had arranged for a crane to meet deputies at Eaton's property. Sheriff Benton located a truck and trailer to haul the car back to Casper. Lisa's Honda rose from its dusty grave about 8:30 A.M. They quickly covered it with a blue tarp and hauled it to the old County Fire building, where it was secured.

Even after the car had been removed, the investigators scooped and sifted. They found another visor from Arby's, but nothing else. Dan didn't want to give up, but the hole was becoming unstable and Sheriff Benton finally ordered him to get out.

The teams took a few days off and then went at it one more time on Monday, August 5th. Could Eaton be hiding other secrets? They excavated an old cabin foundation, areas west of the trailer, a shed near the power poles, and two other suspicious locations. When nothing more was found, they finally stopped and left the remains as shelter for the desert critters.

Dan and Lynn plunged further into the investigation. They sorted through the items found, cleaned them up, took pictures, and prepared to show us the evidence. We didn't have to rake dirt under a scorching sun for four days. They had simplified the process to minimize our pain, and we appreciated their consideration. On August 7th, Dan and Lynn drove to Denver again to meet with Ron, the girls, and me.

We had just moved nineteen miles south of our home in Lakewood.

Only one day before, North American Van Lines had delivered our furniture. Boxes lay unopened, but we managed to clear enough space in the living room to sit on the furniture. Dan and Lynn walked in the door, stepped over the mess and had a seat. We were asked to identify the personal items from photos.

Each item was difficult to look at, but the picture of Lisa's car broke our hearts. It was crumpled and partially rusted from years of being buried. We found out that Eaton had buried the car twice, damaging it extensively. He had access to heavy machinery and equipment through the welding jobs he had worked on in the oil fields and while working for the highway department. He had used a backhoe stored near his property to dig the first "well hole."

After Eaton dug the new septic tank hole, he used a cable to drag Lisa's car from the "well hole." He positioned a large PVC pipe so it was leading into the car then placed part of his trailer on top of the dirt. The thought of him intending to use Lisa's car as a septic tank for his raw sewage made me sick to my stomach.

Before he buried it, he had stripped the Honda of the bucket seats, the radio, wheels, gearshift knob, and anything of value. They found a siphon hose still hanging from the gas tank. The windows were smashed. Only a mangled shell remained.

Dan and Lynn told us it would take two to three months to compile their information and present it to the DA. We also would have to overcome two obstacles. Eaton faced a November 2002 manslaughter trial in Denver for the death of his cellmate in September 2001. He was also in a *federal* prison, which presented its own set of problems and paperwork. Extradition to Wyoming and formal charges would only take place after many legal hoops had been jumped through. It could take a year or more before Lisa's case went to trial.

Lynn and Dan quizzed our family at length about our feelings on the death penalty. Based on what that man did to my daughter, my beliefs are that Eaton gave up his humanity. Somewhere in his life, he had turned into a savage animal. Ron and I knew it might cause controversy, but we gave our blessings to seek the death penalty. The only way we would have relented was if Eaton had honestly shown remorse and given answers to the families of other murdered women in the Great Basin area. Based on the FBI profiling of Lisa's murder and Eaton's behavior during the abduction he was jailed for, we believed more than ever that he had killed before and after Lisa.

Dan asked us to prepare a biography of Lisa to give to the District Attorney. The DA knew *about* Lisa but really didn't *know* her. It took me nearly a month to prepare it because of my fragile emotions. I would work on it a few hours, then cry for many more. How could I describe the joy she brought into our lives and our hurt in losing her? When I prepared the pictorial DVD for our victims' impact statement and looked at Lisa's baby pictures day after day, I often fell apart. I tried to compile the information when Ron wasn't home because it was hard on him, too. Several times he came home early only to find me crying in front of the computer. There aren't words to lessen the pain, but we had learned to comfort and console one another over the course of the years. Long hugs were all we could muster.

CHAPTER 13

A Violent Past

Ron and I knew little about Eaton for several months after the DNA match. Dan and Lynn were busy compiling information from his criminal and employment records, and interviewing family, friends, and coworkers.

We eventually saw his "rap sheet." He began stealing at the age of 16. He was jailed for auto theft, burglary, and assault with a deadly weapon. He was in and out of jail during the 1960s, spending several years in prison from ages 16 to 27. He had been arrested numerous times for assault and larceny. I couldn't understand why he hadn't been locked up for good many years ago.

We found out other tidbits of information. How did he end up in a federal prison? Had he killed others? We had a million questions. We eventually found out details from various sources. The stories are chilling.

ASSAULT ON THE BREEDENS

On Friday morning, September 12th, 1997, Dale Eaton was supposed to be heading for a welding job in Utah. Along the way, he spotted a young couple standing outside a bright yellow van parked along I-80.

Perhaps it represented a tempting opportunity to him. He stopped to check them out.

Newlyweds Shannon and Scott Breeden were returning to their home in California from a trip across the country to show off their four-and-a-half-month-old son, Cody. They had visited Shannon's sister in Washington State, then Scott's family in Michigan, living in a 1972 carpeted Ford van that they had fixed up with a sink, propane stove, and a built-in bed. Because of its black grill and white trim, they had nicknamed the yellow flat-nosed van the "Bumblebeast."

The afternoon before, the engine overheated between Rawlins and Wamsutter, Wyoming, so they drove onto an asphalt parking lot off I-80 that was designed as a pull-off area for truckers. The area was about two hundred feet wide and long enough to fit at least three big rigs. It wasn't a public rest area, just a flat blacktop surrounded by the flat desert plains. Only sagebrush and grasslands existed for miles. The van wouldn't start again, so they made camp where they landed. Except for the occasional passing car, only wild horses, antelope, snakes and other creatures shared the desert with the Breedens as they ate dinner and watched for truckers who could help. They gave up Thursday night and went to sleep.

On Friday, they woke to a warm September morning, ate breakfast, and waited again. A few truckers had promised to call for help, but no one ever showed up. The sun slowly heated the pavement. Eighteen hours of waiting had passed since their vehicle had broken down. They began to get desperate. They were running out of food and water, and they had Cody to feed, along with a six-toed kitten named "Why" and a three-legged dog named "Weasel."

Around nine o'clock that morning, a stocky dark-haired man pulled onto the parking area in a faded green 1985 Dodge van. They planned to speak to him until he lifted his hood with apparent engine trouble. Their hopes were doused, but only for a moment. The man walked over to the Breedens and asked if they needed help. They said yes, and explained their situation.

The man said his name was Dale and that he had a brother about an hour away in Green River who could tow them to town. Relieved, they loaded their things, their child, and the pets into his cluttered van. Dale obviously lived and worked out of his vehicle as a welder, traveling the desolate highways searching for jobs, or other "opportunities." He cooked on a Coleman stove and slept on a cot set up in the back of his van. Scott said he thought Eaton seemed "normal." Eaton was dressed in a button-up shirt and jeans. Shannon said that Eaton sometimes talked to himself, but he didn't say anything loud enough for either of them to comprehend. The couple exchanged looks when he mumbled, but paid little attention because he also carried on a casual discussion with them about the oil fields and jobs in the region. He also expressed admiration for Cody, saying that his sister-in-law loved children, but couldn't have any of her own.

Eaton drove for a short time and then pulled over. He said that he needed to pee and that the engine wasn't running right. He wanted to check under the hood again.

The Breedens didn't object. Scott needed to relieve himself, too, and Shannon needed to feed the baby. She wasn't shy about breast-feeding her youngster, and she was an attractive twenty-nine-year-old woman dressed in a flowing gauze dress, her long, brown, curly hair hanging below her shoulders. Eyeing Shannon, Eaton said he "needed to rest," could one of them drive? (Later the Breedens remembered that he had been "slamming down" coffee ever since he'd offered them a ride. They were mad at themselves for missing that clue.)

Scott's driver's license was suspended, so Shannon took the wheel. She drove for a short time while Scott sat next to her holding Cody. Eaton was in the back, appearing to lie on his cot.

Suddenly the Breedens heard a rifle lever click. Eaton was sitting upright, aiming a rifle at them. The Breedens knew they had been set up.

"This is a .30-.30. Now drive down this dirt road, and I mean it!" The dirt road led into the Red Desert and a vast expanse of oil field, a place where bodies could lay for years undetected. Eaton showed the loaded gun to Scott, indicating there was more than one bullet. First he pointed it at Shannon's head, then at Scott and Cody's.

"What do I do?" Shannon whispered to Scott.

"Do what he says," Scott replied, his eyes wide with fear.

Under her breath, Shannon said something about spinning the vehicle and Scott nodded.

Eaton should have known not to mess with brand-new parents.

Shannon remembered thinking, "If I'm going down, I'm going down right here."

Aiming the van off the road, Shannon jerked the steering wheel hard to one side forcing the vehicle to circle, knocking Eaton off balance. When he lurched for the keys, Shannon screamed, "Scott, take Cody and jump!"

Scott bolted out of the van landing in the dirt. He laid the baby in sagebrush, whispering, "I love you, Cody," before racing to help Shannon as the van halted.

Although Scott was tall, he only weighed 155 pounds compared to Eaton's 230-pound frame. Scott had to fight viciously. So did Shannon. She struggled to get outside the van, but Eaton held onto her. From behind, Scott pulled Eaton off of his wife and out of the van, and they wrestled the gun away from the crazed man. Shannon fired the gun at him, but missed. She used the rifle to hit him but the wooden stock broke. Undaunted, Eaton stumbled back to the van.

"Somehow we ended up behind the van after he came out with a butcher knife." Scott said.

Eaton tried to stab Shannon, but again the couple overcame him.

Scott continued, "That's when I ended up on top of him and stabbed him in the chest. I said I was going to kill him, but somehow he freakin' got up!"

Scott stabbed Eaton, but not deep enough to stop the attacks. Eaton freed himself from the Breedens, reached in his van and grabbed a third weapon, a crescent wrench. Once again, the three of them fought and Scott ended up with the wrench. He began hitting Eaton in the head but Eaton kept coming at them.

"He used different weapons; that was his thing," Scott said. "He had it set up so at any point he could get to a weapon, and he did. I didn't expect him to get up after I stabbed him, but the next thing I know, we're over by the van again. The only thing I thought of was that I was going to stop him one way or another."

Shannon threw the rifle to Scott. "Here, knock that son of a bitch out."

Holding the rifle barrel, Scott beat Eaton's back and head, hard.

Eaton collapsed to the ground, groaning in pain, but he kept trying to get up.

"He was insane, crazy. He was not quitting." Scott said his instincts told him to go for the knees. He aimed the broken butt of the rifle at Eaton's left knee and took Eaton down. Even as Eaton laid on the ground, he kicked at Scott.

Throughout the fight, Cody lay in the bushes screaming.

"That's what kept us going, kept us fighting," Scott said. "Our little baby was over there crying. He'd been asleep and woke up as I was flying into the dirt. We knew that if something happened to us, he'd probably die, too. We were fighting for his life and ours."

After several whacks to the knee, Scott said Eaton finally gave up and said, "Okay, I'm done." Then he looked up at Scott and asked, "Will you leave me a cigarette?" Scott's voice shook as he recalled the details. "That was the last thing that f——-r ever said to me."

Enraged, Scott said, "I wanted to f——-g kill him. I told Shannon to run over his head. She wouldn't." Scott didn't leave until Shannon had started up the van with Cody safely inside. Weasel had hopped in, too. The frightened six-toed kitten "Why" had stayed hidden under a seat throughout the ordeal.

Shannon sped to the first house she saw in a development of four modular white homes, an area called "Patrick Draw." Wyoming's highway department built the houses for road crews and their families near a shed full of snowplows and other equipment, including gas storage tanks for state vehicles. Stopping, she clambered out and yelled for help while Scott comforted their terrified baby.

The Breedens were lucky that someone was home. A female security guard for the Bridger Power plant was watching TV and heard the commotion. She ran outside to find Shannon pacing by the gate, her dress and bare feet caked with mud. Breathless, Shannon told the woman what happened, so she dialed 911. Eaton was injured, but not dead.

Several patrol cars responded to the call over the Sweetwater County Sheriff's Office radio just before 11:00 A.M. They met the Breedens at the security guards house but weren't sure who had attacked whom. Thinking that Scott was the suspect, they quickly cuffed him.

"They didn't believe us. They called us whacked-out hippies," Scott said.

Shannon yelled in protest, "He's my husband. Let him go!"

After calming Shannon down, the officers interviewed her and Scott in separate patrol cars. The security guard also gave a statement that supported the Breedens' story. Other officers had located Eaton and dispatched an ambulance to treat his stab wound. The deputies found the circular tire grooves in the mud and saw pots and pans, tools, and other items from Eaton's van scattered in many directions, confirming the Breedens' version of the story.

Scott said their experience changed them. Once laid-back and trusting of people, even hitchhikers, they became leery and began to rely more on their instincts. If something doesn't feel right, they don't do it. "It cut the trust thing down a lot for us. But sometimes I feel stronger realizing I survived something like that," Scott said. Shannon agreed and added: "I celebrate it as a victory. We got away."

EATON'S VERSION

Based on the investigation and evidence, Eaton was charged with aggravated assault. Eaton had confessed to an officer with odd ramblings. He said that he had hoped the couple would kill him because he had a life-threatening disease, and he didn't have the guts to kill himself. (He was hoping for what, "suicide by strangers?")

Interviewed in jail by Sweetwater County Detective Rich Haskell, Eaton's tale differed from the Breedens' in other ways. Never looking the detective in the eye, he said that when they stopped for a short break, he heard the Breedens "whispering," saying "funny things." Eaton said he thought the Breedens wanted to rob him.

But he admitted that he pulled a rifle on the young couple, opened the breech to show it was loaded, and ordered them to drive *away* from the housing area rather than toward it.

If he were afraid that the Breedens were going to rob him, Eaton never explained why he got back in the van with them and asked Shannon to drive. If he thought they would rob him, why did he pick them up to begin with? Was he planning to rob them? Shannon said that they were obviously poor. She will always be convinced he saw an opportunity and hoped to have "his way" with her.

During the interview with Eaton, Detective Haskell noticed that Eaton acted stiff, as though in pain from his stab wound and beating. He whined about getting robbed. When asked about anything but the assault, "Eaton loosened up and spoke clearer," according to police records.

He tried to rationalize his behavior toward the Breedens. "Here lately I've been on a real short fuse. I shouldn't be around people; I can't handle it. I get up and walk away. I like being by myself." Then he changed the subject. "It's just weird. I'm depressed about a job deal." He went on to say that he can't find a job and that younger men always won out.

He rambled on about losing everything to his ex-wife. He was destitute, unable to work. His brother had committed suicide. For these reasons, he said he should have killed himself.

After a warrant was obtained, the officers found a variety of tools, a Marlin .30-.30 caliber rifle, several cases of live and expended .30-.30 cartridges, two butcher knives, and a key ring with thirteen keys, one broken.

Something else more distressing was found. Handcuffs lay in plain view. When asked about their purpose, Eaton said he'd had them for ten to fifteen years, since a liaison with a former girlfriend who liked handcuffs, and "turned me every way but loose." He added that since his divorce he'd been unable to make love to any woman. He was trying to sell the handcuffs and a vibrator she left behind for extra money, but no one wanted to buy them. He said that he didn't have a key to the handcuffs.

Eaton lied. One of the thirteen keys indeed unlocked the handcuffs, probably the same ones he used on my daughter.

Eaton was free on bail from September 1997 to April 23rd, 1998, when he was convicted of aggravated assault and battery against the Breedens. He was placed on five years of probation and sentenced to two months in jail. Then, due to prison overcrowding, he was paroled to a halfway house in Casper called Community Alternatives of Casper (CAC). CAC *required* Eaton to have a vehicle to drive back and forth to work. He was *given* his van back. The Breedens, the victims, ended up losing their van after the ordeal. Amazing.

Had Eaton served his meager sentence at CAC, he might have gone free for good. But he couldn't resist the impulse to simply drive away after six weeks, on June 16th, 1998. A notice was sent out across the state through the National Crime Information Computer. Warrants popped up left and right. Eaton was a wanted man.

A Lucky Catch

July 30th, 1998, was a clear summer day when Wyoming Fish and Game Officer Bill Long started up his truck for his daily patrols in the Bridger Teton National Forest. He was visiting camps to warn people about safe food storage. Grizzly bears were foraging in the area.

The first camper Officer Long approached wasn't at a formal campsite. A light greenish van was parked on Rosie's Ridge Road, a side road near an access to Togwotee Pass Highway. The side road was built on a meadow ridge overlooking the Tetons. Sun filtered through the lightly wooded area, creating a pleasant, shady campsite.

Officer Long saw a van with its panel doors open. With no campfires or cooking grill, he assumed the van hadn't been there long. A man in casual clothes stood near the vehicle. As he drove closer, Long called in the license plate numbers as part of protocol. Long rolled down his windows and said, "Good afternoon. Everything all right? We've had trouble with grizzly bears, so I'm talking to everyone in the area and making sure you have a clean camp."

The man had acted nervous enough to make the hackles on the back of Long's neck rise.

"I'm only gonna be here a little while," the man said abruptly, his eyes downcast.

He quickly closed the van door, but not before Officer Long noticed a bed in the back of the driver's side corner. A sleeping bag covered something on top of the cot.

"No bear problems?"

"No," the man muttered.

Long nodded. "Okay. Have a good day, sir." He slowly drove away before stopping at a point where he could eyeball the access road the van was parked on. His intuition told him to stay.

The dispatcher's voice suddenly crackled over the radio, informing Officer Long of alarming news. The van was registered to one Dale Wayne Eaton, an escaped felon. Officer Long confirmed the message and asked dispatch to check again. Once the warrant was confirmed, Long called for backup.

Officer Long drove into a position to monitor the access road and block the escape route should Eaton try to flee. About thirty minutes later, two officers quietly arrived on the scene. During that time Eaton had walked away, but was returning to his vehicle along Rosie's Ridge Road. Officer Long and the two rangers approached through the woods adjacent to Eaton's van. His shirtless chest was a welcome sight because they could tell he wasn't wearing a gun around his waist. They nodded to each other and stepped from behind the trees holding their rifles on Eaton.

He was ordered to kneel on the ground with his hands in the air and then lie face down, where he was handcuffed. Officer Long said Eaton hesitated to follow commands, as though considering his options, but he didn't stall long enough to worry the lawmen.

A third Grand Teton National Park Ranger had driven to the scene after Eaton was in custody. Eaton was read his rights, loaded into a patrol car, and sent to the Grand Teton County Jail. The officers found a rifle on Eaton's cot. Felons can't own a firearm, and that's what landed Eaton in a federal prison.

What he did in those six weeks while he was on the run may remain a mystery, but he was certainly resourceful. Where did he get the money to buy food? And most of all, where did he get another rifle? Did someone help him out? Did other victims cross his path? We may never know.

CHAPTER 14

Federal Obstacles

Even though Dan and Lynn compiled a strong case against Eaton by mid-October 2002, we would have to wait before Natrona County could file charges. Eaton faced a trial for manslaughter. On September 3rd, 2001, Eaton killed his prison cellmate with his bare fist in the Florence, Colorado, federal penitentiary.

His trial was scheduled to begin on November 19th, 2002, at the Federal Building in downtown Denver. I decided to attend, hoping to learn more about the legal process that was so foreign to me, although I knew Lisa's case would be different. More importantly, I needed to see the man in person. I felt it would help me prepare myself emotionally for his trial for murdering Lisa.

Ron questioned my wisdom and objected.

I told Ron, "You may not agree with me, but this is what *I* need to do. You do what *you* need to do. I will support you in *your* decisions, but I need your support in *mine*."

Ron reluctantly accepted my choice.

During the first morning of Eaton's manslaughter trial, I sat quietly on a bench, preparing to take notes. After the jury was selected and seated, the bailiffs brought in Dale Eaton. Seeing him for the first time was harder than I expected. I knew he was a big man, but he wasn't tall. He was stout and barrel-chested, with choppy black hair. He had a grim face, haunting dark eyes and large hands—hands that took my daughter's life. I quietly wept, but I had to cry alone. Only the prosecution team knew who I was, and that's the way I wanted it. I intended to remain anonymous. I did not want to create any problems for the prosecution team, nor did I want Eaton to know that I was in the courtroom.

However, I found it difficult to hide since only one other person, an attractive woman about my age, sat in the observation area. She was dressed in nice clothes that flattered her thin figure, and she wore her thick blonde hair long. Her makeup and manicure looked professional. Her gracefulness contrasted with Eaton's heavy features. Knowing she wasn't his wife, I was curious.

Both of us were smokers, so we went outside of the federal building during breaks. I found her to be conversational and pleasant. However, I avoided personal talk that would disclose my name, and she didn't ask. When I spoke with Dan that evening, I discovered the mystery woman's identity. She was Dale Eaton's younger sister, Judy.

Dan told me Judy was a nice woman. When he interviewed her, she had expressed her feelings of sympathy for us for what her brother had done to our daughter. Dan said I could tell her who I was and it wouldn't cause trouble. But I wouldn't do that until the case went to the jury.

According to trial testimony, the problems began when Carl Inman Palmer was assigned to room with Eaton. Palmer weighed much less than Eaton, and some of the other prisoners ribbed Eaton about Palmer's sexual orientation. Eaton said he didn't like homosexuals. I don't know whether Palmer was homosexual or not.

Monday, September 3rd, 2001, the inmates were free to roam among the cells and the common area, where they could play cards, read the newspaper, or watch TV. Palmer was in the common area, and Dale was in the cell they shared. There was a privacy code among the men for personal matters. If a prisoner went into his cell, closed the door, and placed a piece of cardboard or paper over the window, it meant the toilet was occupied. Eaton put the paper in place to do his business.

About 9:30 A.M., an announcement was piped over the facility loudspeakers for everyone to return to his cell for a head count. Palmer obeyed the orders with a guard following him.

What happened next is unclear, but it didn't appear that Eaton was on the toilet. Testimony reported him to be standing up, but Palmer's entrance angered him anyway. Eaton lashed out at Palmer, striking him on the right cheek with his fist, using the strength of his heavy frame. Palmer recoiled. "Why'd you hit me?"

Eaton shot back, "What the f—k? I don't come in when you're on the toilet."

Palmer suddenly collapsed to the floor, and the guard called for help. An ambulance rushed to the scene, but Palmer's condition worsened. As he was carted away, Eaton was said to weep, asking repeatedly, "Is my roomie okay?" He wasn't. Palmer died from a vertebral artery that ruptured when his head snapped from the blow, an occurrence similar to an aneurysm.

After both sides rested their cases on November 21st, the twelve-person jury left the courtroom to decide Eaton's fate. I gave the bailiff a phone number where I could be contacted when the verdict was reached (a service anyone observing could request). Eaton's defense attorney was behind me, but I didn't pay much attention to him because I wanted to catch Judy and finally introduce myself.

I caught up to her just as the defense attorney blurted out, "Excuse me. Are you Sheila Kimmell?"

I turned. "Yes."

"Are you Lisa's mother?"

"Yes," I said.

Judy burst into tears. "Oh, my God, I need to talk to you."

"I was hoping I could talk to you, too," I told her.

The defense attorney expressed his condolences to me as Judy and I left for lunch. We walked across the busy street to an upscale pub in a high-rise building, finding a private booth. We ordered lunch and talked while waiting for the phone call.

We shared a lot of tears. She said she and her family felt terrible for us. Most didn't doubt his guilt because of the DNA match. Judy and her siblings knew Dale had been in and out of trouble most of his life, but what he did to Lisa was incomprehensible. They didn't understand his dark side.

Judy told me that her family had experienced a hard life and that Dale got picked on the most, but he also caused a lot of trouble, like the incorrigible child. Judy remembered him being protective of his younger siblings, and she got along with him just fine. She couldn't understand what went wrong. They grew up in the same house with the same parents. What made Dale so different from the rest of them?

Our conversation didn't last long much longer. Our cell phones rang, and it was time to return to court. The verdict was in.

Eaton was found not guilty. I was disappointed because a guilty verdict might have helped Lisa's case, but I had to agree with the jury's decision because the prosecution couldn't prove that he had intentions of *killing* Palmer—just intentions of punching him. However, Palmer's senseless death was illustrative of Eaton's past. Had Eaton been able to control his explosive temper and careless abuse of human life, Carl Palmer would probably still be alive.

CHAPTER 15

More Legal Complications

On October 26th, 2002, Lynn and Dan had accomplished their goal of building strong charges against Dale Eaton for Lisa's murder. They handed the case over to Kevin Meenan, the Natrona County District Attorney. Ron and I were anxious. We had expected Kevin to review the case during Eaton's federal trial and file charges immediately afterward in November. That didn't happen. His procrastination should have clued us in on what to expect.

In fact, we didn't hear from Kevin during the entire month of November. What was the holdup? Frustrated, we asked to speak with him, but he wasn't available to take our calls. Our frustration increased. Finally he arranged a conference call with Ron, Sherry, Stacy, and me on December 11th, 2002.

Kevin assured us that after January 1st, he would devote his full attention to our case. He had several other cases to prosecute, and the holiday season had arrived. He also needed to work on legal maneuvers to get Eaton out of federal prison and into the county jail. He asked if we could come to Casper for a face-to-face meeting in the middle of January. Despite Kevin's reassurance, it was hard to wait for even one more day. Eaton was due to be released from prison in the summer of 2004 for serving his time on the firearm charge. We didn't want to take any chances that would allow him back on the streets and put other young women at risk.

Kevin was the incumbent DA running for reelection to the office he had held since 1986. He was reelected for his fifth term in November. He had served as Chairman of the Natrona County Republican Party and President of the National District Attorneys Association in the course of his political career.

At that point, we were impressed with Kevin. He was valued in the community and came from a family with a good reputation. His father, Patrick Meenan, was a successful businessman and had served twenty years as a Republican in the Wyoming State House of Representatives. Patrick would ultimately become the Wyoming House Speaker, respected by both parties. He died at the age of 73 on August 16th, 2001, after a year-and-a-half-long battle with lung cancer. That must have been hard on Kevin and his family.

We were looking forward to meeting Kevin in person. Ron, the girls, and I met with him in the Natrona County Courthouse on January 24th, 2003. Kevin seemed to have everything, including an aura of power. He was tall, attractive, polished. But much of the conversation was filled with assurances similar to our conference call in December. The charges still weren't filed, and that bothered us.

On the positive side, Kevin explained the mitigating circumstances straight from the law books that would support the death penalty in our case. Kevin guaranteed that he would have Eaton extradited and the charges filed by the end of February or the middle of March at the latest. Before leaving the meeting, we discussed filing a civil suit against Eaton. Kevin didn't object and said he would give us names of attorneys we might want to contact to handle the matter.

February came and went. Again, we heard nothing from Kevin. When I tried to call him, I could only reach Janeice Lynch, the Victim-Witness Coordinator for Natrona County's felony division. She seemed to be Kevin's shield. I felt as though he was avoiding me. By mid-March, my patience had worn thin. I called Janeice and told her that the waiting had become unbearable; if the charges weren't filed soon, I would go to the press and make my concerns public.

Kevin appeared to dislike the media, because after Janeice passed the message to him, he called immediately. He asked me for more patience, offering explanations of the delays. I told him that his excuses were no longer acceptable. Again he promised that he would file the charges against Eaton soon, but he couldn't give us an exact date because of security issues. I begged him not to make us go through another anniversary of Lisa's death without charges being filed against her murderer. The anniversary week of Lisa's disappearance arrived. Eaton still had not been extradited to Wyoming, and still no charges were filed. I was crushed. Wednesday, April 2nd, marked the fifteen-year anniversary of the day Lisa's body was found. I couldn't take the waiting any longer. I tried calling both Dan and Lynn at the office at 9:00 A.M. They weren't in. I tried their cell phones. No response. Usually I was able to locate Dan or Lynn, day or night, 24-7, but not that day. Something was up.

It occurred to me that they might be transporting Eaton to Wyoming and they weren't allowed to tell me because of that "security issue." I was confident that my intuition was correct, so I called Dan's cell phone and left a message on his voice mail. "You and Lynn drive careful now."

I calculated their travel time from Denver to Casper and added an hour to process Eaton out of federal prison. Depending on the time they left Casper, I expected them to return between 4:00 and 5:00 P.M.

Sure enough, about four o'clock that afternoon we got a call from the DA's office. Dan and Lynn were on the speakerphone with Janeice and Kevin. The two detectives had successfully transferred Eaton. Hallelujah!

Before hanging up, I told Dan he should check his messages on his cell phone. I guess my intuition had worked overtime that day. Ron and I were relieved beyond words.

Lynn told us that Eaton hadn't spoken a word throughout the trip.

Tribune headlines broke the next day pressuring the DA's office further about filing charges: "Kimmells anxiously await justice. Meenan: Much happening behind the scenes." Two weeks later, Kevin finally came through. The capital murder charges were filed on April 17th, 2003.

Despite our relief, reading the harsh legal wording in the documents brought me to tears again. The charges confirmed that Lisa had been held hostage for days.

A few weeks later my family and I drove to Casper to attend the pretrial motions held on Thursday, May 8th, 2003. A preliminary hearing (a "mini-trial") was scheduled to follow directly afterwards. Eaton's defense attorney, Wyatt Skaggs, began by presenting several motions, honing in on his objections to media coverage. An article had been published in the previous Sunday's paper delving into the possibility that Eaton was a serial killer. Part of the 1988 FBI profile was included, and Skaggs thought the article "prejudicial" to his client. Skaggs also requested that he be allowed access to all information the state might have. His other requests included a gag order on all county and state employees, banning them from talking to the media. Finally, he asked the court to dismiss *all* charges based on the media's "prejudicial" coverage. Skaggs called the *Tribune's* speculation that Eaton was a serial killer as "yellow journalism." All motions were denied, so Skaggs angrily waived the rights to the preliminary hearing.

After the pre-motion trial was over, we met with Kevin and the prosecuting team. Skaggs wasn't the only lawyer upset about the media. Kevin did not want us to talk to any more reporters. It was a bit too late. A three-part feature story was about to break in the *Billings Gazette* that focused on Don Flickinger. When Kevin found out, his jaw tightened.

I told him, "We participated to some degree, but this story has nothing to do with Eaton. This is about an investigator who was very dedicated and committed."

Kevin's jaw tightened more. "I don't want any more contact with the media. Period."

"Look, Kevin," I said. "We've learned over the years that if you work with them, it causes fewer problems. And it's already done. I can't stop them."

He remained visibly annoyed throughout the meeting, until he made an odd comment. (Most people put their blinkers on before they make a turn, but Kevin didn't.) He said that if anything should happen to him, other capable people could step in and handle our daughter's case. We didn't know how to respond to his statement, and we didn't ask questions. We shrugged it off and left the meeting.

One week later, Attorney Mark Gifford filed a wrongful death civil suit against Eaton on our behalf. He wouldn't accept a fee and offered his services pro bono. It was another act of generosity for which we were grateful. Then we turned our attention to Lisa's Memorial Scholarship presentation coming up in Billings.

Lisa Kimmell at age 1.

Sheila and Ron holding Lisa at Christmas, 1969.

Lisa was Daddy's little girl while he served his tour of duty in the Marines, 1970.

From left to right: *Lisa, Sherry, Ricky, and Stacy Kimmell, 1974.*

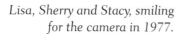

Lisa, Sherry and Stacy, smiling for the camera in 1977.

Lisa Kimmell at three different ages: sitting under the dryer at age 2½, talking on the phone at age 15, and posing for her yearbook photo at age 17.

Lisa in her favorite suit with a touch of lace.

Ron Ketchum,
Natrona County Sheriff
from 1986-1990.

Dan Tholson,
Natrona County Detective
on Lisa's case.

Jim Broz, former
Natrona County Detective
on Lisa's case.

James W. Thorpen, M.D.,
Pathologist and Natrona
County Coroner.

Don Flickinger, retired
Special Agent for the
Bureau of Alcohol,
Tobacco and Firearms.

Darlene and Delores
Gustovich, the psychic
sisters from Great Falls,
Montana.

The 2004 Natrona County prosecution team. Front row: Victim's Advocate Janeice Lynch and Detective Lynn Cohee. Back row: Assistant District Attorney Stephanie Sprecher, District Attorney Mike Blonigen, and Detective Dan Tholson.

Wyatt Skaggs, Dale Eaton's Defense Attorney.

District Attorney Mike Blonigen.

Judge David Park, the judge who presided over Dale Eaton's trial.

Kay Carpenter, the writer who found new information and helped with the book.

Dale Wayne Eaton
(1964 mug shot)

Dale Wayne Eaton
(1998 mug shot)

Moneta,
Wyoming
population
sign.

Dale Eaton's property in Moneta.

Lisa's Honda CRXsi was unearthed from Eaton's property in August, 2002. Dan Tholson is searching for the VIN number.

Lisa's mangled Honda CRXsi after being cleaned up by investigators.

Eaton is suspected of abducting Lisa from this location along Highway 20-26, the Waltman Rest Stop.

The interior of Eaton's Dodge tow truck. The extended cab is where he most likely kept Lisa captive as he drove her to the old school bus where he lived.

The interior of the 1951 school bus where Eaton
kept Lisa hostage for six days.

A close up of the
livestock tank
that Eaton used
as a bathtub in
his school bus.

The Old Government Bridge where Eaton dropped Lisa's body into the
North Platte River, about 20 miles southwest of Casper, Wyoming.

Ron and
Sheila Kimmell
in 2002.

Joe Morian, Lisa's
former boss and long
time friend of the
Kimmell family.

Stacy Kimmell Hoover
with husband Todd Hoover
in 2004.

Sherry Kimmell Odegard with
husband Zane Odegard
and their two sons,
Alex and Trevor .

The scholarship had been successfully awarded for more than ten years. We didn't attend each presentation because the ceremonies were short, and it was a long drive from Denver. Qualified people had stood in on our behalf when needed. When we learned that the presentation was to be held at the same time the three-part feature story was breaking on Don Flickinger and Lisa's case, we wanted to present the award personally. We didn't want to upstage Flick's story, but we didn't want the recipient to feel bad about receiving an award based on a death so graphically described in the newspaper.

I remember the event vividly. The scholarship presentation was held at Billings Senior High in a dimly lit auditorium, much like in a theater. We were invited to sit on the brightly-lit stage with the other presenters. We could hear students whispering excitedly in the audience as they followed the program.

After several presentations, it was our turn to take the podium.

The master of ceremonies gave us an introduction something like, "Many of you have heard and read things in the media about the latest events concerning Lisa Marie Kimmell. In light of that, her parents are here tonight to personally award the Lisa Marie Kimmell Memorial Scholarship Award."

To our surprise, the audience hushed.

I began. "We would like to take this time to shift everyone's focus away from the tragic loss of our Lisa Marie. Now is the time to recognize the good people and our good kids. Tonight is a time to celebrate the good people that came into our lives as a result of our tragic loss. This Memorial Scholarship would not have been possible without the thousands of genuine, caring people who generously contributed to this fund in honor of Lisa. Lisa always wanted to make a difference in life, and as we look upon this crowd of supportive parents, teachers, and now, the scholastic achievers, it highlights the inherent good in all of us. We know that you will go forward and make a difference. You are our hope that you will make this a better world in the future."

Ron took over. "It's a privilege to be here tonight to recognize the communities that supported us for so many years and celebrate our future scholars, contributors to the goodness of mankind. Regardless of the vocation you choose to pursue, our future depends on you. We are

honored, on behalf of Lisa, our family, and the communities that supported us, to come together to recognize another special young person
who will go forward and make a difference, a business major who plans
to attend the University of Oklahoma: Ms. Bobbi Snider!"

The audience gave a hearty round of applause. After we left the
scholarship ceremony, we felt satisfied about our decision to make the
presentation personally.

However, we got fussed at again. Kevin's office was upset about the
article in the *Billings Gazette* about the scholarship presentation. They
said again, *"no more media contact or interviews."* We couldn't understand why Kevin Meenan objected. The article was small and said nothing about Eaton.

Annoyed, I told Janeice, "Tough, it's done. Tell Kevin to get over it."

Six days later we learned about circumstances that put Kevin's behavior in perspective. No wonder he had procrastinated. Our district
attorney, the man who was supposed to bring us justice for the death of
our daughter after so many years, had been under investigation for several months. He was charged with one count of official misconduct and
several counts of felony forgery. Ten counts total. We were stunned.

CHAPTER 16

Disturbing Politics

K evin must have known that charges were forthcoming when he met
with us on May 23rd, 2003. That would explain his odd comment
that if anything happened to him, others could readily step in and
handle our case.

Ron and I were shattered, and concerned about how it would affect
Lisa's case with Kevin as the lead prosecutor. An accused felon prosecuting another accused felon? What a concept! The more we learned,
the more alarmed we became.

Some of the charges included forgery (five counts), larceny by bailee,
official misconduct, unauthorized use of personal identifying information, false written statement to obtain credit, obtaining property by false
pretenses, and unlawful use of a credit card. These were very serious
charges.

Apparently Kevin had received a $55,000 personal injury settlement
in July 1999 on behalf of his stepdaughter. He placed the money in a
trust account and forged her signature. Kevin didn't tell her how much
the settlement was for. Kevin initially said the settlement was only for
$40,000, and then finally admitted the truth. Worse yet, Kevin had *spent*
the money, all $55,000, in ten months.

A little more than a year later, on July 18th, 2001, Kevin opened
a credit card account, forging his stepson's signature. He then illegally

wrote checks against the card and allowed the card to become delinquent. Kevin also opened a credit card account for his stepdaughter in her name without her knowledge, but had made the payments and later closed the account.

If he were to be found guilty of all the charges, he faced up to 95 years in prison and a $100,000 fine. He insisted that it was a private family issue, not a criminal matter. But what was he thinking? I don't know the details about his personal life, but I heard they were complicated, perhaps fueling the problem.

When Kevin was questioned on February 24th, 2003, he said that he had opened credit card accounts for all of his children to help build their credit ratings, and when they became financially responsible, he turned the cards over to each child. Kevin said that the stepson had several "responsibility" problems, so Kevin never told him about his account, or turned the credit card over to him. Kevin confessed to withdrawing money, but couldn't recall what he used it for. He thought he gave some money to his stepson to repair his car. Kevin said he was aware of an outstanding balance, but wasn't able to make payments at the time because he had a "financial situation." Kevin said he never intended to hurt his stepson's credit.

What was Kevin spending all that money on? That's a mystery that may not be solved, and it has nothing to do with Lisa's death. But the repercussions of Kevin's legal difficulties could affect how well he functioned as our lead prosecuting attorney.

Ron and I wanted Kevin off our case, immediately! We wanted no part of the mess.

Ron and I called Kevin on June 20th to discuss our concerns. He was very diplomatic and assured us that he could keep his personal issues separate from managing Lisa's case. He made it clear that he wasn't willing to reassign it to another prosecutor.

We were not convinced. Over the next few days I called a number of people familiar with Kevin and our case. Off the record, each of our sources expressed concerns that paralleled ours. However, they were powerless to act because of the Natrona County infrastructure and politics they faced. Our contacts could lose their jobs or damage their careers if they said anything publicly. We understood. Ron and I had an advantage; Kevin couldn't fire us.

We didn't want to make things worse or hurt Kevin. We decided to try another approach. We thought a peer could act as a mediator to convince Kevin that he would be wise to step aside. Perhaps another lawyer could let him know about our determination to get him off the case. I called Mark Gifford, the lawyer handling our wrongful death suit against Eaton. I asked him if he would talk to Kevin. He agreed, knowing it was a delicate issue. He asked me if I could outline our concerns so that he could discuss them with Kevin. Our outline of the issues read as follows:

Timing. This could not be happening at a worse time for us, with Eaton's trial approaching. The outcome could be tragic if we have to change prosecutors midstream. The sooner he steps aside, the better.

Distraction and attention. Kevin will most likely be distracted by his problems and not give our case his full attention.

Credibility. His status could impair our case when he makes arguments before the court or even a jury.

Selfishness. We know that Lisa's case is not his only case, but we have waited fifteen years for justice. We confess to being selfish when it comes to this trial.

Politics. His political battles are not our concern.

Privacy and Courtesy. If Kevin will step aside, we won't go public with our concerns. This can be handled in a private, courteous, and diplomatic way.

Expectations. We expect him to do what is ethically right concerning our case, by reassigning it and stepping aside.

Mark received my fax, met with Kevin that morning, and communicated our worries. After the meeting, Mark called and said he thought the meeting went well. Kevin seemed receptive to what he was saying. Mark said that Kevin agreed to step aside and reassign our case. However, the changes would take a week or two.

A week passed, then two. Kevin had not acted on his promise.

Frustrated, I called Mark again. Mark talked to Kevin again. Kevin promised to make the changes again, by the end of July. The end of July came and went.

By August 1st, Friday afternoon at four o'clock, still nothing. When I called the office to speak with Kevin, he had left for the day. I nosed around to see if Kevin had acted on his promise. He hadn't.

Ron and I had waited long enough and given him every benefit of the doubt. I had prepared a press release "just in case" and hoped I wouldn't have to use it. Part of it read:

"Given the personal complications that Mr. Meenan is dealing with at this time, we hope that he will step aside as the lead prosecutor in our daughter's case and reassign it. His personal and legal issues seem to be complex and will require a great deal of his focus and attention over an extended period of time. We truly hope that he resolves his legal matters, but we are concerned that these issues may jeopardize the effective prosecution of our daughter's case."

I gathered my list of phone numbers for the media, calmly sat down at my fax machine, and let her rip.

I heard that he was swamped at home that night by phone calls from reporters. He was furious and again refused to back off our case.

The *Billings Gazette* quoted him. "I have worked very hard to keep these matters separate... We have taken every possible step to ensure that the prosecution of Mr. Eaton will continue in due course." He indicated to the reporters that he had no intentions of stepping aside.

Ron and I weren't sure what to do next. In some ways, we felt defeated before the trial even began.

On Monday we got a huge surprise. Kevin relented. He publicly stepped aside and reassigned our case, but wouldn't elaborate on his decision. The Assistant DA, Mike Blonigen, was appointed as our new lead prosecutor. We were relieved. To us, changing lead prosecutors in the middle of a trial would be like changing the head coach in the middle of the Super Bowl. It just ain't done!

Regarding charges against him, Kevin Meenan entered into a plea bargain in December 2003. He pleaded guilty to two felony charges and a misdemeanor charge of official misconduct. He was given two years probation, and a suspended prison sentence of one to three years. He was ordered to pay $300 to a victim's compensation fund (which he did immediately). Only one felony charge will remain on his record when he completes his probation. The other charges were dropped in the plea bargain.

The accusations forced Kevin Meenan's resignation and Mike Blonigen was appointed as the acting DA. In February 2004, Kevin was disbarred for five years. It's a shame that he took such risks with such a promising future. Something must have thrown him off balance. We wish him well and hope that he can pull himself back together.

After Mike Blonigen took the helm, I prayed that nothing else would get in the way. The court date was set for February 2004. Our hopes for justice finally appeared within reach.

CHAPTER 17

Revving the Engines

With the murder charges filed against Dale Wayne Eaton and our case reassigned in August, the newly-formed prosecution team geared up. One of the first items on their agenda was to meet with us. On September 5th, 2003, Assistant District Attorney Mike Blonigen, along with Stephanie Sprecher (another attorney assigned to the case) and Janeice Lynch, drove to Denver to meet with us, the girls, and their husbands. We had never met Mike or Stephanie.

We had always been asked to drive to Casper for our meetings with Kevin, which meant juggling work schedules and childcare for our grandsons. Seeing the prosecution rearranging *their* busy schedules to meet with us was a pleasant switch. I ordered deli trays for lunch and a fruit tray for them to snack on before their long drive back to Casper after our meeting.

Mike exceeded our expectations. He differed from Kevin in many ways. He was shorter, with big brown eyes, a boyish smile, and thinning hair. He seemed more outgoing, open. He was also satisfyingly detail-oriented about the case.

Stephanie was a tall, slender, attractive woman with her long, dark-brown hair neatly pulled back. She let Mike do most of the talking, but I saw her intently listening and processing our discussion.

Our meeting went well. Mike explained legal issues, their strategies, and what we could expect. He also patiently listened to our complaints about our past problems. He said little, but his expression told me that he understood. We sensed he didn't concern himself with politics. He seemed devoted to his job, and he was familiar with Lisa's case even before he was assigned as the lead prosecutor.

Mike began working for the DA's office in 1985. He admitted that he could have made more money in private practice, but seeking justice for victims was his calling. Ron and I liked Mike Blonigen and what he stood for.

As the prosecution continued their preparations, there were many loose ends to tie up. It wasn't unusual to get a call from Dan asking for documents or items. He knew I had a cedar chest bursting with stuff I had kept over the years. For example, he asked for the title to Lisa's car, and I had to track that down.

While sorting through the cedar chest, I ran across a copy of the mysterious note that was taped to Lisa's grave in 1989 from "Stringfellow Hawke."

I called Dan on October 10th to tell him that I found the paperwork, but I had another question.

"Okay, shoot," Dan said.

"I ran across the copy of the Stringfellow Hawke note taped to Lisa's headstone. Do you think that Dale Eaton could possibly be the person who wrote it?"

"Hmm. Why didn't I think about that?"

I laughed. "You've had your hands full, Dan, but that note has always bothered me. It was out of place."

He said he would pull the file and investigate it further. "It might be a stretch, Sheila, but I'll check it out."

I didn't give it much thought the rest of the day, and continued sifting through stuff in preparation for the trial.

Before Blonigen took over Lisa's case, Kevin Meenan had argued in favor of the death penalty before Judge David Park, saying that the nature of Lisa's murder, combined with Eaton's criminal past and other crimes committed during her murder (sexual assault, robbery), supported his eligibility for the death penalty.

On October 23rd, the *Casper Star Tribune* published an article stating that Eaton's defense attorneys were seeking to strike the death penalty as a sentencing option because it was "unconstitutional." The most recent execution was in 1992 of a man who was convicted in 1967.

"When the death penalty is infrequently applied it becomes cruel and unusual punishment," Vaughn H. Neubauer, Eaton's assistant defense attorney, wrote. The defense said that the Wyoming Constitution penal codes should be framed on the principles of rehabilitation and prevention. "While prevention may be a goal achieved by the death penalty, rehabilitation is not."

Blonigen filed a counter-motion stating, "Since being incarcerated in Casper, Eaton has stated he would assault any cellmate placed with him." Blonigen said Eaton would pose a "future danger" to the community. I'm thankful we had a judge with a good dose of common sense. He concurred with Blonigen and kept the death penalty option intact. Defense attorney Wyatt Skaggs's motion was denied.

I want to make something clear. Ron and I do not hold grudges against Eaton's defense lawyers. We understood from the beginning that Wyatt Skaggs and Vaughn Neubauer worked with what they had, which wasn't much. In fact, we *wanted* Eaton to have the best defense possible because we didn't want to go through a trial more than once. I had sympathy for Skaggs and his team. Their work was stressful. Skaggs passionately opposes the death penalty, and because of that, he has defended many hardened criminals in his years in office. I don't know if his hair turned white because of stress or genetics, but I'm betting my hair would have fallen out if I did what he does for a living. I doubt that many public defenders get paid a fraction of their corporate colleagues' salaries, yet Skaggs gave the case 100 percent.

However, Skaggs angered us more than once, and we weren't sympathetic enough to let down our guard. The prosecution fought the defense every step of the way.

We had to deal with their request for a change of venue. At first, District Judge Dave Park did not rule whether Eaton's trial would stay in Natrona County, or whether Eaton would be prosecuted based on the 1988 death penalty law or the current version. Eventually, he ruled that the trial would stay in Natrona County and that Eaton would be tried under the harsher 1988 law.

Judge Park also denied Skaggs' request to block the DNA evidence connected to the blood drawn from Eaton while he was incarcerated at the State Penitentiary in 1998. Skaggs argued that drawing blood for a DNA match violated Eaton's Fourth Amendment rights and qualified as an unreasonable search and seizure. Park brilliantly stated that the rights of criminals are "diminished."

Skaggs didn't ease up filing motions in the months preceding the trial. He disputed the legality of the deputies' searching Eaton's property for Lisa's car. He asked the judge to suppress evidence from the search because investigators did not have probable cause, because they had gone beyond the scope of the warrant when they dug up his property, and because they were overdue in serving Eaton the warrant. Park ruled that Natrona County did not exceed the time limit to serve Eaton and that the DNA match was enough to serve as probable cause.

Eaton sat in on the proceedings and acted as though he couldn't care less. Arguments began on security measures: shackles vs. a shock belt. Skaggs objected to the leg shackles, saying they would look bad and bias the jury. Instead, he proposed a shock belt, which would be capable of sending an eight-second, incapacitating jolt. Blonigen and Sheriff Mark Benton requested that armed deputies be placed inside the courtroom. Skaggs objected. In court documents, Blonigen said that Eaton's escape from the CAC halfway house, his history of violence, and the seriousness of the current charges against him justified extra security inside and outside the courtroom.

Between the fall of 2003 and February 2004, legal disputes between the prosecution and defense popped back and forth like a ping-pong ball. Judge Park unsealed Natrona County Coroner Doc Thorpen's autopsy report. Skaggs was upset about divulging the ligature bruises on Lisa's wrists and said the media would further prejudice potential jurists. The *Tribune* quoted Skaggs as saying, "The media has been very good, in most cases, except for the *Star-Tribune*, who has gone out of its way to sensationalize and stir hatred."

Judge Park's common sense impressed me in many ways. I found out that he had been appointed to the Seventh District Court in the fall of 1998. Park graduated from the University of Wyoming and received his law degree from UW in 1975. He had been involved in general law practice for twenty-three years, representing clients in civil and criminal matters. Park occasionally acted as a special prosecutor in municipal courts; however, he had also acted as a defense attorney. He had upheld both sides of the law, which seemed like a good balance to Ron and me. Park was appointed as a County Judge for Natrona County in 1991. He speaks to kids about the hazards of drugs and lectures at Casper College every year. We were thankful to have him as the judge in Lisa's case.

While the legal proceedings progressed, Dan Tholson and Lynn Cohee continued to gather evidence. Blonigen lined up the witnesses. In October, court officials sent out 750 questionnaires to screen jurors, and everyone was pleased that the jury pool was sufficient so that no change of venue would be necessary.

In December, another motion hearing was scheduled to address, among other issues, whether Ron, the girls, and I could attend the trial proceedings. Mike explained that we were on the witness list to testify and that witnesses couldn't be present during the other proceedings until after they gave their testimony and were excused formally by the court. He knew that we would be upset if we were excluded from any portion of the trial, so he placed a special motion before the court for an exception. He asked us to attend, thinking that it might help us understand the process and that perhaps our presence might make it harder for the judge to rule against us.

Nothing could keep us away from that motion hearing.

It was the first time we had seen Judge David Park and the courtroom. It felt like walking into a church. The brown and white marble walls and floors in the hallways leading to the courtroom were finely polished. The double doors were ornately carved with small sunrises. The ceilings rose about twenty feet; the walls were paneled with warm woods. Janeice reserved space for us in a wooden pew two rows back from where the jury would be seated when the trial began. Oddly, the first two rows were chained off. When we asked Janeice why, she explained that it was because of a "thirty foot rule," so that jurors couldn't hear comments from the audience. An aisle divided the room into two parts, further reminding me of a chapel where the groom's friends and family sit on one side and the bride's sit on another.

Before the motion hearing began, Eaton was brought into the courtroom and seated at the defense table. It was hard for Ron, Sherry, and Stacy to see Eaton in person for the first time. Tears welled up in their eyes, but they wept quietly. Ron leaned forward and gripped the back of the pew in front of him. I bet if I checked that pew today, I would find his fingernail marks. I was glad I had gone to Eaton's federal trial—I was better prepared.

During a brief break in the proceedings, Janeice checked to see how we were holding up. She knew seeing Eaton would be hard. The girls said they wanted to go to the nearest restroom and have a few minutes alone together. Then Janeice turned to Ron.

With the girls gone, Ron let his anger show. "I didn't believe that I could ever the feel the same anger I felt fifteen years ago when we found out that Lisa was murdered, but it all came flooding back when I saw him," Ron told Janeice. "I can't forgive him for what he did to Lisa, and now, for what he's putting my family through."

We composed ourselves after the break. It was time to address the issue of whether we would be allowed to be present during the entire trial. Skaggs didn't resist Mike's motion. Judge Park ruled that we would be allowed to attend the trial proceedings (we would be the first witnesses and would be excused after our testimony). He also made a final judgment that the trial would stay in Casper.

Other legal issues were taken care of over the next few months. The jury selection, planned for February 23rd, could proceed.

The upcoming trial made front-page news on Sunday morning, February 2nd, which was no surprise, but the photo with the article was a shocker. An eerie hangman's noose hung on Eaton's property. My first thought was, "This isn't going to set well with Skaggs."

Ron and I drove out to Moneta that Sunday afternoon, and the noose was still there. We took a picture and wondered who did it. It was obviously crafted by someone who knew how things were done in the old lynching days. Someone carefully fashioned it from a sturdy rope almost an inch in diameter, and hung it from a tall rusty structure welded from pipes, (probably used by Eaton to hoist engines from vehicles). Someone went to a lot of trouble.

Based on the comments we'd heard in Casper, it represented the sentiments of the community. Would Eaton have been angrily lynched in another era? Ron wanted to hang the SOB for what he did to his daughter. I had often wished such a death on that horrible man, but to see a noose that close up made me shudder. Its haunting, emotional symbolism of how others felt struck us so deeply that we decided to use the picture on the cover of our book.

The jury selection was to begin the next day, Monday, February 23rd. As expected, Skaggs was furious about the newspaper's picture of the noose. He immediately brought it up to the court before the jury selection started. He made several motions for dismissing the case, citing bias and prejudice. He accused the media of "staging" the picture to sensationalize the case.

Judge Park remained calm, overruled Skaggs' objections, and said he would order the potential jurors to disregard all media coverage they had seen, including the photo in Sunday's paper.

The next day, the *Tribune* published an article allowing the photographer to defend himself: "No, we didn't set it up. It's completely unethical. I'd never stage a photo. Why would I risk my career?"

The jury selection continued with the reading of each charge against Eaton. As they were read, Ron lowered his head and I cried. It had hurt to read about her suffering in writing the first time, and it hurt again to hear it spoken.

Skaggs then told potential jurors that they would have to view graphic pictures of Lisa's body, and he wanted to know if they could deal with it. A woman raised her hand and broke into tears, saying she wasn't comfortable. She was excused and left the courtroom crying.

The rest of the proceedings were closed to the public, so Ron and I returned to Denver Monday evening. We had practical matters to take care of, and we needed to prepare for our long stay in Casper. We planned to return on Sunday, February 29th. We knew the trial would drag out for weeks, and we knew it would be a bumpy ride.

It was.

CHAPTER 18

The Trial

PREPARATIONS

Before the trial, I made arrangements for Ron and me, and each of the girls with their families, to stay for a month at the Parkway Plaza. It was a lovely hotel just a few blocks away from the Natrona County Courthouse. They offered extended-stay suites that had a refrigerator and microwave so that we could minimize our need to eat out. They also had a business office and Internet access, which was a must for Sherry. She arranged to finish her college courses for that semester over the Internet while attending the trial.

Sherry had quit her part-time job. Stacy and her husband applied the little vacation time they had coming to them to help defray their loss of income. I tallied up the costs of living, loss of wages, and relocating three families for a month. It was staggering. The girls were going through enough emotionally and we didn't want them to suffer financially.

Janeice did the math, too, and was aware that the trial would be a financial burden for us, but she had limited monies to offer from the victims' compensation fund. She pulled strings whenever and wherever she could, but knew that she would only be able to give us each travel reimbursement for our trip to and from Denver and an equivalent of a day's pay for each day we were required to testify. She couldn't guarantee any other help, and she obviously felt bad about it. We understood.

We weren't poor but we weren't rich either—one way or another we would get by. The bottom line was that no matter what the costs, we would be there *every day* of the trial.

Ron and I arrived at the Parkway Plaza on Sunday, February 29th. We had a scheduled meeting with Mike Blonigen and his team. They planned to review our testimony that afternoon—not taking the weekend off. Our girls would join us in the next day or so, depending how the jury selection progressed.

We felt comfortable in the large rooms of the Parkway Plaza Hotel, which were decorated with rustic, western furnishings. When we opened the door to our suite, we found gifts of flowers, food, and a basket of treats awaiting us. Enclosed was a card from the Fuller family and a flyer about a "Casper Cares" foundation that had been set up to help us during our long stay in Casper. The Fuller family? We didn't know them. I was overwhelmed again, much like the morning after Lisa was found, when the two neighbor boys brought us a handmade Easter basket.

Ron and I settled into our "home away from home" before getting together with Mike and his team. The meeting was simple and straightforward. Mike reviewed the questions he intended to ask us on the witness stand. Afterwards, Janeice asked us to come to her office.

She invited us to have a seat, and pulled out a flyer from the Fuller family about the "Casper Cares" fund. I should have known she had something to do with it. She denied doing anything more than complaining about the system to a few people. When the Fuller family learned about our situation, they wanted to help and took it upon themselves to set up money donations, food, and services to help us while we were in Casper. She hoped we weren't offended.

We are proud people and have never solicited charity. We weren't offended; we were humbled. Then she pulled out other donations, including gift certificates from restaurants and one from a local mechanic, Lew Pierson. He enclosed a note saying, "While the Kimmells are here for the trial, they shouldn't have to worry if they run into car problems. I will donate my labor and only charge them for parts at my cost."

I said to Janeice, "I can't imagine needing such a service. All of our vehicles are fine and fairly new." But it was a thoughtful gesture.

The next morning, we attended more of the open jury selection. It was a long process.

That evening I went down to the hotel's business office to inspect the facility and check my e-mail. A man sat at a table in the middle of the room, obviously tending to a heap of paperwork. I assumed he was the hotel's night manager. When I finished checking my e-mail, we engaged in chitchat. I mentioned that I was pleased that they had Internet access and a business office. We would need it over our long stay.

"The staff's so nice and your boss, Sven George (the General Manager), has gone out of his way to make special arrangements for us."

A look of enlightenment came over his face. "Oh, you must be Sheila Kimmell?"

"Yes."

"Nice to meet you. My name's Pat Sweeney."

After chatting a little more, I told him I needed to turn in for the night and let him get back to work so that he wouldn't get in trouble with the boss.

He just smiled.

THE TRIAL BEGINS—
WEDNESDAY, MARCH 3rd, 2004

On March 3rd, 2004 the jury selection was complete and the opening arguments began about 10:30 A.M. Finally! Skaggs tried to delay it, though. He launched into his long list of objections, *again* saying that collecting blood for the DNA match and the search of Eaton's property, etc. were illegal. Judge Park overruled everything *again*.

After Skaggs ran out of objections, the jury filed into the courtroom to hear their instructions. Blonigen gave a well organized opening statement. Skaggs followed by admitting that Eaton was "criminally responsible" for Lisa's death and that the defense felt bad for us that Lisa had died, but that Eaton was grossly overcharged (with the death penalty) for his crime. Giving Eaton the death penalty wouldn't bring Lisa back.

It became clear that the trial had little to do with Eaton's guilt or innocence. It was *all* about the death penalty. Skaggs said they weren't denying the validity of the DNA technology, yet he went on a tangent about the uncertainty of the DNA matching process. I guess he was trying to set a foundation of mistrust.

After the court's lunch break, I was the first witness to testify. Blonigen asked me about Lisa's travel plans, her habits, and her personal grooming. I identified belongings found in the car, including a pair of two-tone Oxford shoes. It was uneventful, although I was a bit nervous about sitting in front of a packed courtroom.

In his cross-examination, Skaggs got hung up about those darned shoes, arguing that I couldn't conclude they were Lisa's. I know that hundreds of shoes like hers were produced at one time in her size, but if they came out of her car and I had seen her wear them, I knew they were hers. We went back and forth until the defense team noticed that his wrangling was creating a negative impression. I saw them gesture at Skaggs to knock it off.

The rest of the day was spent laying the foundation for the prosecution. Ron testified about finding the Stringfellow Hawke note on Lisa's headstone a year after her disappearance. Sherry was next. Her testimony was brief, backing up what Ron and I had said about Lisa's personal habits, such as calling home when in trouble.

Ed Jaroch was called to the stand. He testified about his and Lisa's budding relationship, saying that they were just getting to know each other. He was such a nice-looking young man, with brownish-blond hair. He was working as an accountant in Alaska and was married, with a couple of children. I couldn't help but wonder what he would have been like as my son-in-law.

Emotions in the courtroom had been restrained up to that point, but when Highway Patrolman Al Lesco took the stand and the tape of his interaction with Lisa was played, her soft, youthful voice brought almost everyone to tears. She sounded timid and nervous, understandable when getting a speeding ticket that would cost her $120. That was a lot of money in 1988.

When the detective told her the amount of the fine, she responded with surprise. "You want that all right now?"

"Yes, ma'am."

She said she didn't have that much money. "Can I go to the nearest bank?"

"None of the banks are open," Lesco said.

"Um, how about a cash machine?"

He wasn't sure if there was one in town or not.

"And if I can't get the money?"

"Possibly a telegram."

"I only have $40 with me."

Lisa agreed to follow Officer Lesco to town, but her cash card didn't work. It was too late in the evening to find a way to pay, so Lesco told her to mail the money. She signed a form promising she would.

He asked her where she was going.

She told him Cody. "I was staying with my mom in Denver and I got a phone call this morning saying that a friend was going into cancer surgery Monday, and uh, and I had two days off, so I wanted to see her."

She gave him her address in Billings and Denver. He suggested that she slow down, and he gave her further instructions about sending payment. He told her how to get back on the highway and said, "Good luck." She drove away as he returned to his patrol car and said, "End of stop."

That would be the last time anyone but her killer would see her alive.

During a court break, Al Lesco found us and said he had never forgotten Lisa. His face expressed guilt, and he lamented, "Had I just stayed in the office and had one more cup of coffee, she might have made it safely." He had done nothing wrong. All we could do was give him a hug and thank him.

One of the last witnesses that day was one of the fishermen who found Lisa in the North Platte River. He said he figured the body would be Lisa's after hearing about her disappearance in the media. Roger Means, a highway patrolman, also briefly took the witness stand. He had found Lisa's blood on the Old Government Bridge.

We also met Ashley Fuller, the man who started the "Casper Cares" fund. All of our encounters that day were filled with tears and hugs.

The trial adjourned at 4:15 P.M.

THURSDAY, MARCH 4th, 2004

My family and I were getting ready to head for the courthouse in our separate vehicles that morning. Stacy and her husband, Todd, found a note on their windshield saying, "You're leaking a lot of antifreeze."

They didn't want to be late and decided to drive it to the courthouse and check into it later. In those few blocks the "check engine" light came on. Great.

The trial resumed about 9:30 A.M. The prosecution laid more foundation for the chain of events. Mark Sandfort, another deputy who responded to the police call from the Government Bridge, was questioned. He said her body was found near a fishing spot called "Trapper's Route." His voice cracked when he was shown a picture of Lisa floating in the water. "That's the body." He said her body still had color, as though she hadn't been in the water long.

Dave Kinghorn took the stand to describe the crime scene at the river the day Lisa was found. A nurse from Rawlins Penitentiary was briefly called to verify that the blood she collected was indeed from Eaton. Tilton Davis, from the State Crime Lab, also testified that the blood was processed properly and that it would later match the blood sample that Eaton had given.

During a break, Coroner Doc Thorpen sought us out. He was going to start his testimony that afternoon, and he was concerned about our hearing it. "It's going to be hard, Sheila. Some of my testimony's going to be graphic."

"I know, Doc, but we need to hear it from you, not the newspapers. If it gets too bad, we'll just quietly leave the courtroom."

Ron and I gave him a hug.

Before Doc took the stand, Skaggs put forth a motion to bar autopsy photos because of their graphic nature. Skaggs was overruled.

Doc took the stand only briefly before court adjourned for the day. He would continue first thing on Friday.

After leaving the courthouse, our first order of business was to take care of Stacy and Todd's car. The offer from the car mechanic came in handy. We called Lew Pierson and made arrangements to have it serviced the next morning.

That evening Ron, Sherry, Stacy, Todd, and I joined the Fullers at their lovely home for dinner. Janeice Lynch and her husband joined us. The Fullers and Lynches gave us other donations they had collected, mostly coupons from restaurants, including coupons from Pat Sweeney.

That name rang a bell. I told Janeice, "I remember now; he was the nice night manager I met at our hotel."

The Fullers and Lynchs glanced at each other trying not to laugh. "That wasn't the night manager, that was the *owner*," they told us at once.

Then they told us that he was drastically reducing our room rates for our extended stay. Ron and I weren't going to be charged, and he was only going to charge us a few dollars a day for the girls' rooms to cover his housekeeping costs. Wow.

FRIDAY, MARCH 5th, 2004

Ron and Todd got up early to take his vehicle into the shop. Lew Pierson assured us that he would have it fixed immediately. Ron told him not to rush and not to put off any of his regular customers because he was doing us a huge favor. Lew just grinned. He would call us when it was done. Ron and Todd returned to the hotel to get ready to go back to court.

Doc Thorpen resumed the stand at 9:30 A.M. Friday. His pivotal testimony about Lisa's death captured the audience's attention.

Doc had a formidable presence, with a booming, self-assured voice. Well over six feet tall, he was an attractive man who didn't look his age (he was born in 1929). He attended medical school at the Johns Hopkins University School of Medicine in Baltimore, ranking in the top third of his class. He worked at St. Luke's and the Children's Hospital in Denver before becoming a member/partner of the Central Wyoming Pathologists and a Staff Pathologist for the Wyoming Medical Center in Casper in 1961. Doc was elected Coroner for Natrona County in 1982, and he has held that position ever since.

Not only is his work respected, he engages in his hobbies with gusto. He's been playing the tuba since junior high school and has played in various bands around the state. We would love to watch him in concert someday.

Doc wasn't cheerful on the stand, though. He was dressed in a dark suit as he testified on Friday, his voice unwavering and confident. His medical terms outlined the horrors Lisa physically endured while Eaton kept her hostage.

He said that the bruises and abrasions on Lisa's wrists, arms, ankles, and legs suggested she had been bound with hemp or braided nylon rope. The bruises at the base of her thumbs were consistent with hand-cuffs. Lisa was restrained for most of her captivity.

She was raped repeatedly. When her body was found, the pubic hair that had been shaved showed about six day's growth. Eaton must have shaved her shortly after he abducted her. Was it an act of humiliation? Was it to make Lisa appear even younger? Doc didn't have those answers.

Lisa's body had gone into rigor mortis that had not passed (rigor mortis is a stiffening phase that a body goes through, but it only lasts for a short time). Her core body temperature was 46 degrees F when she was found. Even though the air temperature was 65 degrees that day, the cold water (at 44 degrees) acted as a preservative. Only her fingers showed signs of wrinkling.

Apparently Eaton fed her shortly before he killed her. She had a type of beef stew in her stomach when the autopsy took place. Lisa's blood test showed that she had not consumed any drugs or alcohol.

When Eaton made the decision to kill Lisa, he hit her head from be-hind with such force that it caused a four inch fracture in the left side of her skull. The injury was sufficient enough to render her uncon-scious, but not kill her instantly. However, she would have died in two to six hours from the blow to the head. Eaton didn't wait. He turned her over and stabbed her five times in the chest, carefully avoiding her ribs, each penetrating a vital organ that would cause death within seconds—three of those stabs went through to the spine (5" to 6" inches deep). He also stabbed her once in the upper abdomen, directly piercing her heart. The stab wounds caused massive internal bleeding, which killed her within seconds. She lost so much blood that there was little left in her body by the time the autopsy took place.

The stabs were not performed as part of a ritual; they were the work of an experienced hunter. Eaton knew how to kill, and he wanted to make sure she died quickly.

Doc's description of Lisa's body suggested that Eaton had handcuffed her arms while he drove to the Old Government Bridge. Her arms, po-sitioned like those of a preying mantis, probably went into rigor mortis during the ride, which would have taken about an hour and a half on the back roads.

Lisa's body left other clues. Her hip was fractured during the fall from the bridge. He left two of her gold necklaces in place, and two diamond stud earrings in her ears. She was dressed only in pink underpants and dark blue socks. Her wristwatch had stopped at 9:40 due to contact with water, but that clue wasn't helpful because it could have taken many hours for the water to seep into the mechanism, nor did the style of watch indicate either A.M. or P.M..

When her body was found Saturday afternoon, rigor mortis was still present, which suggested she had been killed somewhere between 36 and 48 hours earlier—most likely, Thursday night. Doc was hesitant to say exactly when she was killed.

I knew all along in my heart that Lisa was killed Thursday night. Evidence continued to support my vision that she had called out to me from the foot of my bed the night she died.

The jury viewed the autopsy pictures knowing that we were seated directly behind them. They were careful not to let Ron, the girls, and me see the horrors. Despite their concerns, we grimaced during Skaggs's cross-examination of Doc when Skaggs suggested that Lisa would have been unconscious when Eaton stabbed her and that she therefore would not have suffered when she died. We were upset, but the audience (particularly two women seated behind us) reacted dramatically, gasping at various times. Skaggs complained to Blonigen, and my family was cautioned to avoid any "outbursts." Skaggs is damned lucky we remained as composed as we did during that part of the trial.

When Doc left the witness stand, he looked sad and drained. Everyone in law enforcement has a few cases that they can't forget. Doc has told me that Lisa's case was one of his. He wanted the killer caught, and I think that's one of the reasons he worked so hard to make sure the DNA found on Lisa survived long enough for the technology to catch up. My family is beyond grateful for Doc's dedication to his profession.

The only other witness on Friday was Chris Reed, the audiovisual and fingerprint technician for Natrona County. She discussed the search of Eaton's property and showed a videotape of the procedure, including lifting the car out of the hole. The primary goal of the video was to show that Natrona County conducted the search properly.

During one of the breaks that day, Ron heard a story that a Natrona deputy was sent to the county jail to bring a juvenile to another courtroom. The deputy gave the jailer the juvenile's name, but the jailer led him to the wrong cell and opened it. Instead of finding the juvenile, he found himself facing Eaton. The deputy looked Eaton square in the eyes and, without missing a beat, he said, "You are the most evil son-of-a-bitch to have ever walked this earth." Then he walked out, asking to be directed to the proper cell.

Eaton filed a complaint with Skaggs, saying that he was being harassed. The deputy was summoned to appear before Judge Park, who asked if the deputy had said those words. The deputy responded, "Yes I did, and just what part of that statement isn't true?" The deputy wasn't disciplined, but was strongly cautioned to not let it happen again.

The kids had to return to Denver on Friday after the trial was convened for the weekend. They planned to come back to Casper Sunday night. Saturday, March 6th, was my birthday. It was a hard day. I did laundry and cried a lot. Ron and I ate at a nice restaurant that evening, but I felt sapped of any energy to celebrate.

Sunday, we got a call from Lew telling us that Todd and Stacy's car was ready for them. On a Sunday? We were stunned.

"That's great, Lew, but I hope you didn't rush it or work over the weekend," Ron told him on the phone.

Lew *had* worked over the weekend, but he seemed happy to help. Lew also added that someone donated the water pump to fix the problem, so there was no charge.

Before Ron could even say thank you, Lew added, "I hope you don't mind, but I also noticed that their windshield was cracked, so we replaced it, too."

Tears streamed down Ron's cheeks. After he hung up, he put his head in his hands and wept, overwhelmed by Lew's generous gift of help.

CHAPTER 19

A Procession of Witnesses

MONDAY, MARCH 8th, 2004

The trial resumed at 9:00 A.M. Monday. The witnesses featured were Dr. Robin Cotton, from Cellmark Labs, and Kim Clement, from Bodie Labs. I expected to be overwhelmed by charts and scientific statistics that would bore me to tears. However, the testimonies were quite interesting and educational; each witness was unflappable about her facts.

The findings of the DNA tests were complicated so I won't attempt to relay them. Plenty of other books can explain laboratory procedures in the DNA field. The point is that each lab came up with the same conclusion using slightly different tests. The DNA in the semen found on Lisa belonged to Dale Eaton. The chance that it *didn't* belong to him was something like 1 in 240 quadrillion.

The main event Monday involved a juror who kept nodding off to sleep during the trial. A closed emergency-motion hearing was held that afternoon, and court was adjourned for the day. The "sleepy" juror was excused from duty for "personal reasons," and an alternate replaced her.

TUESDAY, MARCH 9th, 2004

Ten witnesses were called to the stand in a procession that made it a long day. Before the attorneys got started, Skaggs complained about the first witness, a prisoner who had been jailed in a Casper cell next to Eaton, and the jury wasn't allowed in until the matter was settled. Skaggs didn't want him on the stand. However, Joe Dax was allowed to testify.

Joe Dax claimed that Eaton had "confessed" to him when they did time together in the Natrona County jail. As soon as the man was brought in, Eaton yelled out, "You f——r, don't point at me! You don't even know me!"

After Eaton calmed down, Dax told his story. It was similar to the statement he gave Dan and Lynn before the trial.

"I had already been sentenced for possession of firearms in relation to a burglary charge that happened out in Natrona County when I met Mr. Eaton," Dax said.

The two struck up a conversation about their crimes, and Dax complained about his lawyer. It appeared that Eaton wanted to talk to someone, too. Dax said that Eaton was worried about a car found on his property. What Dax told us was, "He said, 'I can't figure out how they found this,' and uh, he was a little bit concerned. He said that somebody from Colorado must have told them (the detectives) where the car is, or he was wondering if they just found it by an accident."

The next time they talked, Eaton called Dax to his cell. "He had a newspaper article about him and, uh, he started telling me basically that the newspaper article was mostly bull——t, um, that he wasn't worried about it. He said 'the chick was really nice to help me out,' that's exactly what he said. ... He said, 'she seemed like a nice girl.'"

Eaton's version of the story was that this "nice girl" gave him a ride, but she became "snotty" when he suggested that she have dinner with him. "She 'got really kind of nervous' is the way he put it and that she said she wasn't interested... He said he put his hand over on her leg. ... He said she just locked up the front of the car and slammed on the brakes, pulled over to the side of the road, and was screaming. He said she was screaming really loud, she told him to get the f——k out of the car, he was lucky that he even had a ride and that she was acting like he was a like a f———-g pervert and, uh, he said, 'Hell no, I ain't getting out of the car; you can take me to where I'm going.'"

"He said that she kept f———-g screaming and she was going to get out of the car, and that he grabbed her and, uh, he said, just kind of lost control. He said he didn't want her to get out right there on the road. The only thing that was flashing through his mind basically was, 'what am I gonna do?' He said he knew right there and then that 'I had to do the bitch,' that's what he said. He said if he would have planned this thing it would have been a lot easier.

"He said the whole thing was really hard. And then the other thing, he asked me a question, he goes 'Well, what the hell would you have done? Would you just have jumped out of the car in the middle of night?' I'm like, well, yeah, probably. I would have got out of the car but I doubt if I would have gotten into the situation either. He goes, 'but she was yelling and screaming and she pissed me off and then she started to go out of the car and I grabbed her.'

"He made one comment that he didn't want to leave the car out there and he couldn't let her get out to the highway. He said he just grabbed on to her and held her and told her to f———-g drive. And he goes, 'Yeah, I don't think anybody would miss her anyway, she was a lousy lay,' or a lousy piece of ass."

Eaton supposedly said again that, "If he would have planned it, it would have been a lot easier; it turned out to be a lot of trouble. He wished that this wouldn't have even happened and that, uh, he felt, he thought it was her f———-g fault for freaking out. He was trying to make me think that it was all right, what happened." Dax finished up his testimony and left the stand.

We were in shock.

Dax's testimony was disturbing at first. When Ron and I had time to think it out, I questioned whether Eaton was talking about Lisa or another girl. I've heard that the minds of killers sometimes get their victims mixed up. I *know* Lisa would not have given a ride to a strange man late at night. She wouldn't act the way he described. When Eaton said he couldn't let her get out to the highway, was he referring to a later escape attempt?

To me, Dax's testimony only proved that Eaton confessed to a horrendous deed. I think the scariest thing Dax said was, "If he would have planned it, it would have been a lot easier." To us that implied that Eaton had planned other abductions. There had to be some truth in what Dax said, but we'll never know how much.

Eaton's son, Billy, was the next to take the witness stand. His testimony was pivotal, but for another reason. He had seen parts from Lisa's Honda in the summer of 1988 when he lived with his father.

In an earlier statement, Billy told Dan and Lynn that while he lived in Moneta, there was a wooden workshop across the highway near an old motel that had burned down (where Lisa's car could have been hidden). Billy wasn't allowed to go near the shed or the "well hole" that Eaton was digging. Billy's eyewitness account of seeing the Honda parts made his testimony important. The following is from Billy's statement to Dan and Lynn that Billy repeated on the witness stand.

Interview with Billy Eaton

Dan: What was the deal with the seats?

Billy: Uh, my dad had the seats and the stereo laying around, so we put the stereo up on the top of the cab and the seats in the front. (Speaking of a truck that Eaton gave Billy.)

Dan: And what kind of seats were they?

Billy: Uh, bucket seats, black and kind of gray, maybe gray stripes. I can't really remember; they were pretty, pretty fancy. They were out of a Honda.

Dan: How do you know that?

Billy: The stereo was out of a Honda. Just 'cause I'm into cars.

Dan: And how did you put the seats in there?

Billy: We just bolted them in there. And he made some kind of bracket. I don't know if to make them sit up a little bit, but they pretty much just fit right in there.

Dan: What's the deal with the wheels?

Billy: Uh, the Honda wheels that was out there was melted down.

Dan: How do you know that?

Billy: 'Cuz he told me he was going to do that. Just to, they weren't worth nothing, he was going to melt them down for aluminum; that's what he did as far as I know.

Dan: How did you know they were Honda wheels?

Billy: They had Honda on them; the hubcaps had the little H. And actually there was only the Prelude and the CR, or the CRX that had that wheel.

Lynn: When you said that they were just laying out there when you got there, the seats and the hubcaps?

Billy: Yeah, they were in the back of that bus or on the side of the bus. They were there around that bus somehow. And he told me he had just had them laying around and was going to let me fix the interior [of the truck], and the interior was, it was pretty nice, but it could have been nicer, so that's what he had the seats and the stereo laying around for, he said. Just to fix it up a little bit, since the outside looks so good and he could make the inside look good.

Dan: Did you see him melt the wheels down?

Billy: Uh, I was trying to remember. I think, I think I was there when he did that. He melted quite a bit of stuff down there.

It saddened me to hear Billy's testimony. He was only fifteen years old in the summer of 1988. Eaton constantly had car parts and flea market finds lying around. Billy obviously had no idea that his father had killed Lisa and stripped her car, offering his son part of the plunder to enhance his pickup truck. I met Billy and his mother in the hallway during a break. He looked so sad.

The rest of the day was filled with a variety of witnesses. A woman who worked with Eaton during 1988-89 said she saw him digging the "well hole." A man who installed electricity on Eaton's property in 1988 took the stand and described the hole and the messy condition of the land. Another woman testified that she had witnessed the blood sample being taken from Eaton when he was in prison on federal charges.

Three more people took the stand to say that they had worked with Eaton or knew of his using a backhoe to dig holes on his land.

An interesting piece of testimony came from "Mary Franklin," a woman who worked at the Community Alternative Center (the halfway house), and had known Eaton since 1989. Eaton was a friend of her husband, and she worked at the CAC during the short two months Eaton served time.

According to her testimony, Eaton began asking her out when she and her husband were apart. She refused, even after he gave her son one of his trucks, an odd gift when "courting" anyone. He was persistent, sending her more gifts. He gave her a ring, a coat, flowers, and a pair of red gloves (nothing belonging to Lisa). She still refused to date him.

Mary described Eaton as someone who rarely showered. While he was sentenced to CAC, he told Mary that he had pulled a gun on a young couple, hoping they would take the gun away and kill him. Mary remembered a comment Eaton made to her around 1991. He told her never to stop at a rest stop or along a highway because women get raped and killed doing that.

Mary's husband testified that he, too, saw Eaton digging a hole on his land with a backhoe. Another man, who knew Eaton had access to a backhoe, took the stand briefly.

Lynn Cohee was up next, and she began her story about the DNA hit, her interview with Eaton, and the search of the Moneta property. She discussed the "well hole" findings before court adjourned for the day.

WEDNESDAY, MARCH 10th, 2004

Lynn took the stand again first thing Wednesday morning, and evidence was carted into the courtroom. Lynn aligned pieces of Lisa's car found in the first "well hole" to life-size pictures of the car's front and rear bumpers. Lisa's personal belongings were brought in and shown to the jury. I sensed the case growing tighter with the physical evidence, but seeing Lisa's things again after so many years was rough.

Lynn also clarified some of the things the investigators found in Lisa's car, specifically "dated" items they recovered. They found a jar of Carmex that Lisa used on her leg rash. Lynn was *very* pleased that Skaggs asked her that question. (She later said, "It took me nearly a damn month to track that one down.") She had gotten in touch with the Carmex company's owner's grandson, and he was able to pinpoint the dates the batch was made, sold, and distributed. His facts confirmed that the Carmex was bought before Lisa was murdered in 1988. Lynn's testimony assured me that the investigators hadn't ignored even the smallest detail in preparing for the trial.

Several rapid-fire witnesses came forward. A neighbor said he saw Eaton digging the second hole late at night. Another man from the power company confirmed when Eaton was legally hooked up to electricity. Detective George Jensen got up and talked about the Stringfellow Hawke note from Lisa's headstone.

The next witness lightened up the dismal mood. Doris Buchta was Eaton's neighbor when he moved to Moneta. Her late husband, Buck, helped Eaton work on cars, and Eaton spent a lot of time with the elderly couple, eating dinner and shooting the breeze.

Tiny, sharp-witted Doris was an important witness because she kept a daily diary. It provided evidence that Eaton was preoccupied from March 25th to March 31st of 1988.

To prepare for Doris' appearance in court, Janeice had helped Doris dress in a nice suit and comfortable shoes, and fixed her short gray hair. Doris needed to have an oxygen tank with her, so it was quite a logistical achievement simply to get her on the stand.

According to the trial transcripts, Blonigen questioned her first.

"Could you state your name for the record, please?"

Doris looked at the judge. "I can't hear. He has to speak louder."

Judge Park leaned closer and said loudly, "What's your name? "Doris."

"And your last name?"

"Buchta."

Mike resumed his questioning. "Did you ever live in Moneta, Doris?"

Doris looked at the judge again. "I can't hear him."

Loudly, Judge Park repeated the question, "Did you ever live in Moneta, Doris?"

"Yes."

Mike asked if he could come closer to the witness stand and Park said yes. Doris piped up. "All right. I got my hearing aid in, too."

Judge Park said, "We'll do the best we can, Mrs. Buchta."

Mike and the judge finally established that Doris had lived in Moneta, that she wrote in her diary every day for thirty years, and that the diary included mention of people who visited her and what the weather was like.

Mike asked if she could remember what she wrote without looking in her diary. At first she said yes. Mike became more specific. "Do you remember everything you wrote down in 1988?"

"I don't remember what I did yesterday," Doris retorted.

People in the courtroom burst into laughter. When it calmed down, Mike directed her to specific days. He had to approach the bench.

Doris said, "Hearing and vision going, too."

That brought another round of chuckles.

Judge Park asked, "Ms. Buchta, how old are you?"

"Ninety-one-and-a-half."

"Ma'am, I've put some green arrows by those areas. Do you see those?" Mike asked.

"Where is the green arrow? I don't see a green arrow."

Janeice then brought a flashlight and a magnifying glass as big around as a paper plate in case it was needed to "shine some light on the situation."

Then Judge Park leaned over and pointed. "Right here."

"Oh, it's so big, I couldn't see it."

Again, we laughed.

Skaggs interrupted and said he didn't mind if Mike got on the stand with her. Mike did that, but they still had to turn on a flashlight to help her see. Mike pointed to the entry on March 24th, 1988.

"Where am I? Oh, right here. I got the mail and burned all the papers. My, how exciting."

The crowd laughed again and Doris grinned. I think she was enjoying the attention.

"And breakfast. What does that say there? I watched the guy?" Judge Park said, "It says 'quiz shows.'"

"I watched the quiz show, yeah. That's the only thing I watch on television. Helped, oh, Buck, my husband, oh, Dale Eaton worked on the car and so forth. That's Thursday, March the 24th."

She had recorded the snowstorm on Wednesday, March 30th. Mike pointed out one last entry, on April 1st, 1988.

"Oh yes, I see. I don't feel good that day. How about that?"

He pointed out the rest of the entry.

"Dale. Oh, yeah. Dale visited."

"So Buck and Dale were visiting that day?"

"Yes."

Mike and Skaggs discussed the pages and submitted them into evidence. Before dismissing Doris, Judge Park asked Skaggs if he had any questions.

Skaggs said he had no questions, then turned to Doris, "Do you remember me?"

"Yes," Doris said.

"I have no questions."

Doris blurted out, "I thought you did a good job."

Skaggs said, "Pardon?"

Doris repeated her compliment.

"Thank you very much. I hope you are doing well. Are you doing okay?" Skaggs asked.

"Oh, fine," Doris said.

"You still got that sense of humor," Skaggs said.

Doris looked at the judge.

Park repeated loudly, "He said you still have a good sense of humor."

"Might as well be dead if I don't have."

Everyone in the courtroom laughed again, including Judge Park. He directed Janeice to come get Doris. She made one last comment about how "young and handsome judges are these days." Judge Park blushed.

I hope I'm that spunky when I'm ninety-one-and-*a-half*.

After a recess, the proceedings resumed a serious tone. Jim Broz, one of the original detectives, took the stand. He had become a certified handwriting expert. Although he had moved to Denver to work for the U.S. Mint, he had stayed connected to the case, which he said had always haunted him. Before leaving Natrona, Jim made Dan promise to call him. "I want to know who did it before I die."

Ironically, Jim was recovering from a heart attack when he got the call from Dan telling him, "We got our man."

Jim reminded Dan about his promise. "You cut it kind of close."

On the stand, Jim said that he reviewed hundreds of Eaton's handwriting samples before concluding that Dale Eaton had indeed written the Stringfellow Hawke note.

Jim's statement infuriated Eaton. He turned to his defense attorneys and blurted something out like, "You f———s. I told you where I was that day, and you don't do nothing about it."

I think that portrayed Eaton's distorted thinking. He had dated the note 11-13-88. That was a Sunday. He probably had an alibi for that day. Didn't he understand that just because he wrote down a date, that doesn't make it true? As I mentioned before, we had been to Lisa's grave, and even Ron could tell the note wasn't weathered. After Eaton's outburst, Judge Park dismissed the jury, called a recess, and had a conference with Mike and Skaggs.

Jim Broz resumed the stand after things calmed down, finished his testimony, and was not cross-examined by Skaggs.

Dan Tholson was up next. Dan's testimony was powerful. He showed slides of the crime scene that included the weather conditions. The pictures of Lisa's fresh blood on the bridge made it clear that she had *not* been in the water for long. It was further evidence that Eaton had held her captive for six days.

When Lisa's car was found, another important piece of evidence was added to the case. Dan told the court that her trip-meter read 215.8. We knew Lisa's habit of getting gas in Cheyenne, Wyoming, and resetting her trip-meter. Ron had trained everyone in the family to do that so that we could keep track of our gas mileage. Depending upon which gas station she used, the mileage would have put her near the Waltman rest stop. (Remember that Mary Franklin had testified that Eaton warned her about the dangers of rest stops.)

After Dan was finished, Mike Blonigen rested his case. Court was adjourned for the day and would not resume until Friday, when the defense's only witness would fly in from Florida.

That evening, we met with some of the prosecution team in the hotel lounge and let our hair down. I could tell that they were glad to have this part of the trial behind them after so many months of preparation. They showed little concern for the forensic pathologist the defense was bringing to the stand to dispute Doc's findings.

Thursday was a day off for Ron and me. I spent the day catching up on laundry and other chores. Ron got a treat when Lew, the mechanic, brought his restored white Lamborghini to the hotel to take him for a spin out on the highway. Lew even let Ron drive it back to the hotel, but Ron wouldn't confess how *fast* he drove it. He just smiled when I asked.

I said, "Janeice said she'd take care of any tickets we got while parked at the courthouse during the trial, but I don't recall her saying she'd fix our *speeding* tickets."

FRIDAY, MARCH 12th, 2004

The first and only witness of the day was Dr. Daniel Spitz, a forensic pathologist from Tampa, Florida. He was a polished man several years younger than Doc Thorpen. Dr. Spitz had an impressive résumé. In fact, Skaggs devoted hours to reviewing his credentials for the jury, including Spitz's education, his books, and the classes he taught. The list went on and on. My mind screamed, "I got it already! Let's move on!"

I realized that Skaggs was trying to build up Dr. Spitz's qualifications in an effort to minimize Doc Thorpen's. Dr. Spitz agreed with most of Doc's findings on Lisa's autopsy, but disagreed with a few "minor" issues. Minor? Ha!

His opinion was that Lisa died from acute blood loss after being stabbed. He acknowledged that the head trauma was a significant injury, but he said it could have come immediately *after* the stab wounds. In his summary letter to the defense, Spitz wrote, "Based on the blood evidence and the appearance of the scalp laceration, the head trauma was likely caused by an impact against the edge of the curb on the bridge over the river where the body was found… The head trauma likely played little or no role in her death."

For this to have happened, Lisa would have to have been stabbed on the bridge and instantly thrown over. The stab wounds were smooth, performed without a struggle. There were no defensive stab marks on her arms. Did Spitz think she was asleep or something? Everyone knows that knocking someone out allows a person control of the victim. Then Dr. Spitz offered another conclusion: that Lisa was *not* stabbed on the bridge because of the pattern of blood on the bridge. Huh?

Dr. Spitz also said that the time of Lisa's death was impossible to determine. Doc had narrowed the time frame down to 36 to 48 hours before she was found in the water, because rigor mortis was still present in her body. Dr. Spitz focused on the cold water, which was about 44 degrees Fahrenheit. "A cold environment such as this would significantly retard the process of decomposition, making it possible that the decedent was in the water for as long as five to seven days after her death."

Did Dr. Spitz ignore the evidence of Lisa's *fresh* blood on the bridge?

He also argued that the small abrasions and contusions on Lisa's arms and legs were "common in bodies recovered from moving water."

I guess the defense was trying to diminish the idea that Eaton had had six days to plan Lisa's death (tying in with the premeditation and kidnapping charges). The defense's strategy didn't work. In my opinion, some of the evidence contradicted Dr. Spitz's "opinion."

Court adjourned early that day because the defense rested its case at 1:30 P.M. We spent the rest of the weekend trying to unwind.

MONDAY, MARCH 15th, 2004

Mike Blonigen and Wyatt Skaggs gave their closing arguments Monday morning. Ron and I thought Mike's argument was impressive and articulate. He reviewed evidence and witnesses' testimony that supported my theory that Lisa was killed Thursday night. He stressed that she had been held for days in "sheer and abject terror," knowing her fate. "He had choices to make, and Dale Wayne Eaton chose, with premeditated malice, to end this young girl's life."

Skaggs gave it his best shot, denying that the kidnapping, robbery, and rape were committed at the time of her murder, but again he didn't deny Eaton's guilt. He tried to discount the DNA testing *again*, said that Eaton didn't write the Stringfellow Hawke note, and he called Eaton's fellow prisoner Dax a liar. Et cetera, et cetera.

The jurors received their instructions and began deliberations. At about 2:00 P.M., the jury sent a note to the judge asking how to handle the fact that Skaggs said Eaton was guilty in his opening statements. It appeared obvious that there was little to be discussed. We later heard that one of the jurors wondered whether that was a violation of Eaton's rights.

The jury was excused for the night around dinnertime and expected to meet again the next morning.

We thought it would be a slam-dunk case, but our worrying wasn't over.

CHAPTER 20

The Verdict

TUESDAY, MARCH 16th, 2004

Tuesday was a disaster. We found out at 10:40 A.M. that a juror had driven to the Old Government Bridge over the weekend to see where Lisa was dropped in the river. Why? After being reminded by Judge Park several times a day for nearly two weeks *not* to seek evidence outside what was presented in court, why would a person jeopardize the entire trial? We couldn't endure another trial if that occurrence resulted in a mistrial. We wouldn't have the emotional energy, time, or resources. Not to mention that thousands of taxpayers' dollars were at stake.

When Sherry and Stacy heard the news, they came to our room and cried with us for hours. Janeice showed up and shed tears of frustration, too.

Around noon, we found out that the other jurors had had the good sense to report the incident immediately. The offending juror was released and an alternate replaced him. Because of their quick action, Judge Park did not declare a mistrial. We spent Tuesday afternoon recovering from the possible trauma. It could have been one of the biggest disappointments of our lives.

We waited and waited. Time felt so cruel. At 5:00 P.M., Janeice called to tell us that the jury had adjourned for the evening.

WEDNESDAY, MARCH 17th, 2004

Deliberations resumed Wednesday and we waited again by the phone for the verdict. The hours dragged. My ailing Dad, ill with cancer, my brother, who had joined us the previous week, and the rest of my family watched TV, walked the dog, checked e-mail, or restlessly paced the floors of the hotel. I couldn't focus my attention on anything except for the minutes ticking by. It reminded me of the eight days when Lisa was missing.

At 2:30 P.M., the calm exploded. The verdict was in.

Ron and I rounded everyone up, hopped in the cars, and rushed to the courthouse. Janeice made sure the announcement waited for our arrival. She met us at the back door and told everyone to take a deep breath.

"Are you ready?" she asked.

We nodded, and then followed her through the basement hallways to the elevator. When the doors opened, the media met us head-on. Several reporters with flashing cameras and spotlights opened fire, but politely stood far enough away to allow us dignity. We walked into the courtroom amid hushed whispers. The courtroom was packed with observers, reporters, and extended family and friends.

We rose for the judge and again for the jury. Once, we even rose mistakenly for a court clerk. Nervous laughter rolled through the courtroom. When the judge received the verdict from the jury foreman, he briefly stepped into his chambers to check the wording, and then returned. Satisfied, he gave it to the court clerk to read. The room quieted.

The clerk began to read off the long list of charges against Dale Wayne Eaton. On first-degree premeditated murder: *guilty*, aggravated kidnapping: *guilty*, aggravated robbery: *guilty*, and first-degree sexual assault: *guilty*. Eaton was also found guilty of three counts of first-degree felony murder, which were determined to have been committed during the separate crimes of sexual assault, robbery, and kidnapping.

A collective sigh resounded throughout the courtroom. Ron, Sherry, Stacy, and I hugged, deeply relieved, yet not happy. We had waited almost sixteen years for that bittersweet moment, but the justice served would not bring Lisa back to life. We hugged everyone else who had made the journey with us as court adjourned for the day.

Janeice ushered us out of the courtroom, passing the line of cameras again to a private waiting room that serves as a hiding place for victims and their families to regain their composure after emotional court events. Awaiting us were more thoughtful gifts of treats and refreshments from the contributors to "Casper Cares," which reminded us again that acts of kindness try outweigh the evil in our world.

When we had had time to catch our breath, we returned to the hotel. Everyone agreed to meet in the lounge for another gathering. I won't call it a celebration because no one wins in a murder trial, but it was a chance for everyone to let off steam. Sixteen years worth of steam. It was March 17th, St. Patrick's Day. A lot of green beer flowed that evening among the detectives, the attorneys, friends, and family. Ron and I again expressed our gratitude to everyone for giving Lisa justice. The only disappointment was that Doc didn't bring his tuba. We were hoping to hear him toot his own horn.

CHAPTER 21

The Penalty Phase

THURSDAY, MARCH 18th, 2004

The guilty verdict had already been handed down. Thursday opened the penalty phase, which is almost like a second trial. In a Wyoming death penalty case, *only* a jury can decide if someone gets death. The attorneys spent time that morning arguing over how much evidence about Eaton's volatile past the prosecution could deliver in the penalty phase. Not much, we discovered.

The jury was brought in, and opening arguments began with Mike Blonigen asking for a "full measure" of justice for Lisa by giving Eaton the death penalty. Skaggs countered in his statement that Eaton was a product of an abusive childhood.

Mike called his first witness, Shannon Breeden, but all she was allowed to do was identify Eaton, say he assaulted her with a weapon, and name the weapon. Red-faced and obviously frustrated at not getting to tell her story, she glared at Eaton as she left the witness stand. He shaded his face again, as he had during much of the trial. After being excused, she vocalized her anger in the courthouse hallway to anyone who asked: "He's still a sick son of a bitch."

After that, Detective Rich Haskell, who handled the Breeden case, testified. Anthony Howard, the prosecuting attorney, also testified with only a few words. Mike's hands were tied as to what and how much he could ask.

That was it.

Our side wasn't allowed to tell how dangerous Eaton really was, because it might negatively influence the jury. I may be stupid when it comes to this aspect of the law, but if a jury has to decide on a penalty, why couldn't they be allowed to know the full extent of Eaton's violence? It didn't seem fair to me. We were allowed three brief witnesses, and the defense would be allowed ten or more.

The defense never denied Eaton's guilt. I had to remind myself that this trial was about the death penalty, not his guilt or innocence. The defense saved their best efforts for this phase. The defense was trying to prove mitigating circumstances, a fancy term for "excuses" that might persuade the jury to spare Eaton the death penalty.

Skaggs brought in a parade of witnesses to accomplish that goal. The first witness he called was Dr. Kenneth Ash, a psychiatrist in private practice from Ft. Collins, Colorado. Dr. Ash spent the morning explaining his credentials as a doctor who specializes in treating addictions. He's board-certified in general psychiatry, addictions, and forensic psychiatry.

Once the doctor got past the resumé and awards, which were all impressive, he gave the court a mini-lesson about diagnosing people with emotional problems.

He finally began describing Eaton's background. He had studied Eaton's medical records and spent more than twelve hours with him, face to face. During that time, he made observations and entered assessments into a computer program that determines a step-by-step diagnosis. Dr. Ash asked Eaton about his life history as a child, a teen, and an adult. He said he did a neurological evaluation, but only based it on "self-report." Self-report became a pivotal issue in the trial because it means that information is gathered from what someone says, not necessarily from the facts. How can anyone trust the words of a career criminal who lies? Evidence revealed that Eaton had lied about many things.

"There is one consistent finding throughout all of his medical records, and that consistent finding is depression," Dr. Ash explained. He described the symptoms of depression: lowered energy, lack of concentration, problems with eating and sleeping, and feelings of hopelessness and suicide.

Untreated depression, according to Dr. Ash's testimony, can cause brain damage. "The brain damage occurs in the area of the hippocampus of the brain, which is especially important in terms of stress regulation, memory, and new learning."

Dr. Ash did his best to portray Eaton as a man under extreme duress after his ex-wife left him and took the children. "In fact, the night of— of the murder, he had called, wanting to have his children with him at Easter time. He called and he talked to his wife. His wife said no, but it was the way that she said no. She said, according to Dale, that, 'No, these aren't even your kids.' And she laughed. And then she let him know that she was with another man."

Dr. Ash explained that this event took place the same night Eaton "encountered" Lisa. He was depressed and distraught after his conversation with his ex-wife. This was supposed to give Eaton a rational excuse for abducting her? The story became more pathetic as Eaton had obviously convinced Dr. Ash of misery that the facts didn't support.

Ash continued. "He was earning a living by two ways. One was he was going to different dumps, getting the cans. The other was he was going to mines and finding copper wire that he would take and then sell at the flea markets. He would make up to five hundred dollars a month on a good month," Dr. Ash explained.

Dr. Ash admitted that Eaton had problems dealing with people. "He—he has a very explosive personality; intermittent explosive disorder is what we would call it in psychiatry."

Dr. Ash continued to try to build sympathy for Eaton by showing how much stress he was under while in Moneta with a "stress scale." Please. I've seen those kinds of quizzes in ladies' magazines. According to stress tests, Ron and I should be dead, considering what we've been through.

Ron and I listened to the testimony without much sympathy. After Dr Ash had spent almost two hours explaining Eaton's mental problems, Skaggs suddenly asked Dr. Ash questions we weren't expecting and were totally unprepared for.

"I want to ask you precisely how this—how this homicide came about. And so the first question I have for you—I think we already broached it—was: he [Eaton] essentially had gone into town, made a phone call, right?" Skaggs said.

"That's correct," Dr. Ash said.

"And did he encounter Lisa Marie Kimmell?"

"Yes, he did."

"And where did he encounter her?"

Ron, the girls and I held each other's hands.

Dr. Ash spoke softly. "Mr. Eaton said he encountered Lisa as he was driving towards his land."

"Okay. And she was parked there alongside the road, then?"

"Her car was parked there. And when he got there, he felt someone was again, breaking in, robbing his bus, and so he was angry. He was already in an angry state, but he got angrier. And he felt that Lisa was not alone, that there were other people there."

Rob him? Of what? He had nothing of value. He didn't even have water, electricity, or a toilet that flushed. My rage surged.

Skaggs asked if Eaton confronted Lisa with a gun. Dr. Ash said yes. Skaggs asked the doctor to explain.

We couldn't hold back our tears.

"Well, he had a gun. And he took it out and walked up to her car."

"Okay. And basically, did he get her out of the car at gunpoint?"

"Essentially."

Mike Blonigen objected about leading questions. Skaggs backed off and asked what happened next.

"He realized she was alone. And so he then proceeded to take her down to his bus. And he said he realized the moment he started taking her down to his bus that he was in trouble."

"And did he have occasion to keep her?"

"He kept her there, he said, for a few days. During the time that he kept her there, well, when he was walking down, he said to himself, he's not going to be alone for Easter. He kept her there; he forced her to have sex with him. He was, during the entire time, expecting the police to come at any moment. He was thinking whether or not to let her go, whether or not to keep her. And then he decided that he was too afraid of what would happen to him if he let her go."

Everyone around us was in tears. His words were excruciating, but there was more. Skaggs asked what happened next.

"What happened was that at a point after a couple of days—and this is not entirely clear—he decided he was going to kill her, and walked up from behind her and hit her in the back of the head with a pipe. She fell to the floor, unconscious. He realized that she was—her heart was still beating. And then he proceeded to stab her until her heart stopped beating."

Skaggs asked how he disposed of her.

"He said he had some plastic material from old mattress wrappings, and that he wrapped up her body in that and then put her in his car and took her to the bridge."

That would explain why the pool of blood found on the bridge had a long straight edge to it. It must have spilled out of the plastic.

Dr. Ash continued. "He said, this probably sounds screwed up, but I, she had said she wanted to be home…" Dr. Ash choked up and had to take a breath. "Excuse me… with her family by Easter. He took her to the river and threw her in the river. He said he knew there would be fishermen that would find her."

By this time, we could barely contain our sobs. Janeice leaned over, put her arm around me and asked if we were okay.

I whispered, "No, we're not."

She led us out of the courtroom so we could have a good cry.

We didn't miss anything. Mike and Skaggs began arguing over whether Dr. Ash could apply mitigating circumstances to Eaton's situation. Judge Park asked the jury to leave while they worked out the details.

We were deeply shaken. But when we discussed the confession, it didn't make sense. We saw his property. There is no way Lisa would have stopped in the middle of the desert. The driveway to his trailer wasn't directly off Highway 20-26. And why would he think others were with her in a two-seater car? He knew cars very well. Additionally, her trip-meter reading placed her at the Waltman rest stop —not as far as Moneta.

When we returned to the courtroom, Mike had begun his cross-examination of Dr. Ash. He focused on the alleged phone call Eaton made the Thursday or Friday before Easter to his ex-wife. Eaton had abducted Lisa a week before Easter. His lies were clear.

Mike attacked the aspect of Eaton's "self-reporting" to the doctor. Mike turned Dr. Ash's testimony against the defense.

"In listening to your testimony, it sounds as if Dale Eaton's self-reporting played a very important role in your conclusions. Is that an accurate statement?"

"It's an important part, yes," Dr. Ash said.

Mike brought up Eaton's past brushes with the law and his psychiatric evaluations, which were primarily based on Eaton's self-report, too. It became evident that Eaton had embellished every chance he could over the years to evoke sympathy or to avoid legal consequences. Eaton learned how to use the system to his favor—exaggerating when necessary.

The line of questioning led Mike and Skaggs to the judge's bench several times in disagreement. But Mike didn't back off.

Mike Blonigen also attacked Eaton's claim of total isolation, showing Doris Buchta's diary as proof that Eaton visited with his neighbors often and for hours at a time. For example, on April 11th, he was at the Buchtas' for six hours. Mike had documents showing that Eaton was running a welding business, countering his whining about lack of jobs. Mike showed Dr. Ash that Eaton owned three trucks.

Dr. Ash hadn't called Eaton's ex-wife to find out whether the alleged phone call had actually occurred. Mike concluded his questioning by showing Dr. Ash a calendar of 1988. Dr. Ash didn't know that Lisa had been abducted March 25th and that Easter was nine days later.

Mike concluded his questions, and then made a simple statement that spoke volumes. "Doctor, a diagnosis is only as good as the information it's based on, isn't it?"

"That's correct," Dr. Ash said meekly.

Dr. Ash was excused from the stand.

For the rest of the afternoon, the defense tried to show that Eaton could be kind to his family and the few friends he had. They also tried to show that Dale had been severely abused as a child. Dale's elderly aunt and uncle took the stand, two of the few people who refused to believe Eaton could murder anyone.

Dale's Uncle Loren was in a wheelchair; I guess he was supposed to kindle sympathy with the jury. In my opinion, the testimony produced sympathy for no one, not even Eaton's family. The uncle couldn't remember details. The only specific episode of abuse he recalled was a time when he found the pantry empty. He bought the Eaton children a sack of lunchmeat to feed them. Supposedly it wasn't good enough for Dale's dad, so dad went to town and spent what little money the family had on a steak for himself. Oh, and Dad's abusive behavior included hiding a box of candy in his car because he didn't want to share it with his children.

I've heard a lot worse stories than that, and they didn't lead to murder. I thought, "The defense needs to come up with something better than this."

Then Skaggs called two friends and two neighbors to testify that Eaton was good to them. Most obviously missing was testimony from his siblings. Some of them have told Ron and me that they were devastated by what Dale did, and in my eyes, they became victims of his crime, too.

FRIDAY, MARCH 19th, 2004

The defense began their grand finale on Friday. Skaggs called Dr. Linda Gummow, a highly-accredited psychologist, to the stand. She stated that she had spent two days in June of 2003 interviewing and evaluating Dale Eaton. She conducted a "historical record review" (a fancy way to say that she read his old records). Dr. Gummow agreed with Dr. Ash that Eaton suffered from a major depressive disorder in addition to possible brain damage. She produced an elaborate time line of significant events affecting his life prior to killing Lisa.

According to her findings, Eaton's failed marriage was a big factor in his depression. Eaton had told the psychologist that the problems with his marriage began on his wedding night, when "Marie" wanted a divorce. The marriage went downhill from there, although the couple stayed married for sixteen years. He told Dr. Gummow that when he moved to Moneta, he "needed to get away from people," and he called his bus "the hideout." She said that his few friends would take their own food when they visited because Eaton's idea of dinner was to throw frozen venison into a dirty frying pan and eat it with his hands. His hygiene was poor. He was known to bathe in a car wash or at friends' houses.

Dr. Gummow showed the court a slide presentation about how a "normal" brain works compared to a depressed brain. She displayed MRIs and PET scans of dysfunctional brains. Interestingly, she didn't show pictures of Eaton's brain. When asked why not by the prosecutor, she explained that she wasn't a doctor and couldn't order those kinds of tests. No one explained why Dr. Ash didn't issue those orders. Perhaps someone had conducted tests on Eaton and found nothing unusual.

Her testimony suggested that Eaton's mental instability resulted from his abusive father, deep depression, possible brain damage, and "stressor" factors, including the suicide of a younger brother.

Eaton told Dr. Gummow that he blamed himself for his mother's mental illness, and for his brother's death. He owed his brother money. He lamented that he hadn't been able to keep a good job and pay his brother back; perhaps, if he had, his brother would still be alive.

While Dr. Gummow testified, I saw Mike furiously taking notes with a scowl on his face. I wasn't sure how much longer he could remain quietly in his chair, waiting to cross-examine her. Finally his time came — and thank goodness, because at times it seemed as though that woman's long-winded psycho-babble was about to give me brain damage.

Mike Blonigen questioned Dr. Gummow's analyses, also mostly based on Eaton's self-report. His questions were tough. He finally confronted Dr. Gummow about the brother's suicide. "You said you always checked things out carefully; is that right?"

Dr. Gummow said, "I try."

"You said, when you were standing up here with this time chart, that one of the most significant events in Dale's life before the homicide was the suicide of his brother, Darrel, is that correct?"

"That was my statement, yes."

"And that was listed as occurring on January 1st, 1987; is that correct?"

"That's an approximate date. I only had the year. So when I have something like 1/1/87, it means that I don't know the exact date and I put the year."

"Both you and Dr. Ash talked about this being an event that was affecting him at the time of the homicide, as part of his depression, isn't that true?"

"No, I didn't testify to that."

Ron and I were taken aback. What? That's what she just implied. Everyone heard her. Or did I need a hearing aid?

Mike didn't hesitate. "Well, Doctor, did you ever bother to get a death certificate?"

"No."

Mike whipped out a paper in what I call a "Perry Mason moment." "I would like to show you Exhibit Number 1003, a simple thing to check on, a very simple thing to check on."

"Not for me. I'm not an investigator. I wouldn't even be able to get authorization to do this."

"Doctor, what day did Mr. Eaton's brother commit suicide, from that document?"

"October 10th, 1988."

"Well after the Kimmell homicide, isn't that true?"

Dr. Gummow glared at Mike and handed the paper back to him. "That's true."

Eaton's brother committed suicide more than six months after Lisa's death.

Skaggs objected and Mike said he had no further questions.

Wow. If I were Dr. Gummow, I would have felt as though I had just been through a paper shredder.

Lynn Cohee was recalled to testify again. This time she discussed the interviews she had conducted with other Eaton family members. Lynn said Eaton and his dad had gotten into a fight or two. Nothing sounded horrible enough to excuse him for murdering Lisa.

The defense rested their case at 11:45 A.M., and court would be in recess until nine o'clock the next morning. That gave the attorneys time to prepare their closing statements and Judge Park time to prepare the final jury instructions.

I couldn't help but reflect on the morning's events focusing on brain damage and abuse. I had met and come to know members of Dale's family. I didn't see evidence of severe abuse.

I do realize that almost every family has its share of dysfunction, from verbal arguments to physical temper tantrums. Maybe Eaton's dad lost his temper at times when he was a young father with seven active kids—anyone might snap with that many children. Maybe Dale was a difficult kid. I don't know what happened in the Eaton household. One of his brothers committed suicide, but I was told he had gotten himself into deep financial problems. Whatever happened in that family did not give Eaton an excuse to kill Lisa, and some of his family has said the same thing. How many thousands of people survive a tough childhood and grow up to be productive citizens? Thank God most people do. None of Dale's siblings, raised by the same parents in a similar environment, turned into killers.

Later that afternoon, Janeice called to tell us that the judge had polled the jury to see whether they wanted to work over the weekend or take a recess until Monday.

The jury wanted to continue on Saturday. I was glad. We were all tired from the emotional drain of the week. Waiting until Monday would have put everyone on hold for two more days.

SATURDAY MARCH 20th, 2004

Saturday morning, Judge Park read instructions to the jurors, and then Blonigen and Skaggs gave their closing arguments. The jury was allowed to have lunch before starting their deliberations about whether or not to give Eaton the death penalty.

We were nervous, even though Mike had put forth an excellent case throughout the trial. All twelve jurors would have to agree to give Eaton death. How much stock would they put in the mitigating circumstances? The brain damage? The depression? The childhood abuse? Would there be more problems like those we had had with the two previous jurors? How long would this process take? It made our heads spin.

At 3:15 P.M. we got a call from Janeice. I expected to hear an update or my worst fear, that we had another problem. Not this time.

"The verdict's in," she said excitedly.

"Oh, my God! We'll be right there!"

The jurors had taken a little over two hours to decide Eaton's fate.

We piled into our cars and raced the few blocks to the courthouse. Once again, we encountered a barrage of cameras and a courtroom packed beyond capacity.

We took our reserved seats. Judge Park entered the courtroom and summoned the jury. Silence blanketed the room. The jury foreman handed the verdict to a clerk to let the judge to review before handing it back to the clerk to read. Everyone held their breath.

The verdict? Death.

Skaggs asked that each juror be polled, and each person confirmed that was indeed his or her verdict.

The judge dismissed the jurors after thanking them for their service, and court was adjourned.

Tears and hugs flowed among family, friends, the prosecution team, and people we didn't know who had followed the trial.

Before leaving the courtroom, there was one last thing I wanted to do. I went to the table where the defense team sat. They were quietly packing stacks of files into boxes and their briefcases. I asked them if I could speak with them for a moment. A puzzled look came over their faces, but they nodded.

"I know you had a tough job to do and did the best you could, given what you had to deal with," I said. "I know it must have been very hard for you, too. All I can say is that you did your job and you did it well. I thank you."

Their faces looked tired, but appreciative.

Expressing Our Gratitude

On March 21st, Sunday morning, we met the press in a patriotic conference room at the hotel. Mike Blonigen began by thanking the investigators and prosecution team for making sure a fair trial was held. "Good cases are like houses—they're built on good foundations. Mike Sandfort, Jim Broz, and Dan Tholson built that foundation—we might not have known it for fourteen years, but they did everything that made what has happened here possible."

Ron, Sherry, Stacy, and I sat in front of the reporters and tried to maintain composure, but it wasn't easy. Ron read from our prepared statement first. We wanted to make sure we said our important messages before the press began firing questions at us.

Ron began. "For our family, the words 'thank you' are very inadequate to express our gratitude to so many. We would like to thank the media.

We had no jurisdiction to help us when we learned that Lisa was missing nearly sixteen years ago, and we turned to you for help. Without exception, you were here for us from the very beginning of this tragedy and stayed with us for these many difficult years. We know you have a tough and sometimes controversial job to do by trying to balance news, your job, and respecting our privacy. We confess it has been difficult at times, but by and large we have been treated with concern and respect, and we truly appreciate it."

"We would like to thank Mark Benton, Dr. Thorpen, and all of the investigators who have labored over this case with us for so many years. With special thanks to Don Flickinger, Lynn Cohee and Dan Tholson, and there are many more. They have cried with us, they have anguished with us and for us. They were there for us in our times of deep despair. Even during the times we felt hopeless, after many years had passed, they never gave up."

I spoke next. "We would like to thank the prosecution team, Mike Blonigen, and Stephanie Sprecher. Not only did they do their civic duty, but they were passionate about it. They sacrificed family, friends, and personal time for months preparing for this trial. They wanted justice for Lisa, for our family and for you, the concerned citizens who have suffered from Dale Eaton's actions. We would like to thank Janeice Lynch, our Victim-Witness Coordinator. We had no idea what her job entailed until we saw her in action. Her tasks are multiple and not just limited to attending to the victims of a crime. She not only gave us practical support, but also emotional support to cope throughout this ordeal."

Sherry thanked the defense team and jury. "We want to thank the defense team. As odd as that may seem, we're grateful that they tried to defend Mr. Eaton to best of their abilities. We respect them for performing their civic duty. They were handed a difficult task, and we know this wasn't easy for them, either.

"We would like to thank the jury. We know they invested time and emotion to make this very hard decision. They painfully endured a glimpse of Lisa's tragic death. We are certain they had to deal with many of the same inner conflicts we have had as they decided Mr. Eaton's fate. We admire their strength and courage to give Lisa, our family and the community justice.

Stacy concluded our statement. "I'd like to thank the community. We are so humbled and touched by the generous kindness that has been extended to our family during this very trying time. It seems as though a legion of angels were dispatched to brace us and embrace us, to give us the strength to get us through each agonizing day. The support came in many forms, from prayers, financial gifts, services, food, flowers, and housing accommodations, to hugs or a shoulder to cry on. Your support and kindness has given us the strength to endure this difficult time. It is true that Casper cares.

"Lastly, there are so many others we would like to thank by name, such as Pat Sweeney and his staff here at the Parkway, the Fuller family, Lew Pierson, and the list goes on."

The four of us held up pretty well at first, but questions from the press tapped into our emotions.

A young woman reporter asked, "What was Lisa like?"

Sherry's eyes watered and her voice cracked. "At sixteen years old and eighteen years old, you know, you always have that sibling rivalry and fighting. I wished I still had the opportunity to become friends—Stacy and I, we talk every day."

Ron told the press that Lisa had always been one step ahead of us because she was so independent. We were learning to be parents with Lisa, and she boldly led the way.

One of the hardest moments came when a reporter asked, "Where do you guys go from here?"

"Home!" I blurted out. "This is something we will never get over, but must get past. We need to get on with our lives. There are jobs to return to, children to raise, and grandsons to spoil. But we will never forget what happened to Lisa."

Ron added, "I relate it to a Reba McIntyre song. The world doesn't stop for my broken heart." His chin quivered as he tried to keep from breaking down. "Life goes on, and we need to do that as a family."

CHAPTER 22

Man of Many Faces

THE EATON FAMILY'S PERSPECTIVE

I'll be honest. I didn't want a chapter about Dale Eaton in my book. I wanted to focus only on the consequences his acts had on innocent people, but I realize that many want to know who he is and why he killed. I can't answer *why* he killed, but I can explain some of his history. The following portrait of Dale Eaton was compiled from conversations with his younger sister, Judy, and her husband, Gary Mason.

Judy Mason is insightful. She spoke candidly about her brother, saying she believes what he did was wrong and that he should pay for his crime, but he's still her brother and she will always love him. She and I have become friends since his federal trial in Denver. She's a delightful woman, married to her husband for thirty-nine years. She's active in her community, dotes on her numerous grandchildren, and looks about half her age.

Dale Wayne Eaton was born February 10th, 1945. He was the second child born and the oldest son of Merle and Marian Eaton. The Eatons would have eight children, losing a daughter at birth. Merle and Marian weren't highly educated—few rural folks were in those days. The family was poor and moved frequently in the Rocky Mountain region. Merle was said to have a hot temper and didn't keep jobs for long, but he mellowed as he aged, and now he's close to most of his kids.

Judy said Marian was a loving mother who treated the kids fairly. She sewed all of their clothes and made sure they attended school. Despite her efforts to provide for her children, she struggled with mental illness. She was diagnosed with schizophrenia, but Judy's not convinced she got a correct diagnosis.

Dale possibly inherited his depression from his mother. Several members of the family commented that he definitely inherited his dad's temper, that he's just as bull-headed as Merle. The two clashed often.

"I do think my dad was hard on him," Judy said.

Judy looked up to Dale because he protected his younger siblings. If one had trouble at school, he rounded up the family and they went home together. He was bigger than other boys his age, developing a thick, muscular body from chores and jobs on farms. His size both helped and hindered him. He was teased about being big and poor. He'd whip another kid in an instant when they harassed him or his siblings. He developed a tough hide and a mean stare with his deep-set, dark eyes.

Dale had a younger brother born with cerebral palsy. Dale carted Allen to school in either a wagon or on a sled, and Dale got into scraps when other kids made fun of Allen's disability. When the kids were allowed time to play on snowy days, Dale tucked Allen in with him and headed down the hills on their homemade sled.

In 1960, the Eatons lived in Meeker, Colorado. Merle worked as a gas station attendant, and Marian was a maid. Judy said that her mother's depression was worsening. Some days the freshly-cleaned house smelled heavenly with baking bread. Other times, her mother had slept all day. The kids foraged for themselves and cleaned the house, making sure Mom got a bath before Merle came home. He wasn't patient with her mood swings.

Marian didn't drink. No one knew what was wrong with her.

One afternoon, the children came home from school to the frightening sight of a towering fire truck in their driveway. Men in a dark sedan took their mother away.

Marian had tried to burn down their rented house.

Merle happened to arrive before the fire destroyed the house or their possessions, but what damage was done to the kids we cannot know. Anyone watching his or her mother whisked away would be traumatized.

Judy thought it hit Dale pretty hard because he was very close to their mother.

No one called the family together and explained that she was going to a psychiatric hospital. Back in those days, mental illness was treated with shame. The children didn't get to see their mother for six months. They might have thought she didn't want to see them, when, in fact, the doctors wanted to regulate her before letting the family see her. Part of her treatment included electroshock therapy, so she must have been in bad shape.

Shortly after Marian's breakdown, Merle moved the family to Greeley, Colorado to be near her and the doctors who were caring for her.

Dale hated the move. He loved Meeker, and he loved his mother. She was the buffer between him and Merle. Dale was only fifteen years old when his mother was hospitalized, but he shouldered a lot of responsibility, even if no one asked him to. Judy remembered a time when young Dale took it upon himself to provide the family with food. He killed a porcupine, skinned, cleaned, and cooked it, showing pride that the family had meat that night.

Dale acted out his anger after leaving Meeker. The move had ripped him away from a town he liked and separated him from his beloved grandfather. He and his granddad had hunted and fished together often. Dale took up with a rough crowd in Greeley, Colorado.

It's interesting to note how important fishing and hunting were to Dale. Judy said that the last time she saw her brother, he wanted to talk about the fun the family had in Meeker. A fond memory was fishing with their mother; she took the kids to the river more than Merle did. Dale reminded Judy of the time their mother caught a huge fish. When Judy tried to reel it in, she accidentally dropped it and the fish got away. Hunting- and fishing-related issues appear often in Dale's background.

Shortly after Dale turned sixteen, he began getting into trouble with the law. Judy didn't remember precisely what happened in September 1961, but she did remember that Dale needed shoes for gym class and Merle said they couldn't afford them. Dale stole either pumpkins or watermelons from a neighbor lady to sell so that he would have the money for the shoes. When the woman confronted Dale, he snapped and stabbed her.

The woman didn't die. He was charged with burglary, assault with a deadly weapon, and auto theft. I'm not sure how auto theft was involved, but he ended up in the Golden, Colorado Lookout Mountain School for Boys, a reformatory.

Dale did well in a structured environment, and he learned to weld. Judy said he seemed to get his act together around the age of nineteen. He was out of prison and had found a job. He met "Rose," a young woman still in high school. She was about sixteen or seventeen. Judy said the family loved Rose, and they hoped she and Dale would get married someday.

"She was a sweetheart. Dale acted so normal around her," Judy said. Judy also thought Rose resembled their brown-haired mother in looks and in personality.

Marian was out of the hospital by then and on medications. Life seemed to stabilize for Dale. Dale and Rose became engaged, but she was still young. While Dale worked out of town and commuted weekly to his job site, she did what many teenagers do. She found a new boyfriend closer to her age. She broke up with Dale and broke his heart, according to Judy.

Shortly after the breakup, he was arrested for grand larceny and was sent to the Buena Vista Correctional Facility in Colorado. He spent nine months there before getting paroled. He couldn't stay out of jail during the 1960s. He was in and out of Buena Vista several times for grand larceny and parole violations.

In the late 1960s, Dale met another young woman I've been calling "Marie." By then, Dale was twenty-five. Marie was only sixteen. They got married, but Judy said they fought constantly. "They never got along from day one. I never saw them happy. She was always on his case about something. I've seen her slap the crap out of him and kick him," Judy said. "One time they were at the grocery store. She wanted to go to the liquor store to get some wine, even though he didn't drink. He told her that she didn't need that, and she slammed his hand in the car door."

Judy viewed Dale as the family guardian and said that keeping family together was important to him. Perhaps he blamed himself every time it split apart. Merle once left Marian and moved to Arizona. Judy and Dale paid the rent, utilities, and grocery bills for their mother until Merle came back.

In 1979, Marie filed for divorce the first time and took the children. I don't want to hurt the three Eaton children, so I will not discuss their situations with either parent. I will say that many family members and observers have commented to me that they felt sorry for the kids, thinking they had a bad home life given Dale and Marie's unhappy relationship.

The couple was separated off and on from 1979 to about 1983. They reconciled, but not for long. Marie divorced Dale in 1986, and it wasn't amicable. The police were called in. He talked about suicide, and that got him admitted to a psychiatric hospital where he was evaluated, treated, and released when they thought he had calmed down.

In 1987, Dale moved a 1950s era school bus out to the desert on the Moneta property his uncle gave him. He became reclusive and rarely bathed. Without electricity and plumbing, he let himself go. Judy said when he'd drop by her home, she wouldn't let him in until he agreed to take a shower. While he bathed, she washed his clothes. She'd make him clean up his vehicle, too.

He became a scavenger, stealing anything he could find to sell at flea markets. Not only did he steal things, he stole lives. Somewhere along the line, I think something stole his soul.

I felt bad for Judy. She was never in denial about Dale. It devastated her to know what he did to Lisa, and she cried many times over it. How could she claim to still love him? Judy is a nurturing type of person and dwelled on his good side, overlooking his faults. Her memories of Dale are of the good things he did when they were growing up. That's the only side she knew, or perhaps wanted to know. She didn't understand the depth of his dark side.

Not all family members share Judy's point of view, including her husband Gary. He told Ron and me, when we met before the trial, that he wanted to be supportive of Judy's feelings about her brother, but quite frankly he "couldn't stand the guy." He shared many stories about Dale's mean and dishonest behavior. Gary has known Dale since 1965.

"Dale had an extremely hot temper. The minute something would go wrong, he couldn't handle it. At work, he'd either hit someone and get fired or he'd quit."

Gary said he witnessed Dale's frightening temper, and it troubled him. "His temper goes instantly. He'll go from being just fine to being a raging bull in one second. He's a very scary person, and when he hits somebody, it's like a sledgehammer. I saw him once in Greeley, in a bar. He picked me up from work, and he wanted to stop and have a beer. Somebody came in he'd known from years back. He says, 'Hey, Victor, come over here.'"

"So Victor walks over there and Dale says, 'Where's that money you owe me for bailing you out of jail?'"

"The guy says, "I don't owe you any money.'"

"Dale says, "Let's go outside.'"

"When Dale goes outside with somebody, he's not going to talk. He jumped on this guy from the back before he even got through the door. He was on top. He went right for the back of the neck and busted his face into the pavement and just kicked him half to death. I was grabbing at him, trying to get him off the guy." Gary's comments would not be the only reference to how Eaton attacked people's necks or faces.

Gary also thought Dale had a strange view of the world. It was "all backwards" from Gary's perspective. "If he wanted something, he would find a way to get it without paying for it," Gary said. "One time he drove up to our house in this big piece of junk with stars in his eyes. And it was the biggest piece of crap you've ever seen in your life."

"He was always stealing stuff from farmers, the mines, the railroad— you name it—and selling it at flea markets."

Gary recalled other incidents. "If his old car would break down, he would walk into town to find another one just like it on a car sales lot. He'd ask to take it for a test drive, take it to where he was broken down and swap over the parts he needed. He'd drive off, then call the dealer and tell them that their car broke down on the test drive and tell them where to go get it."

Then Gary told me something that struck a chord. "He told me years ago, after he'd been in prison a few times, he would probably end up back in prison." His strategy of surviving prison was to find out when he first got there who the tough guy was. "He'd go over there and hit him. Smack him in the face and get a fight going right then and show him who's the boss. And Dale was extremely strong."

After hearing that, I reflected on the death of Dale's cellmate. Eaton dealt a fatal blow to Carl Palmer's jaw. The testimonies made Dale's

SHEILA KIMMELL | 193

actions sound impulsive, but I began to wonder if his actions were premeditated to some degree. Even though Palmer was half his size, perhaps Dale wanted to show Palmer who was "boss" when he got the chance.

Gary made other comments about Judy's dad, Merle, who had problems with his temper and holding a job, but Gary didn't blame Merle for Dale's actions. "He's actually a pretty nice ol' guy. The family had its share of problems," he admitted, "but what family doesn't? What happened to Lisa was totally Dale's doing. You can't blame the father, then his father, and the list could go on and never stop. Dale, and Dale alone, was responsible for what he did."

I tried to process the information Judy and Gary shared with me. Their comments left me with more questions than answers.

Dale was raised in impoverished conditions (as were many kids of that era). He came from a large family. His dad was tougher on him than on the other kids. Was it because he was an incorrigible child and they both had strong wills? His mother suffered from mental illness. He had many disappointing relationships with women in his life. What man hasn't? He had three children. He needed to control people.

Was his childhood or environment that much worse than other people's? If so, I don't see it.

CHAPTER 23

Details Not Presented
During the Trial

I didn't know how many people Dan and Lynn interviewed until after the trial. I was given a chance to read statements and transcripts and listen to a few of the interview tapes. It wasn't out of morbid curiosity. I was searching for answers. I knew *how*, but I didn't know *why* Dale Eaton killed Lisa.

I never found all the answers. Dale was like a chameleon, adapting to the company he kept. He was a master of manipulation, showing his family, friends, and the many psychiatrists who evaluated him only the sideof himself that he wanted them to see. Some saw through his charades, others didn't.

One of Dan and Lynn's first stops after getting the news of the DNA match was CAC, the halfway house where Eaton was incarcerated for the Breeden assault in 1998. CAC's goal, then and now, is to offer felons and transitional offenders a structured environment. They hope to promote positive self-development and help the "residents" prepare for independent living. Residents are required to seek employment. They are required to drive their vehicles back and forth to work and sign in every day. Eaton was given back his Dodge van.

That doesn't sound like much punishment to me.

Note that none of these writings of Dale Eaton have been edited for grammar, spelling, or punctuation.

Eaton would later write to friends from prison, "One of the resons I took off from CAC was because of the health hazards." He said he tested positive for tuberculosis. "If I have caused any one to Come Down with TB I would feel so Bad. … Also the way the sewer smell came into my Room from the septic tank when the windows where open it would fill the Room so Bad with sewer gas you would gag. … Also locked in Room with 4 other guys where if 2 was standing the others had to Be Laying Down every one there always had cold or something"

Dan and Lynn continued to research his past, collecting almost ninety names and statements before the trial.

"Kathy May," a one-time girlfriend of Eaton's, told Dan by phone that she met Eaton around 1991 at a restaurant where she worked. He bugged her until she agreed to go out with him. He was nice to her, and her family liked him. She moved to Nevada and said that Dale "found her there." Eaton moved to Utah, but continued to write or drive to see her. She said that he helped her father build a driveway with his back-hoe. She got the impression that Eaton enjoyed assisting people, once sending her money so she could go on a cruise.

He sent Kathy a card in 1993—of all the holidays, he picked Easter. The front features a vase of tulips and reads, "Easter Wishes for a Special Friend. I think of you as family." The inside poem says, "It's all decided for us who our relatives will be, But in a special way we get to chose our 'family,' For if we're very lucky, certain people whom we meet Will care about us deeply and help make our lives complete. We'll think of them as family and we'll love them that way, too. I know this from ex-perience—that's how I think of you." "This is singed Dale W Eaton."

I had to stop reading because my hands shook with anger. An Easter card, thoughts of love and family? He was a free man then. He could walk into a store and buy a sentimental card for his "family" after stealing part of mine. Every Easter we suffer from the memory of what he did, but he had obviously gotten over his actions pretty quickly.

After I composed myself, I read two more letters to Kathy. I was sur-prised at how normal he sounded. Besides his poor handwriting and spelling, I wouldn't expect a murderer to express feelings of love. Did he truly *feel* love, or had he learned that certain words manipulated other people into liking him? In a birthday card he wrote, "I still care very much wether you lik it or not, I sure hope you don't think I am a weirdo But know one has ever kept me spell Bound as you have."

In another letter, he told Kathy that he knew she didn't want to be far from her family. She had a daughter, and his words suggested he was fond of the child. He even offered to buy Kathy a car so that she could "run Back and forth" to see her family.

I stumbled upon words in another letter that made me wonder if he had convinced himself that he had never killed Lisa, or was he deliberately lying?

"I have Been single since 87 or 86. I am scared of getting hurt But I cain't get you out of my mind. I never played around any in 15 years of marriage. My family was the world to me I belive in doing things to gether and playing to gether Belive it or not I stay home most of the time watch Movies Ect. Bad house Keeper Bad Letter writer But won't try and Become auther I Love Kid's But scarde of getting attched since my Devorce haven't really cared if the sun Rose or not so will have a Lot of changing to Do. And will piss you off a Lot. But will do my Best By you and your's." He signed the letter, "Yours for the asking, Dale Wayne Eaton."

Kathy eventually broke it off with Eaton, and he didn't pursue her. She's lucky.

Dan and Lynn interviewed other people who liked Eaton. Lynn talked to "Jake Hooper" by phone; he had known Eaton for thirty years. Jake was Eaton's foreman on many jobs. Eaton had also worked for Jake's sheep-shearing business. Sounds like Eaton skillfully pulled the wool over his eyes.

Eaton lived in an old recreational vehicle on Hooper's property for a short time. Jake commented, "God, it was clear full of stuff. He worked in swap meets. I always got along good with him. I drove a truck with him."

Lynn asked, "Did you ever see Dale get mad or upset or anything like that?

Jake said yes, but only once when another truck driver accused Eaton of doing something he didn't do. "That guy was a bully he self, and uh, when he pushed Dale, Dale just followed him around trying to get the guy to fight, and this guy, after he found out that Dale wouldn't back down, why then he didn't want to fight. I told Dale, come on, get in the truck and forget about it."

Jake shared other memories. Jake said Eaton borrowed money from him that he never repaid. And he borrowed a spinning reel, fishing basket, and a tackle box that he never returned.

Lynn asked Jake if he had any last comments; Jake threw out his opinion of Eaton's innocence in Lisa's case.

"It's hard for me to think that, uh, Dale would do anything like that, 'cuz he wasn't no guy that uh, favored sex, put it that way."

Lynn sounded startled. "He what?"

"He wasn't a guy that favored sex," Jake said bluntly.

"Did you guys ever have any conversations about sex?

"I been around, you know, people, all my life, and he just, he didn't pay any attention to women. He didn't go around like all them guys. They'd all leave them filthy books, you know laying around, in the, in the change shack and Dale never would look at anything like that… Some of them guys, God, they lived on that s—t." Jake said when he was a supervisor, he didn't let the truck drivers bring pornography into the change shacks. He saw dirty magazines in their rigs, but not in Eaton's. (I guess he never saw the dildo, handcuffs, and rope that Eaton kept in his welding truck.)

Jake added, "He was always was super around me. Put it that way. He was always more than polite around my wife. Other than he didn't bathe often enough. There's a lot of times when you ride with him, you had to ride with the window down, but that was just Dale, mechanic grease all over him all the time."

Dan and Lynn spoke to several others who confirmed that Eaton had a bad temper, and stole from people. Doris Buchta recalled that he stole things from her and neighboring properties. Many people commented about Eaton's poor hygiene.

I came across the letters he had written to the "Smiths." They were the nice couple trying to help Dale out by storing some his of belongings while he was in prison. They turned over his possessions to Dan and Lynn, along with four letters they had received from him. After reading the letters, I didn't know what to think. Again, did Dale have caring feelings, or was he trying to manipulate them, knowing that the Smiths were Christians?

In the first letter, it was obvious Eaton had read the Bible desperately to find out if he could get into heaven. "Lately have run into problems that have me worried I give you the verses because I don't know as I can be for givein." He listed fourteen chapters from the Bible with two pages of scriptures that suggest a variety of requirements. Several say all he has to do is "knock" and the door will be opened. Hebrews 10:26-27 is less lenient. "If we deliberately keep on sinning after we have received the knowledge of the truth, no sacrifice for sins is left, (27) but only a fearful expectation of judgment and of raging fires that will consume the enemies of God."

Eaton said he wished he could be more like the Smiths and be accepted by the church. He seemed to recognize some of his problems. "I know that I should be Different with my temper and feelings and I'm not I shouldn't have to have this meds to make me feel good because Knowing Christ should do that for me." He asked the Smiths to write back about his chances of getting into heaven. "please tell me what you really think because am really worried about it." He added a note to the bottom. "It took week to write this."

In the second letter, Eaton wanted to let the Smiths know he was witnessing to his cellmates. He apologized for causing the couple any trouble. "don't know how or when but will try to make it up to you. This is not a promise But a hope that I can I sure need to Learn to Controll my temper Am getting Better But my Bibbile tells me I should change automatically or something in that order and most days am starting to see change But sill fly off handle once in a while I do not Blame any one But my self for Being here as I have Brought it on myself I know that. Talk about changing things and reading everything it Looks Like I would change over night yet still have Bad thoughts once in awhile"

In the third letter, Eaton was less philosophical. He complained for two and a half pages about the living conditions at CAC, as though that excused him for escaping.

The fourth letter was written almost five months after Eaton had been in the Wyoming State Penitentiary. He focused on his bad health more than ever, telling the Smiths that they could not get TB from his letters as he thought previously. He told them that he liked having a cell to himself. He'd bought a TV and watched religious channels, leaving his Bible on top of the TV so other prisoners could read it.

Eaton revealed a strange sense of humor in this letter. He said he went to work in the prison print shop. "they won't Let me print what I wanted to. all I ask to print was 50 & 100s. every night we play a game of spades. the other night they caught me with all the spades in my hand, they said, and we trused you. I told them that If they would read there Bible It tells you to trust in God and no where dose it say trust in Dale."

I read and listened to other stories that horrified me. One young woman's encounter with Eaton stood out.

Dixie Brewbaker, a woman from Riverton, Wyoming, who knew the Eaton family, had contacted Dan after hearing that Eaton was charged with Lisa's murder. Dixie said that Eaton had assaulted her around 1971, when she was a teenager. Her testimony wasn't needed in the trial, but her description of Eaton illustrates his hair-trigger temper and how he kept some people from pressing assault charges.

Dixie's father and stepfather worked with Eaton at one time. Dixie's mother and Marie also became friends, and later roommates, when Marie and Dale were separated.

Dixie said that her memory of Eaton "comes back vividly." The assault happened when her mother and stepfather went on vacation. They had asked Eaton's young bride, Marie, to housesit, cook, and baby-sit their five kids. Eaton was working a night shift in the Gas Hill mines. The arrangement would keep the children and Marie from being alone at night. Dixie liked Marie, who had just found out that she was pregnant.

The happy mood in the house changed when Eaton lost his job.

"He moved in with us. I was terrified of him. He would argue with Marie, and he would hit her." Dixie's bedroom was across the hall from the room the Eatons stayed in. "One time I saw him hit her in the face with his fist in the hallway during the day."

Dixie told her school counselor about Dale, but nothing was done. Dixie said she wanted to leave, but she had a little sister to protect. Eaton stayed at Dixie's house for more than a week before he attacked her.

Dixie relived the nightmare. "One day I came home from school, and

Marie had prepared a pork roast. It smelled differently than what my mother had fixed. I opened up the oven door and pulled out that roaster. And I saw garlic cloves had been inserted into the pork. All I said was, 'Mom doesn't fix it like that.'"

She didn't know Dale was there. He burst into the kitchen. "The evilness in his eyes, the look on his face. He looked so powerful, very controlled in what he was doing. When I saw him coming at me, it scared me to death." He didn't scream, but his voice rose.

"He grabbed a hold of me, took me over to the table, took my head and hair and kept ramming it down into the plate that was on the table. And he said, "Eat it, you'll eat every bit of it. You hear me, you'll eat every bit of it." She remembered yelling, "There's nothing there to eat!"

After shoving Dixie's head into the empty plate, Eaton pushed her into a kitchen chair, grabbed her throat, his raging dark eyes boring into hers as he choked her with his large hands. His force leaned the chair back. Dixie said. "I remember thinking, 'I'm dying.' Everything was going dark. I felt like a dishrag, powerless."

Marie yelled, "Leave her alone! Stop it, Dale! You're killing her!"

He let go, and Dixie came to, hearing Marie's screams.

"I'm going to tell my daddy," Dixie cried.

He grabbed the heavy, old-fashioned telephone receiver and said, "Go ahead and call your daddy.'" He smacked her jaw hard. Dixie recoiled, crying harder. "He had a thing about the face. He didn't hit me anywhere else."

She and her father filed charges, but when her parents returned, apparently Dixie's mother and stepfather dropped the charges because Dixie's stepfather was still a friend of Dale's. I can't help but wonder if the stepfather was afraid of Eaton.

At one point in the tape, Dixie remarked that she and her mother thought Marie was lucky that Eaton didn't kill her. "My mother knew of Marie's beatings at his hands. Everybody knew it."

Thank God that Marie, Dixie, and the countless others he assaulted survived. I can't help but wonder about other unknown victims.

CHAPTER 24

A Serial Killer?

I am not the first to publicly say that I think Dale Eaton is a serial killer. I think he has trolled deserted highways at all hours and possibly killed women over a period of almost three decades. I hope to help other families discover the truth and find whatever peace of mind is possible.

PROFILER'S COMMENT

In November 1988, Special Agent Ron Walker, an FBI criminal profiler in Quantico's Investigative Support Unit and Violent Criminal Apprehension Program (VICAP), wrote a profile for Natrona County at Dan Tholson's request. Ron and I did not know about the profile until recently.

The profile was compiled in November 1988, before Ron discovered the Stringfellow Hawke note in March of 1989. The profile suggested that a serial killer could have murdered our daughter. I'll repeat the key statement:

"This is not likely to have been the offender's first crime of this nature. He may have successfully avoided detection for similar offenses in the past. If so, it is likely that he will continue to assault until apprehended."

We know it's hindsight, but we wish Natrona County had used the "proactive" methods taught by VICAP. One VICAP method is staking out a victim's gravesite close to an important anniversary, such as a death or disappearance. If a law enforcement agency had done that, Eaton could have been caught on the spot when he taped the Stringfellow Hawke note to Lisa's headstone.

Had we known about the profile in 1988, it would have confirmed our worst fears that Sheriff Ron Ketchum's office was not using all of its resources. The profile fit Eaton well (although we realize it fits many sexual predators).

For example, in the category of describing the "offender traits and characteristics," the FBI profile suggested that the killer would be a white male. The offender was suspected of being in his mid-twenties or older. "Research into similar crimes supports the conclusion that this assailant is no inexperienced youngster." This suggested the possibility that the man had committed other crimes.

The crime was described as "not overly sophisticated," but the profile suggested that the man was in full control at all times. He had the "ability to think rationally, to premeditate his offenses, and to act methodically in a calculated fashion and without panic."

Furthermore, the offender was described as having "immature expectations" of his relationships with women, probably choosing younger women to dominate. The man was thought to be familiar with the area surrounding the crime scenes—probably having worked nearby in a "blue-collar" or "semi-skilled" occupation. The assailant showed that he was familiar with the criminal justice system in the way he used ligatures and disposed of Lisa's body and evidence.

Other descriptions fit. "Rather than being described as an unsocialized loner, he is more probably a 'lone wolf' who prefers to be by himself." The profile suggested the killer didn't have a lot of friends, perhaps living as a hunter-recluse.

The detectives would have to hunt him down.

VICAP supported "proactive" investigations to flush out killers. For example, they often published their profiles in newspapers and printed handwriting samples of suspected killers, sometimes on bulletin boards. They sought unconventional help from every psychological avenue available, including the media. Reportedly, Ketchum wouldn't authorize unconventional methods. Dan and Jim didn't have a moment to spare, and they weren't trained in VICAP methods.

The FBI profile wasn't the only reference to a serial killer. The media speculated that Lisa's killer had murdered others. On May 6th, 2003, a Casper Star Tribune reporter wrote about her conversations with Dr. Robert Keppel, the lead investigator on the Ted Bundy case. He wouldn't draw conclusions about Lisa's case because he didn't have enough information about the crime scenes, but the Tribune quoted him, saying he thought "Kimmell's killer displayed sophistication on a few levels."

Another person quoted by the newspapers was Greg Cooper, a former Special Agent FBI profiler from Quantico. Greg and a former Utah Department of Public Safety Law Officer, Mike King, coordinated the Utah Criminal Tracking Analysis Project in 1996. Greg had proposed the tracking project after he became the Provo City Police Chief and heard about unsolved murder cases in the region. He wanted to create a Utah criminal tracking program on a par with the FBI's national level.

They studied eleven Great Basin murders that took place between 1983 and 1997, Lisa's murder included. The project and a conference attracted the attention of agencies in several states. Cooper and King initially believed that at least two different perpetrators were involved in the eleven murders.

I decided to speak to Greg Cooper and find out if he could offer a more comprehensive opinion of Lisa's case if he were given more details. I found him working for CRISNET, a company that has been helping provide law enforcement agencies with the latest information technology in software training and support.

According to their web site, CRISNET designs and develops software applications for national "incident-based" law enforcement. Greg and Mike now head up a new division in the company (acquired by Motorola) to offer investigation software, training in profiling, and consulting services.

Good for them! Perhaps their services can help law agencies overcome the territorial bickering that hindered Lisa's case for fourteen years. Jurisdiction wasn't just a problem for Natrona County. It has been a problem for law officers probably since the dawn of civilization.

Greg Cooper agreed to write up his opinion based on the information provided to him. His response exceeded my expectations.

From Greg Cooper

I have been profiling violent crime cases since 1990, when I was assigned to the FBI's National Center for the Analysis of Violent Crime as a criminal profiler in the Investigative Support Unit. I subsequently served as the National Program Manager of the Violent Criminal Apprehension Program (VICAP) and finished my career with the FBI as the Unit Chief of the Investigative Support Unit. This unit's work became famous when dramatized in the motion picture *Silence of the Lambs*. That Academy-Award-winning production generated numerous motion pictures and television programs illustrating the concepts and principles of criminal investigative analysis, which have proven to be effective in analyzing, investigating, apprehending, and successfully prosecuting violent serial rapists and killers.

After leaving the FBI, I have continued as a profiling consultant and expert witness, and I have instructed police around the globe in the art and science of criminal profiling. My colleague Mike King and I have continued to explore the minds of violent criminals by studying their crimes and interviewing them in prison. We have shared our research in classrooms and publications. These experiences drew me into the abysmal and perverse nature of criminal thinking. Particularly disturbing and haunting are the thoughts and behaviors of violent serial offenders, especially the serial killer.

In all of my experience and the thousands of cases that I have reviewed, I have never witnessed a more distressing anomaly of humanity than the serial killer. I suppose the most disconcerting aspect of this freak of nature is that the terrifying attributes generally associated with fictional monsters have been transposed into human form, but they eat, sleep, talk, and walk just like you and me.

The major difference is that they don't think or feel emotions like you and me, especially empathy, compassion, or love.

The suffering that they create for their victims and victims' families is devastating. Little is comparable to that level of grief and despair. When tragedy strikes, we are compelled to understand the cause responsible for the effect. Identifying that link can help us cope with an otherwise unbearable pain.

The human heart and mind can more readily accept loss of life, even on a massive scale, through catastrophic events of nature or accidents. It is almost incomprehensible for us to understand why the life of a loved one is snuffed out by the malicious acts of another person. We want to know *why*? How can another human being commit murder out of such base emotions as power, domination, and ultimate control over another person?

When I speak about serial killers, I am often asked, "How do you emotionally reconcile the existence of both sociopaths and good Samaritans in society?" How is nature sufficiently compatible for such extreme types of human beings to co-exist on the same planet? I came to the realization that these human predators are the exception, not the rule. They are emotionally dysfunctional creatures who occasionally surface and inject their narcissism into a generally stable world. Fortunately, they represent only a tiny fraction of the population.

Understanding the serial killer is even more difficult because we presume that they are "like us." They are not "like us." They don't think or feel like you and me. They regard other people as things or possessions for the taking and satisfaction of their own selfish and distorted needs. They have no sense of responsibility to society and are completely void of empathy. Society at large becomes the host, and they are the parasite. They perpetually feed off of the naiveté and trust of other people.

Another common error we make when trying to understand this predator is to project our value system into theirs and seek common ground. We must recognize that there is no common ground. This type of offender is akin to a piranha among a school of guppies. The nature of the piranha is to seek out and destroy. The guppy will never change the piranha's motivation.

Lisa's case has haunted me since I first became aware of it in

1998. Mike King and I facilitated a Multi-Agency Investigative Task Force in Bountiful, Utah on the Great Basin Murders. Approximately thirty law enforcement representatives attended a conference from four states, including Wyoming, and Lisa's case was one of eleven murders that we reviewed.

I have always felt an affinity toward Lisa, probably because I have a daughter her age who has similar personality characteristics: she's full of adventure and independence. I have never forgotten Lisa's case, and it has troubled me through the years knowing that she was a prime example of a perfectly innocent victim caught up in an extraordinary series of random events that resulted in her premature death.

It is with this background and frame of reference that I have been invited by Sheila Kimmell to provide a characterization of Dale Wayne Eaton's background and the method and manner of Lisa's death.

Law officers often determine that a person has contributed to their own victimization because they recklessly and negligently placed themselves into an environment or circumstances that elevated the probability of a hazardous outcome. For example, a runaway, hitchhiker, or prostitute increases the risk of becoming a crime victim when he/she willingly places himself/herself under the control of a stranger. We consider such persons as living a "high-risk" lifestyle where the probability of being victimized has increased and the odds are against them for favorable outcomes. The more the person engages in such activities, the higher the probability that he or she will eventually be victimized. Furthermore, if a victim's lifestyle is high-risk, the more likely it is that the victim and the offender will be strangers. This is indicative that the victim became a victim of opportunity.

There are exceptions, as in Lisa's case. Lisa lived a very low-risk lifestyle because she worked full-time at a respectable job, never hitchhiked or accepted rides with strangers, had a strong supportive family, and was what we generally call a "productive citizen." Her chances of being victimized were low. However, the night of March 25th, Lisa was on a highway in an environment and circumstances that she was not familiar with.

It was late, and she was alone in an isolated area. If she had had car trouble or stopped at a rest stop for a quick break, she would have been vulnerable to anyone who saw her and had a malicious interest. Although I don't know how Eaton first came into contact with Lisa, considering her lifestyle and personality, I am confident that Lisa was low-risk. Due to the unfamiliar circumstances, she became a victim of opportunity. For Lisa, it was the wrong place at the wrong time. For Eaton, it became the perfect opportunity, and Lisa became the perfect victim.

Eaton either initially abducted Lisa against her will or he used a con to lure her into a vulnerable position where he could overpower her. I know that Eaton had the ability to seize Lisa's vehicle after taking control of her because of the one-ton dual-wheeled tow truck he drove. Although stealing her car opens up the possibility that there could have been two abductors, judging from his nomadic and lone-wolf lifestyle, Eaton most likely acted alone. Eaton would not have wanted to share the spoils.

Eaton was a thief; he basically pillaged, burglarized, and sold loot to pawn shops or unsuspecting persons to sustain himself, while only working sporadically at temporary manual labor jobs (this is probably why he stole the car, too—for the valuable parts). Eaton towed Lisa's vehicle without concealment and on the open highway, suggesting that he was familiar with the general area where Lisa was abducted, and that he knew that the possibility of being seen before he reached a safe haven was unlikely. For that reason Eaton was comfortable in the area proximate to the abduction site and would be taking both the vehicle and Lisa to a predetermined location that he knew would be isolated and secure from interruption or detection. It would also be a location that only he had primary or exclusive access to. Finally, it would be a destination that he could travel to while risking a minimal amount of exposure to witnesses while en route and subsequent to his arrival.

The coroner estimated that Lisa had been dead for 36 to 48 hours before her body was discovered, and suggested that she was in captivity for several days. Her stomach contents were consistent with having consumed dinner within hours before her death.

Additionally, there were ligature and binding marks on Lisa's wrists, arms, ankles, and legs. Hence, it is evident that Eaton was prepared to capture and keep a victim for a significant amount of time even before he targeted Lisa. It was also apparent that he had a predetermined location, and a plan to detain the victim indeterminately. He would therefore have required a location that confidently provided personal control and exclusive authority to preside over his victim. This was consistent with Eaton's makeshift residence in an old school bus that was located on his property in a remote, desolate area.

Lisa's autopsy indicated that her pubic hair had been shaved and that she was subjected to numerous sexual assaults. The method and manner of the assaults, the restraints as well as the style of her incarceration, are suggestive of an offender who is playing out an extensive fantasy that he created in his mind and/or acted out repeatedly. It was an effort on his part to perfect the fantasy or improve on previous failed and/or unsatisfying experiences.

The method and manner of death and disposal of Lisa's body also reflect elements of practiced deadly skills and familiarity with the disposal site. Lisa was hit from behind with a determined, intentional, and focused amount of blunt-force trauma. This type of assault was not a superficial or hesitation wound. It was a mortal wound that would have been lethal in two to six hours. It was purposeful and intended to cause death.

The amount of force involved suggests that Eaton was frustrated or angry at the time the blow was inflicted. He may have been frustrated knowing that he could not sustain her indefinitely without being discovered. Additionally, he may have been getting bored, wearied, and/or fatigued while attempting to support Lisa, conceal her abduction, and prevent her from escaping. It is also likely that he was disappointed and becoming angered that his fantasy exceeded reality. The fact that she was hit from behind suggests that Lisa may have been trying to escape from Eaton.

Eaton's intent to keep Lisa in captivity longer may also be implied by the contents of her stomach. He fed her a type of beef stew two to four hours before her death. There was no purpose to feeding her if he intended to kill her in the immediate future. The force of the blow and the subsequent six fatal stab wounds to ensure Lisa's death are indicative of a possible disturbing event that triggered Eaton's vicious assault.

I would expect that part of Eaton's fantasy included a "legitimate" relationship with Lisa that he pretended would last. Perhaps he was beginning to trust her to "stay" with him, and at some point removed her restraints. Removing her restraints would have validated in his mind her willingness and even a desire to remain with him.

Based on Eaton's past behavior with women and his medical records made public during his trial, he was known to display an impulsive and explosive temper. He obviously did not trust women. If he let down his guard and Lisa attempted to escape, it would have shattered his fantasy and precipitated a spontaneous reaction of rage. Therefore, after he delivered the killing blow to her head and stabbed her until her heart stopped beating, he may have angrily placed or replaced the handcuffs on her wrists before he disposed of her body.

It should also be noted that a note authored by Eaton was discovered at her gravesite a year later. This behavior and the contents of the note are consistent with his lingering fantasy about being "in love" with Lisa and how he perceived their relationship.

Finally, the placement of her body at the disposal site is significant. It was remote, at night, yet also a popular fishing spot for local fisherman. It was located within a reasonable distance from Eaton's residence. Eaton was a known hunter and fisherman. He was obviously familiar with the location and had probably fished there before. He knew that he could dispose of Lisa with minimal risk of detection, yet knew that fishermen would discover her. Eaton admitted to a psychiatrist that he wanted Lisa found in time for Easter. This intent also supports his emotional interest in Lisa. However, he probably knew the water could serve as an agent to destroy forensic evidence. Eaton's history of criminal activity and time in prison certainly educated him in the ways of avoiding being connected to a crime by physical evidence.

The method and manner of this crime support the conviction that it was a culmination of pre-planning and methodical cunning to either live out a fantasy or improve on previous failed attempts at the fantasy. The preparation and ability to carry out this crime to the very end with sustained control and domination reflects experience, determination, and absolute commitment to an ultimate goal. Other murder cases have shown those goals to include wanting supreme power, domination, and control over their victim, and having a legitimate relationship with the type of woman fantasized about. Eaton was constantly on the hunt and determined to find prey. There is no doubt in my mind that Eaton is a human predator and by all indications was involved in similar crimes before crossing Lisa's path, and certainly after she was stolen from her family.

The approach that he employed with Lisa and subsequently with the Breeden family in 1997 lends credibility to my opinion that Dale Wayne Eaton is a serial killer.

UNSOLVED CASES

How many people has Dale Eaton murdered? He traveled so often to so many states that no one may ever learn the truth. After numerous long searches on the Internet for missing people and unsolved murders in Wyoming, Utah, Nevada, Colorado, and Montana, I found almost two dozen women missing or murdered who were young, small-framed, possibly isolated, and alone.

There are probably a lot more missing persons who haven't been reported or whose bodies have been found but not yet identified. The desert is a big empty place. Except for Lisa, the bodies that have been found were only found by chance.

Am I saying that Eaton killed about two dozen women? No. The Internet doesn't produce enough evidence to make that connection. However, there are four cases in Wyoming that make Eaton look highly suspect. I was told by law enforcement to avoid using names in case it might prejudice a future jury. Eaton has already gotten the death penalty,

SHEILA KIMMELL | 213

plus a life sentence, plus fifty years for killing Lisa. He's not going free even if he is tried again and found innocent of other crimes, if in fact he's responsible.

The following are cases that cause me concern. I will use the victims' names, if for nothing else, to give these women a voice they no longer have.

Naomi Lee Kidder

The first case that caught my attention was Naomi Lee Kidder, an eighteen-year-old who was last seen alive on June 29th, 1982. I met Naomi's mother, and she still blames herself for Naomi's death. Naomi was going through a rebellious stage, as teens often do. She experimented with drugs, and she had a child. Her mother was raising the baby. However, just because Naomi wasn't perfect doesn't mean she deserved to die. I told her mother that "Naomi is a precious life, too." Who knows how she would have turned out? People change after they grow up. Naomi didn't get that chance.

Naomi, a petite girl, less than five feet tall, with long brown hair, had taken a trip with friends to Rawlins, Wyoming, earlier in June. The friends went back home to Buffalo, Wyoming, but she stayed. By the time she was ready to return home, she ran out of money. She called her mother to ask for cash, but her mother refused. Naomi had pulled that before, and Mom was trying "tough love" for a change.

Naomi left Rawlins on June 29th to hitchhike to Buffalo. Two days later, when no one had seen her, Mrs. Kidder reported her missing.

On September 10th, 1982, the mummified remains of a young female were found near a remote dirt road to a fishing area off Bucknum Road in Natrona County. She had been strangled with a bizarre, twisted wire ligature that was still in place. Whoever killed her may have done so in a rage because the wire was savagely twisted four times to tighten it. What horrors had Naomi endured?

She was nude. A silver necklace was found nearby, as well as shotgun and .357 caliber metallic casings.

Natrona County wasn't able to identify her, so "Jane Doe" was buried. Somehow communications had lapsed in the 227 miles between Buffalo and Rawlins. Mrs. Kidder found out that Naomi's dental records weren't in the national computer system on March 10th, 1994. She insisted they get entered into the system. On March 14th, Naomi's dental records were matched to the Jane Doe.

Because Naomi's body had been exposed to the elements for so long before she was found, there was no DNA available to test, and few other clues remained. Hopefully at some point, technology can give the case a boost. Until then, unless her killer is willing to talk, the case will remain unsolved.

Belynda Mae Grantham

Less than two months later, another unsolved case emerged on Friday, August 6th, 1982 when "passers-by" found the body of a young woman floating in the North Platte River near Glenrock. A rope attached to the victim's neck was tied to a thirty-three pound rock. Her 102-pound body had been in the water from two to five days, and it was badly decomposed from the hot sun and warm water. Someone had strangled her, using a rope and/or their bare hands. She had multiple traumatic injuries to the neck and base of the skull. She suffered bruises on her right jaw consistent with a fall or assault. She was nude except for her bra and a blouse that was buttoned, but turned inside out. Her jewelry was left on her.

No one knew her name for three weeks. Friends then saw her composite picture in the newspaper, and she was identified as Belynda Mae Grantham, a twenty-year-old woman who had last been seen at the Casper Fair.

The Casper Star Tribune printed a short article about Belynda. She was possibly a troubled young woman who started running away from home at an early age and had been a ward of the state of Wyoming several times. The last time she ran away, she was said to have joined a carnival operating out of New Mexico. Some of her friends had not seen her since the previous June, saying she planned on moving to Kansas.

She was pretty, with green eyes, shoulder-length brown hair cut in the "shag" style so popular in the 1980s. She left behind a baby girl, only sixteen months old.

Eaton was reported to have lived on Monkey Mountain Road during the early 1980s, less than a mile from where Belynda's body was found.

Janelle Johnson

According to a report on the Internet from the National Organization of Parents of Murdered Children, only six months after Belynda's body was found, a pretty young woman named Janelle Johnson left her home in Riverton, Wyoming, to interview with the Vannoy Talent Center in Denver. It was the day of her twenty-third birthday, February 16th, 1983. She probably had high hopes, with her thick, long curly brown hair styled for the interview. I don't know if she was accepted or not by the agency, but her roommate was reported to have said that Janelle had called and was on her way home.

She left Denver around 5:30 P.M. and hitchhiked as far as a truck stop in Sinclair, Wyoming, a few miles east of Rawlins. She was last seen around nine o'clock the evening of February 17th. When she didn't make it back to Riverton for several days, a missing person report was filed with the Riverton Police Department on February 2nd.

On March 1st, 1983, Janelle's body was found by a county employee on the Muskrat Creek Road near Shoshoni, Wyoming—a road traveled mostly by oilfield and agriculture workers. The county worker was repairing storm damage and saw her legs. She had been buried, but flooding had partially uncovered her. The autopsy report states her cause of death as "mechanical strangulation" with a wide ligature, such as a belt. The attacker had raped her and left bite marks on her shoulder. She was nude—no jewelry or partial clothing.

Her time of death remains a mystery. The cold conditions preserved her body, but there is a chance that if Janelle had been abducted the night of February 17th, she might have been held captive before she was killed. In 1982, the technology that could have established the facts didn't exist. I will point out that her body was found 4_ miles south of Shoshoni, only about twenty miles away from Moneta. Although Eaton didn't live in Moneta in 1983, he must have been familiar with the area (the Moneta property was owned by his uncle). Eaton had worked in the nearby oilfields. Dan Tholson recently told me that a newspaper clipping about Janelle's death was found in Eaton's trailer when his property was searched for Lisa's car.

Amy Wroe Bechtel

The most recent murder that pointed to Eaton as a "person of interest" is the Amy Wroe Bechtel case. Her disappearance, on July 24th, 1997, triggered an onslaught of publicity, as did Lisa's. Why? She was a pretty blonde, 5'5" tall, blue eyes, about 110 pounds. She was a runner, a marathon competitor.

Thursday morning, Amy told her husband, Steve Bechtel, goodbye, and set off to run errands around Lander, Wyoming. Her husband, a professional rock climber, went on a climb 75 to 90 miles north of town with a friend. Amy was last seen at a camera store at about 2:30 P.M. She was helping organize a 10K race, and authorities think that her next stop was to drive out and check the route.

Steve came home about 4:30 P.M. knowing Amy had a lot to do. He socialized with friends, ate dinner, and moved items into the new house he and Amy had just bought. When she failed to turn up by 9:00 P.M., Steve began looking for her. He called the police around 10:30 P.M. when no one could find her.

A massive manhunt ensued. Amy's car was found at 1:00 A.M. Friday, off of Loop Road near the Shoshone National Forest. Her keys were hidden under her "to do" list on the front seat of her white Toyota station wagon. Hundreds of people volunteered to search, and by the end of the week, they had covered 500 square miles of the forest and the Wind River Mountains.

The family encountered problems similar to ours. People initially assumed Amy had been the victim of a hit-and-run accident or hurt in a fall from one of the paths. The volunteers and friends who came to help also contaminated the scene around Amy's car. Volunteers destroyed footprints. It took law officials four days to assign an investigative officer.

Only two clues surfaced. A pen was found on Loop Road, but not near her parked car. It didn't match ink on her notes in the car, so it was dismissed. A Timex Ironman watch was found six years later, in June 2003. Amy owned one, but the one found turned out to be a man's watch and not hers.

My heart goes out to the Bechtel family. Amy has never been found. I pray someday her family can bring her home. I understand how they feel.

THE NOMAD

After the trial, Dan Tholson reluctantly allowed me to look at Eaton's timeline that Natrona County had compiled based on their interviews, receipts found in Eaton's belongings, and papers found in his trailer and in his other vehicles. Dan was reluctant because few items are verifiable. I promised him that I would use the timeline wisely. He's right—it only proves a few things, but one issue is important.

Dale Eaton traveled—and a lot.

He drove the highways in the Great Basin area constantly. If he has killed others, his victims could be hidden forever in the wilds of Colorado, Wyoming, Utah, Nevada, Kansas, and possibly all the way down to Waco, Texas, where he worked briefly as a welder.

The timeline begins with his birth in Bay Springs, Mississippi on February 10th, 1945. The 1960s document mostly his arrest records. He appeared to have had fewer altercations with the law after getting married. The timeline listed mostly job referrals from his welding union during the 1970s and 1980s. There is no proof that he showed up for the various jobs, but the timeline suggests that he traveled extensively even while he was married.

He apparently worked in Wyoming, Colorado, and at Utah power plants. Based on interviews, I know he worked for the Gas Hill mines south of Moneta during the early 1970s. He was sent to Greyrocks Dam, Stauffer Chemical in Kemmerer, the Husky Refinery in Cheyenne, and Big Horn Construction in Rawlins. He registered for a P.O. Box in Mills, Wyoming, in September of 1994.

His divorce from Marie took place in Goshen County, Wyoming, in 1986. The job referrals stopped coming from his welding union in 1984, and he settled into his school bus in Moneta in September 1987. Doris Buchta's diary then became the primary source for tracking Eaton. When he first moved to Moneta, he only visited with the Buchtas about once a month. Doris didn't see him at all between January 15th, 1988, and March 8th, 1988. In March, he suddenly began spending a couple of hours or more at their house, and the Buchtas had four visits from Eaton that month. He made sure to be at their house on April 1st, the day after he killed Lisa (to establish an alibi?). From then on, he showed up in Doris' diary about three times a month until he began to visit seven to eight times a month during the summer of 1988. Billy was living with him then, which might explain the additional interactions.

Doris recorded Eaton's wanderings when she and her husband fed his cats. She said Eaton and his son went to Salt Lake City, Utah, on January 3rd, 1989. Billy stated in a separate interview with Dan and Lynn that they started out staying in Clearfield, Utah for about two weeks, and then moved to Elko, Nevada, where he attended school. They didn't return to Moneta from traveling until April 1989. Doris wrote on April 20th, "Dale and Billy here—brought me 3 pkg Marlborough cigs and sweat shirt—Just as full of BS as ever. Billy has a car of his own."

Dale's grandmother was buried in Lander, Wyoming, on January 20th, 1989, but it wasn't clear whether Dale attended the funeral. It certainly gives him a link to Lander.

Eaton's pattern of coming and going to and from Moneta and visiting the Buchtas continued through 1992. Doris wrote about a few of his travels to Gas Hills, Jeff City, and Denver. However, she and her husband were aging and needed more care. They moved to Casper in April of 1993, and she quit writing about Eaton.

After the entries from Doris, the timeline listed the many gas receipts and vehicle registrations found in Eaton's belongings. He was apparently buying and selling cars and trucks, probably after swapping parts from mechanically sound vehicles, as his family described. His various addresses and store receipts put Eaton all over the map, especially in Wyoming. For example, in January 1994, he bought a red Ford truck in Riverton. He set up a phone in Evanston on 1/30/94. His insurance policy shows a Lyman address on 2/9/94. Detectives found various receipts from Ft. Bridger Travel Stop dated 2/22/94, gas in Sinclair dated 2/26/94, Big A Auto Parts in Mountain View dated 3/1/94, two receipts from Kallas Automotive Supply and Wal-Mart (for hair color "X6") in Evanston on 3/3/94. He apparently visited Mt. View and Evanston a lot in March 1994. Later in the spring and summer he could be placed in Worland, Casper, and Thermopolis, Wyoming. In the fall and winter of 1994, he bought propane in Idaho Falls, Idaho, sold stuff to a recycling center in Mills, Wyoming, and bought supplies from the Exeter Drilling Company in Denver the day after Christmas.

How was he making money? Some people speculated he was stealing from farmers and others. He received unemployment benefits on April 8th, 1995. He continuously traveled the desert highways from Moneta to Casper, Shoshoni, Powder River, and Mills, Wyoming; Milford, Utah; Denver, Colorado; and Las Vegas, Nevada during the 1990s, until April 23rd, 1998, when he was finally convicted of aggravated assault against the Breedens.

But he had been free on bail for seven months. He only spent six weeks in the Casper halfway house before he left and spent six more weeks as an escapee. He wasn't completely off the streets and highways until July 30th, 1998. How many other young women did he kill when he had the chance? He was certainly given plenty of opportunities.

Interestingly, the Utah Criminal Tracking Analysis Project suggested that the Great Basin murders stopped around 1997. That's about the same time Dale Eaton went to prison.

Is Dale Wayne Eaton a serial killer, or are these incidents coincidental? I'll let you decide.

CHAPTER 25

Fitting the Pieces Together

B efore, during, and after the trial, Ron and I learned details about Lisa's abduction that devastated us. We've processed the information over and over, trying to understand what happened. We've heard the various theories. People speculated that Eaton might have run Lisa off the road, or that she may have had car trouble (although the car only had 10,000 miles on it), had a flat, or pulled over after hitting an animal.

We still don't have all the answers, but based on witness testimony, the evidence from her trip-meter, and knowing Lisa's personal habits, we believe that Dale Eaton abducted Lisa from the Waltman Rest Stop. Eaton may have been driving toward Moneta at his own pace when he neared the rest stop, or perhaps he was already there, laying in wait for a victim. Either way, he probably couldn't believe his eyes when he spied Lisa in her Honda, alone.

I'm convinced that Lisa drove past Casper and needed to use the restroom as everyone must do when traveling long distances. The Waltman Rest Stop isn't a dark, ominous area far away from the highway. It's a clean, red brick building with hefty streetlights, and it's as close to the road as any gas station. Benches, picnic tables, and plenty of parking beckon travelers. It was probably a welcome sight to Lisa because it appeared safe and convenient. She could dash in and out of the bathroom and continue on her trip. She most likely pulled up around 11:00 P.M., hurried into the restroom, and then back to her car. She may have turned on her overhead light for a moment to check my atlas and confirm her route.

I don't think Eaton seized Lisa as she emerged from the bathroom. He told Dr. Ash that he forced her out of her car at gunpoint. We believe that what Eaton told the psychiatrist is the closest to the truth we'll ever get from him, but he lied about parts of the story. I know Lisa. She wouldn't have stopped on his land because she wasn't a person to dawdle. My theory is that he saw an opportunity and acted quickly. Eaton appeared to carry his "rape/murder kit" with him when traveling. I think Eaton looked for women alone in the desert much like a hunter seeks his prey, as Greg Cooper described.

I think Eaton picked people he thought he could easily subdue. All of the women who have been murdered in that region were small- or average-sized. None could have defended themselves against a large, muscular man like Eaton. Even the Breedens may have fooled Eaton at first because Scott was so tall and thin.

Whoever Eaton's victims have been, there's an element that appears to be unique to Lisa. I think Eaton convinced himself that he fell in love with her. The Stringfellow Hawke note taped to her headstone expressed this "love." I think she became part of his fantasy world.

When Eaton abducted Lisa, a lot had happened in his life. Divorced, often unemployed, and broke, Eaton lived in self-imposed squalor. He was diagnosed with depression in 1986. Isolated in the middle of a desert with no plumbing or electricity, his destitution may have further warped his already troubled mind. Perhaps dwelling on his sexual fantasies helped him escape his dreary existence. For many serial killers, killing people is part of their fantasy, and it's a "fix," according to researchers.

Ron and I believe that Eaton was determined to get a "fix" the night of March 25th, 1988, by overpowering a victim. Detectives found a .30-.30 rifle casing in Lisa's car when it was excavated. When Eaton approached her in the Honda, had Lisa locked her doors and refused to come out? Did Eaton blast a window to scare her out of the car? Lisa didn't carry a gun.

Once he gained control of her, there was little she could do to escape him in that barren desert. He carried handcuffs and flex cuffs. He probably clamped them on her and ordered her into his truck.

The detectives agonized over the details of Lisa's abduction. How could one person have managed to kidnap Lisa and her car? Why take the car at all? At one point, the officers thought two people were involved, and so did we. But for Eaton, it was easy. His 1979 Dodge one-ton dually had an extended cab and a winch. After he handcuffed Lisa at gunpoint, he probably pushed the bench seat forward and ordered her to climb into the back.

The extended cab compartment was the perfect size for a victim. Once Lisa was tied up, laid out in his secret place, and the bench seats were upright, she couldn't escape. Eaton could lock his truck doors, back Lisa's car into position, and hook it up to the winch at his leisure. I doubt that he wasted time though, in case other drivers spotted him. Once he got the car secured, it was a short twenty-two mile drive to his school bus, the pigsty he called home.

What did that monster think about as he drove? He probably figured he could hide the car in the old shed near his elderly neighbors, the Buchtas. Doris would later say she saw a small dark vehicle in the shed, but figured Dale was hiding it to keep it from being repossessed.

Evidence of Lisa's trip-meter supports our opinion that once Eaton concealed Lisa's car, the Honda was never driven again. However, people still wonder why there were so many car sightings. I've mentioned two theories. Lisa traveled between Denver and Billings several times after she bought her car. I'm sure people saw her, but they got the dates mixed up. Additionally, the Wyoming couple who owned the other black Honda CRXsi traveled frequently, and at a glance, the young woman resembled Lisa. Also, one of the composite drawings of a male reported to be seen in Lisa's car resembled the woman's husband.

After Eaton hid Lisa's car, he held her hostage for six days. Why six days? He apparently became infatuated with Lisa in his perverted way. But I'm sure she used every angle she could think of to survive, and I'm sure she tried to escape. During those six days I'm certain he realized how important her family was to her—family seemed to be important to him, too, by some accounts. He even admitted disposing of her body in a place where he knew fishermen would find her so that she'd be home with us by Easter.

Did Eaton set her up subconsciously, by removing the handcuffs, knowing that she would try to escape and that he would have to kill her?

Was he tired of keeping her, as Greg Cooper suggested? Was he living out a fantasy that made him feel like Stringfellow Hawke? We don't know.

Ron and I believe that we've put the big picture together, but there are missing pieces of the puzzle that may never turn up.

CHAPTER 26

Long-term Effects of Crime

After Eaton was given the death penalty, we returned home on Monday, March 2nd, 2004. We had lived at the Park Plaza hotel for so long, I had almost forgotten our home phone number! We were glad to be home. A few days after we returned, we got a call from a juror. She wanted to express sympathy for our family and tell us how the trial affected her and the others. The jurors planned to meet at the Old Government Bridge on April 3rd to leave flowers for Lisa. They wanted to meet us when we came to Casper for the formal sentencing in May. We agreed. We wanted to meet them and thank them for their hard work.

We hoped life would return to normal (whatever that is), but it didn't. One week after coming home, Ron's father had a stroke. A week later, my Dad (ill with prostate and bladder cancer) suffered congestive heart failure. Ron headed south and I went north to Montana. We spent our thirty-sixth wedding anniversary 950 miles apart caring for our parents.

A month later, in April, we learned that we had "won" the civil suit against Eaton, almost a year after we filed. We were granted $5 million— $4 million for compensatory damages and $1 million for punitive damages. District Judge W. Thomas Sullins granted us the full amount by default judgment because Eaton never responded to the lawsuit. The $5 million is supposed to draw interest at ten percent a year until paid. Yeah, right. Obtaining Eaton's property will end up costing us money, but it's the principle.

We knew the man didn't have money. We could claim and sell his junky vehicles, but those are in police custody. His property in Moneta is worthless dirt—the Casper Star Tribune reported, "The 6,000-square foot property is valued at $1,400, according to an official with the Fremont County Assessor's office." We wanted to strip him of everything he owned and rid Moneta of the evil, haunting reminder it stood for. We've asked the nearby volunteer fire department if they will use it in a training drill and burn it to the ground. They've agreed. Others have offered their help to clear the debris afterwards.

Lisa's life was priceless. Five million dollars doesn't compensate us for her death.

Also during April, an investigator for Natrona County asked Ron, the girls, and me to write down how Lisa's death affected us. Our statements were for the "pre-sentencing investigation." A PSI is information that Judge Park would review before making his final decision regarding Eaton's punishment. The PSI would include Eaton's past criminal history and how his crimes affected various people. This file will follow Eaton throughout his prison sentence.

Sherry and Stacy worked hard on their statements, and they're hard for me to read. I get upset knowing how much my girls still hurt inside, and I wish I could erase their pain. However, Ron and I must step back and let our daughters grieve at their own pace and find their own way to deal with the loss, but support them in it. Forgive me for repeating myself, but that's the most important lesson we have learned from our tragedies.

From Sherry Kimmell-Odegard

The effects of Lisa Marie Kimmell's murder on me are enormous. It is difficult for me to put into words how Lisa's tragic death has changed my life. I will briefly share the difficulties that hurt me the most today.

First, I will never know Lisa with a husband and family. I felt so much pain on my wedding day nearly thirteen years ago because Lisa should have married first. Then nine years ago in August, I gave birth to my first son, Trevor. I could not share that joy with my older sister. Again, I feel the pain that she should have had children before me. And today, the deepest pain I feel is that my children will never know their Aunt Lisa, or the children she probably would have had. My boys know that they have an Aunt Lisa and that she is with the angels. They will never have the opportunity to hug Lisa or to feel her gentle touch. They will never hear her voice.

During the trial my boys stayed with me and saw me cry for Aunt Lisa. They understand that she died at the hands of a *very* bad man. If Lisa were alive today, my boys would not have to know such awful things at such a young age. I have talked to Trevor and Alex about Aunt Lisa nearly every day since they could talk. I have pictures of Lisa and tell them about my memories so that through them, they can know who Aunt Lisa was. Lisa will not be forgotten when I am gone, because Lisa's legacy will live on through my boys and through their families in the future.

I hope that one day Dale Eaton will understand that he didn't discard just a life. He discarded Lisa's future. Lisa's life had just begun. She would have married and had children. It's one of the things she talked about often.

Thank you for the opportunity to share the pain I carry every day with the loss of my sister, Lisa. She is very much loved and missed by all of her immediate family and her extended family who never had the opportunity to meet her.

From Stacy Kimmell-Hoover

1) How did Lisa's death affect me?

I turned 13 on May 24th, 1987. I was the typical 13-year-old; I thought I knew everything. I was selfish and a brat. I think most people can look back and realize that about themselves as teenagers, especially as a "new" teenager. Around March 15th, 1988, I was told that my older sister, Lisa, was coming home on March 25th for a visit; I was not happy about it. Why? Well, she was going to stay in my room while she was home. I was very upset by that because I did not want to share my space, my room being the only space I had, with anyone else. I told my friends I did not want her to come home, that I didn't even like her, all because I didn't want her in my space.

On March 26th, 1988, I went skiing with my parents. We got home and found out that Lisa never made it to Cody, WY to pick up Ed, her boyfriend. She was missing, although we could not report it to the police since she had not been missing long enough. Lisa was a very dependable person and always had been. She was very conservative, rarely even wore jeans. I thought she was a nerd because of that. As soon as we found out that she had not reached Cody, we *all* knew something was wrong.

We started searching for her right away. It began with phone calls, trying to piece things together, then a full-out search. My parents searched between Denver and Billings to find anything associated with Lisa or her car. They found nothing. A nationwide bulletin went out for her and her car.

On April 2nd, 1988, Sherry and I went to a convenience store to get out of the house and buy candy. As we were walking up the sidewalk, near our house, we saw the police car and suddenly heard screams. We ran into the house, but were quickly sent to the basement. Once the police left, my parents gathered themselves together and retrieved us from the basement to tell us the terrible news that Lisa's body had been found. She had been murdered and dumped in a river.

I will never forget that day: the shock, disbelief, the immediate feeling of loss and pain. That was the day I thought what a terrible sister I was for not wanting her to come home. It was as if I caused this to happen to her by feeling that way. After Lisa's body was found, Sherry and I didn't go to school. I do not remember the month that I was out except for a vague memory of her funeral.

There is an entire month of my life, my childhood, missing. I can also say that the month that's missing must have been the month that I grew up. I lost the chance to say, "I'm sorry" for not wanting her to come home, for being a bratty little sister. I have carried much guilt for that. I didn't get the chance to tell her that I loved her. At 13, you don't say that to anyone.

And lastly, I didn't get the chance to say good-bye. As for now, sixteen years later, I truly believe that Lisa's death has made me the person I am today. I am conscious of other people's feelings, and think I do pretty well at not taking them for granted. I make sure that I tell my family and friends that I love them often, because I understand that you never know when you will never see them again. My guilt has since changed to sorrow, as Lisa missed out on so much of life and we missed out on hers. She was 18 when she died, and even though that seemed old to me at age 13, she was so young and deserved so much.

2) How did the trial affect me?

When Dale Eaton was finally caught for killing Lisa, it was difficult for me to handle. After sixteen years without her, I learned to cope with the loss. I went through life calling Lisa my guardian angel. I always asked her to watch over our family, knowing that she was looking down on us with just as much pain, seeing what her death did to us. When we were told that the DNA match was discovered, I was scared. I didn't know how to process that. I had already convinced myself that the day would never come when we would hear those words. I had been telling myself for years that it was okay if the killer was never caught because he would burn in hell and that would be justice enough.

It was difficult to hear some of the things at the beginning, but nothing compared to what I heard at the trial. As the trial neared, I became increasingly distraught. It consumed my mind, and I felt like she had died all over again. I knew what it felt like when it happened, and I didn't think there was any way I could go through it again. Somehow, with the help of my family and friends, I managed to make it to the trial. There were so many things that I had never been told, nor should have been at 13 years old.

It was difficult, yet awesome, to hear her voice after 16 years. How many people can say they have had that chance? To hear the things that Eaton did to her through the autopsy and his psychiatrist's testimony was extremely difficult, impossible at times. I continue to replay those testimonies in my dreams nearly every night. The sorrow I feel for my sister is different because I now know what he did to her. I can only imagine the terror she must have felt during the torture that Eaton put her through.

In brief summation, it is very difficult for me to say *how* this has affected me, because it is my life. I live it every day and it will never go away.

CHAPTER 27

Formal Sentencing

The trial was over, but we had one big hurdle left to deal with: Eaton's sentencing. Ron and I geared up for the sentencing on May 20th. It was a formality. The jury had already decided on the death penalty, and Judge Park could not overrule that. However, there were separate charges for which Eaton was found guilty, and Judge Park would need to assess those charges a penalty.

During the penalty phase of Eaton's jury trial, we were told that we could not give a victims' impact statement until the formal sentencing. I spent months preparing a statement and a DVD video pictorial of Lisa's life. The DVD included a selection of music to help us express our feelings. The music was important to me—I felt as though it reflected the joy she brought into our lives and the deep sadness we felt at her loss.

Two days before the sentencing hearing was scheduled, I got a call from Ron on my cell phone.

"Where are you?" he asked cautiously.

"I'm at the pet store getting ready to pick up Missy." Our dog was at the groomer, and we needed pet supplies.

"You need to go find a seat somewhere."

"What? I'm in the checkout line."

"I'm serious. Get out of line and find a seat."

I could tell something was wrong. I braced myself by leaning against a nearby pillar.

"What's up?"

"Janeice just called me and said that the Judge won't let us play the music with our video."

I exploded. I started hollering (and cussing too) so loud that it caught the attention of almost everyone in the store. Not wanting to make a bigger scene, I stepped outside.

"Ron, if we can't say how this crime has affected us our way we're just not going for the sentencing! What's the point? That music is half of our statement!"

I continued to rant and rave. Ron asked me to calm down, to come home, and we would talk. I went back inside the store bawling my eyes out. I paid for the supplies and collected our dog. I'm sure people thought I was a crazy woman.

I cried all the way home. As soon as I got through the door, I called Blonigen and Janeice and yelled some more. I told them that we were not coming to the sentencing. It was a waste of time, money, and emotions. "Victims have no rights!" I shouted.

They begged us to come.

We had waited sixteen years to confront Lisa's killer. We took the high road whenever possible. Suddenly our way of communicating our pain was being ripped out from under us. We wanted Eaton to realize who Lisa was and how much damage he had inflicted, but most importantly, we wanted to touch what conscience he had.

The defense said the music in our video would be "prejudicial." Prejudicial to what? The jury had already handed down their decisions without hearing from us, and they would have no part in the formal sentencing. According to the *Tribune*, Judge Park commented that "We have to be careful this doesn't turn into a memorial." Park told the attorneys, "Strike the music. I'll watch the pictures."

Eventually we calmed down and made the trip. The evening before the sentencing, one of the jurors, Lori, planned a potluck dinner for the other jurors and our family. If it hadn't been for that dinner, we would have stayed in Denver.

I'm glad Ron and I went. It was a special evening for us in Lori's tidy, comfortable home. Almost every juror showed up. We met teachers, college students, and a paralegal. They were from all walks of life, and they had two questions for us. Who was Lisa? Did we want Eaton to get the death penalty?

They had a sense of what kind of girl Lisa was, but wanted to know more about her personality. I shared stories about Lisa's childhood and teenage years. They shared their reactions during the course of the trial. The experience was hard on them, too.

I told them that if they wanted to know more about Lisa, I had pre-pared a slide show on a DVD for our victim's impact statement and would play it for them. Lori invited everyone to watch it on her TV set. As the music played and pictures of Lisa and our family filled the screen, most of them cried. When it was over, a juror commented, "Now I know for sure we made the right decision."

We told the jurors about the judge ruling out the music, so we wouldn't be showing the DVD at the sentencing scheduled the next day at 3:00 P.M. The jurors tried to persuade me to show it whether the music was allowed or not. Being stubborn, I said that, if I couldn't show it in its entirety, I wouldn't show it at all. I hoped our words would be enough to get through to Eaton.

The day of sentencing arrived. We had breakfast with Judy Mason and her husband, Gary. We were all a bit jittery, but Judy showed a remark-able strength for what she was facing. I could tell she still cared about her brother. No matter how bad family can get, love remains.

Sherry and Stacy weren't able to attend the jurors' dinner the evening before, so we arranged to take them to the courthouse early to meet the the jurors. To our surprise, several anxious people, including Dan Tholson, greeted us at the elevator.

Judge Park had reversed his ruling about the music!

"It's too late, Dan," I said. "I canceled the arrangements with the AV tech."

"Don't worry, Sheila. I took care of that. He's in the courtroom now, running cables."

Good old Dan. He always comes through.

Then I turned to Mike Blonigen and asked, "How in the world were you able to pull this off?"

Mike responded, "I didn't do a thing; it was because of what you did."

"I didn't do anything except cuss and holler a lot."

"Well, it must have worked," he said, grinning. "I'll see you in the courtroom."

We were ushered in, and I was surprised at the number of people packing the courtroom. Again—standing room only.

Judge Park spoke. "Prior to your making your statement, I would like to make a comment to the family. During the trial which you attended and many of the pretrial proceedings that you also attended, you had to listen to some terrible things. And you all sat there, maintained your dignity, your presence. Your ability to experience what you had to hear and see is a comment not only on your devotion to your daughter, but on your courage. And I acknowledge that. You've waited a long time for this, and I understand there was some distress over my earlier ruling (regarding the DVD). Sometimes things that I believe to be self-evident may not be so obvious, so I want to explain part of the reason for that decision."

"This case, by its nature, will be subjected to intense and very close scrutiny by the Wyoming Supreme Court, and potentially by federal judges. My mission since this case was assigned to me was to ensure that whatever verdict was ultimately reached would withstand that scrutiny, and in part, this was done by my attempt to meet every procedural and substantive safeguard."

Judge Park discussed the Wyoming statutes and how careful he wanted to be to not prejudice his decision. He had not thought the music on the video would add additional information to the case and might build "error" into the record.

"However, since my ruling, the parties have agreed that the background music may be present. And to the extent that Mr. Skaggs had any objection, he has withdrawn that objection. Now, in all fairness to Mr. Skaggs, I believe primarily the objection was mine and not his. But in view of their agreement that this music may be presented when you get to that appropriate point, you may present the DVD as it was prepared, including background music."

Ron, the girls, and I were then allowed to take the podium in the center of the room. We stood together as a family, and I acted as the spokesperson. I was nervous but determined to deliver a message that conveyed our real feelings. It would be the first and only time that we would be allowed to confront Eaton face to face.

Although this may repeat material which has appeared earlier, this is the statement in its entire form.

Victims' Impact Statement

We would like to thank your Honor, Judge Park for allowing us to address the court and Mr. Eaton. Your Honor, with your permission, we would now like to direct our comments to Mr. Dale Eaton.

Mr. Eaton, through the course of this trial you have learned more about Lisa, but you really don't know who Lisa Marie Kimmell was.

She was born in Covington, Tennessee, on July 18th, 1969. We named her Lisa Marie because Ron's mother expressed her desire to have a granddaughter named that. We granted her wish, and over the course of time her grandma often referred to her as "my little miss Lisa Marie," from which came the nickname, "Lil' Miss."

From an early age, Lisa was very independent, inquisitive, creative, and smart. Lisa was a good student and never a problem for her teachers. Shortly after Lisa turned fourteen, she went to work part time at Arby's.

When Lisa was barely sixteen, she wanted to buy a waterbed and asked us to co-sign for her so she could establish credit. She made all the payments, on time or ahead of time. In less than a year she had established good credit. While going to school and working part-time, she maintained good grades, her financial obligations, her focus and independence. My mother would often tell me that Lisa was really a thirty-year-old disguised as a teenager.

After graduating from high school, Lisa decided to put off college for a year to explore her options and her future. Shortly afterwards, she bought her new Honda CRX. She did it all on her own. She didn't need a co-signer because she had established excellent credit years before.

So, *who* was Lisa Marie Kimmell? She was our daughter. She was a sister. She was a granddaughter. She was a niece. She was a friend to many. She was a good student and employee, and was motivated to excel. Lisa was mature beyond her age but still had a naïve and innocent quality about her. She had a strong set of personal values and ethics. Lisa loved her family. Lisa loved people. Lisa loved animals. Lisa loved *life*. Lisa loved to be in love and to be loved. Lisa was dearly loved by her family, friends, and ultimately by extended friends across the country who came to know her through this tragic ordeal.

Now, Mr. Eaton, we ask you to think about the *"What ifs?"* What if Lisa had been allowed to live? What would her life be like? Career, husband, children? *What if?*

Sherry and Stacy, her sisters, both have done well for themselves and have been daughters to be very proud of in their continued education and careers. *What if?* Would Lisa be running some big company today?

Then there are two fine men, Zane and Todd, we are proud to have as son-in-laws. *"What if?"* Who would Lisa have married? Then, there are two other fine young men we are so proud of, Trevor and Alex, our grandsons. They never knew their Aunt Lisa, but when they see her picture they know who she is and will say, "that is our Aunt Lisa and she lives with the angels." *"What if?"* Would we have other precious grandchildren? The *"What ifs?"* have haunted us for many years.

Lisa never had the chance to become a wife, a mother, an aunt or a sister-in-law. The harsh reality is that we will never know because Lisa's life was cut so short when you brutally murdered *her* and took her away from *us*.

Lisa was not your *only* victim, Mr. Eaton. Nor is this just about Ron, Sheila, Sherry, and Stacy standing at this podium before you here this day who have been affected by your hideous crime against Lisa Marie Kimmell.

Here today are many friends, concerned citizens, law enforcement personnel, and yes, even members of the media who have been affected by your crime. And, no, it doesn't stop there. There are even members of your own family who have become "abstract" victims because of your crime. They have cried many tears because of you and for you. They have wept for us and wept with us because of what you did to our daughter. They will bear the undeserved stigma and shame of your actions, though it is *not* of their doing and our hearts truly go out to them. We would like to reassure them, that our family will hold their deeds and actions in life, separate and apart from yours and pray that others will, too.

Look behind us. These people are not here out of morbid curiosity; these are people that have also wept and grieved over Lisa's tragic loss. Words of comfort are difficult to find at times like this but we want to acknowledge their grief and express our gratitude for their support.

Mr. Eaton, your crime against Lisa Marie Kimmell wasn't an accident or error in judgment. It was *EVIL*. Can we ever forgive you? The answer is no. How can we forgive someone who has never asked for it? We are not vindictive or cruel people. You made the decision to abuse your God-given gift of free will. Even if you were to ask for forgiveness and take responsibility for what you have done, we maintain and pray that you will be punished to the maximum extent in your present life. We know God will honor that, and we know that God will also deal with you in the here and after.

As the court painfully ponders your fate, Mr. Eaton, I would like to remind you and the court, that nearly sixteen years ago to this day, *you*, Mr. Dale Wayne Eaton, pronounced *your* death sentence upon Lisa Marie Kimmell.

With that said, on March 25th of 1988, Lisa set out on a journey to explore more of life's adventures, a Pilgrimage in a sense, seeking her future, direction and purpose. Because we are at a loss to further express ourselves, we have prepared a special pictorial video to present to you, which was very difficult to do. How does one express the joy Lisa brought into our lives, the deep sadness we still feel about her loss and send you, her killer, a personal message on Lisa's behalf?

Mr. Eaton, pay very close attention.

The ten-minute DVD played, and almost everyone in the room wiped away tears. Eaton stared at the defense table, showing no emotions or remorse. When asked if he had any comments, he shook his head. We'll never know if we got through to him or not.

Judge Park signed Eaton's death warrant and gave him an additional life sentence, plus fifty years in connection to the numerous charges surrounding Lisa's murder. He set the execution date at June 25th, 2004, but the appeals will most likely drag it out for years. The *Tribune* quoted Judge Park as saying, "It was a murder that touched the community. Her violent death shattered illusions of peaceful lives." He then read Eaton's complicated sentence.

Judge Park finally dismissed us, but it took a long time to leave the courtroom with all the hugs from everyone.

The ordeal still wasn't over. We were about to meet the press, and Judy Mason was prepared to give her courageous statement on behalf of the Eaton family.

Judy wasn't used to the press. Her voice shook as she began reading her statement. She said she was representing her father, two sisters, and a younger brother. She disputed a number of claims that Wyatt Skaggs made when trying to defend Dale.

She said her family felt betrayed by the defense attorney's claims that their father was an alcoholic who picked on Dale. It hurt Merle to know what his son did; to be blamed for it was unbearable.

The *Tribune* quoted Judy as saying, "It's been really hard. I love my brother, but it is with sadness that I have to support the death penalty in this case."

She said that Lisa has been in her thoughts every day since she and I met at his federal trial for killing Carl Palmer.

Judy told the press, "I was in shock during the testimony. This is not the family I grew up in. We love and support our father. Yes, Dale was disciplined, as were the rest of us when it was deserved. Our father was not to blame for the way Dale turned out. His actions were his own."

Judy said that the family was also upset about their mother's emotional problems being used as another excuse. "She was a wonderful and caring mother, and we loved her dearly." Judy said her mother's troubles were exaggerated.

She was also angry that the defense lawyers didn't interview her to get her side of the story, and she believed they told Dale that she no longer cared about him. She wasn't allowed to talk to her brother during the trial and the letters she mailed to him were returned unopened.

Judy told the press that if she could speak to him, "I would tell him I loved him… but he took away a life. What he did was not right."

After the press conference, another round of hugs was shared. It had been a tough day.

CHAPTER 28

Conclusions

Ron and I returned to Denver after Dale Eaton's formal sentencing, but we didn't have long to relax. We had to start packing for a move closer to Ron's parents. Our new house would be ready soon. Life must go on. I got touching notes from the jurors. One said the following:

> I just wanted to write you and let you know how much I enjoyed meeting you and your family. It was a relief to know that we had done the right thing for you. I also wanted to thank you for sharing the video and stories about Lisa and also about your son, Ricky. It was wonderful to meet your two beautiful daughters. I wanted to let you know how much I admire you for the strength and courage you have had throughout the last sixteen years. I feel that you did a wonderful job yesterday with your speech, and you had a tremendous impact on everyone there.

Facing grief wasn't over with Eaton's trial and sentencing. Sadly, we had to face yet another chapter of sorrow for two months starting at the end of July. We found out that my dad's health was deteriorating rapidly and that he only had a short time to live. Ron and I wanted to be with him and let him die in dignity in his own home. We were glad he had lived to see justice. Sometimes I wonder if he didn't keep going for that reason.

After two difficult months during which my brothers, Ron, and I tended to his last needs, Dad passed away from cancer on September 14th, 2004. We weathered the trial, moving to a new house, and Dad's death within one year. How much can a family endure? A lot, if they let themselves grieve and grow past it.

When things settled down, I wondered how to end this book. I wrote a long story about my Dad's suffering and his excruciating death. I wanted to tell the world how unfair it was for him to suffer horribly from natural causes—how unfair it was for Lisa to be terrorized for six days by a man she must have known would kill her. Life also seemed cruel to take my son at such a young age. By contrast, Dale Eaton will receive a shot that will end his life in a few relatively painless minutes.

Dealing with my father's death presented another test for Ron and me to apply our experience and let each other grieve in different ways. It also gave us insight into the hope of eternal life after our earthly suffering. We heard my father speak to the "other side" frequently during his last days, and it wasn't scary or mystical. Hearing his side of the conversations, it sounded practical. For example, he asked if he had to walk to heaven and was comforted by an apparent answer that he didn't. He wanted to know if dogs go to heaven. He was assured they did. That consoled him and us.

The most agonizing, bittersweet journey of our lives began Saturday, March 26th, 1988, when we learned that Lisa had disappeared. Our journey may never be over. We continue to hear about shocking sexual homicides, but we continue to meet good people who shower us with loving support.

In concluding this book, Ron and I hope that our readers have gotten to know Lisa and our family better. We hope that the way we coped with our emotional and spiritual pain may help others who face what may to them seem insurmountable suffering.

We pray each day that law enforcement agencies will cooperate with each other and forget about jurisdictional issues. Solving a crime should be everyone's goal. We're still encouraging law enforcement to work together harmoniously on other unsolved murders, including the cases of missing young women in the Great Basin region.

Our hope is that law enforcement agencies will someday set up a standardized system of recording and connecting violent crimes so that dangerous killers like Dale Eaton can be caught faster. We also hope that modern technology can help solve more cold cases, particularly those involving victims of violent crime who are now without voices.

We have said that there is no closure for us, or an end to the grieving process, but we are moving on with life. We hope our readers are uplifted by our stories about the amazing people who gave us the strength to endure this tragedy. Thank God for their goodness, perseverance, love, and dedication.

And thank God justice prevailed.